I0605674

# The Architecture of **Wesley Clark Dodson**

*Publication of this book was assisted in part by generous funding from the Summerlee Foundation of Dallas.*

# The Architecture o

# Wesley Clark Dodson

## LEGACY OF A GOOD NAME

**Mary Helen Dodson**

TEXAS A&M UNIVERSITY PRESS COLLEGE STATION

First edition

∞ This paper meets the requirements of ANSI/NISO Z39.48-1992 (Permanence of Paper). Binding materials have been chosen for durability. Manufactured in China through Martin Book Management.

Library of Congress Cataloging-in-Publication Data

Names: Dodson, Mary Helen, 1940– author.
Title: The architecture of Wesley Clark Dodson : legacy of a good name / Mary Helen Dodson.
Description: First edition. | College Station : Texas A&M University Press, [2026] | Includes bibliographical references and index.
Identifiers: LCCN 2025020716 (print) | LCCN 2025020717 (ebook) | ISBN 9781648433153 (cloth) | ISBN 9781648433160 (ebook)
Subjects: LCSH: Dodson, Wesley Clark, 1829-1914. | Architects—Texas—Waco—Biography. | Public buildings—Texas—Design and construction—History—19th century. | Courthouses—Texas—History. | LCGFT: Biographies.
Classification: LCC NA737.D63 D63 2026 (print) | LCC NA737.D63 (ebook) | DDC 720.92 [B]—dc23/eng/20250619
LC record available at https://lccn.loc.gov/2025020716
LC ebook record available at https://lccn.loc.gov/2025020717

*To my brothers*

*Charles Henry Dodson Jr.,*

*Thomas Bruce Dodson,*

*and*

*Durrett Blake Dodson,*

*who knew the importance of family,*

*and to my grandchildren, who I hope*

*will learn to appreciate it as well.*

*I never knew one of the Dodson family to be hung, go to jail, or the penitentiary. They are peaceable, amiable and industrious. 'A good name is a great fortune.'—Proverbs 22:1*

—Rev. Elias Dodson, "Genealogy of the Dodson Families"

County Government Building, Cleburne, Tex.

# Contents

# Preface

## Pursuing My Family's History

Pursuing my family's history has been one of my lifelong interests. Growing up, my brothers and I often heard stories of our heritage. We were intrigued by possessions our great-grandparents passed down to us. My father showed us the tableware that was used to set the table at Great-Grandfather Thomas Roane Blake's ranch in Texas, the five-dollar Federal Reserve note found in Great-Grandmother Mary Ellen Bacon Blake's purse the day she died, the Civil War medal that Great-Grandfather Wesley Clark Dodson had treasured. My mother often shared stories of her family. We learned that when her father was only four years old, he stood on the family plantation in North Carolina and watched General Sherman's army march across the family's land. It was on its way back from burning Atlanta, leaving a path of destruction in its wake. The family had buried its silver and farm implements and hidden hams in the rafters to keep the Union soldiers from taking everything. As a result, even as children, we were aware that our ancestors were real people with important stories to tell.

Then, more than thirty years ago, my brother Rhett began doing genealogical research. He shared some of his early discoveries with me, and soon I joined him in digging further into our family's history. Initially, we focused on finding the missing branches on our family tree. Our direction changed about ten years ago, when we stumbled across *Historic Brazos County*, a Brazos Heritage Society publication authored by Robert Borden. To our amazement, the book devoted an entire chapter to two early settlers in Bryan, Texas, our Great-Grandfather Wesley Clark Dodson and his wife, Sarah. The chapter contained photographs of them and letters they had exchanged. Borden put us in touch with curators of the Texas Collection at Baylor University, enabling us to access a valuable stash of our great-grandfather's papers. In addition to the photographs and letters between Wesley and Sarah, the collection contained Wesley's memoirs, which he had written when he was in his eighties. The documents contained such extensive detail and told such a compelling story that, as an American historian, I thought I had to write a book about Wesley's remarkable life.

I began to track down information about Wesley's architectural career, finding the courthouses, jails, schools, and churches that he had designed. As I gained an appreciation of the importance of his work, I focused more on it. I discovered the advances in technology that he pioneered. I saw the way his designs evolved as he was the first to modify the courthouse floor plan to accommodate a ground-supported masonry central tower and how he was the first architect to top a Texas courthouse with a dome, the twentieth-century symbol of governmental authority. I investigated his efforts to establish architecture as a profession and to establish, then serve as president of, the Texas State Association of Architects.

As I got deeper into the project, many kind people, some at county historical societies, some at university libraries, and some in county government offices, provided me with information and pictures. Previously unknown cousins helped locate graves and shared information from their own research efforts. Surprisingly, many of the people I contacted seeking an answer to one question put me in contact with others who provided information that enabled me to answer other questions. My daughter Carolyn was indispensable as a reviewer and editor, sharpening and clarifying the organization and the writing.

Wesley Clark Dodson wrote his memoirs because he wanted his children and grandchildren to know something about his "ancestors, whose character and worth are their heritage." In the spirit of this sentiment, I have put this book together to share not only with family but also with others interested in learning the story of a remarkable man who survived the tumultuous period of the Civil War to become one of Texas' foremost post–Civil War architects.

# Acknowledgments

A book such as this does not get written without the cooperation, help, and kindness of many people. I wish to thank those who generously shared their time and their knowledge with me. Many people at county historical commissions, others at county clerks offices at the various courthouses, and others at genealogical societies, libraries, museums, archives, and universities expressed enthusiasm that the history of their courthouses would be made known. I have tried not to overlook anyone, but if I did, I apologize.

Robert Borden, the author of *Historic Brazos County*, put me in touch with the Texas Collection at Baylor University and with the family of Mary Alice Hall, who had donated Wesley Clark Dodson's letters and papers to the Texas Collection. Amanda Mylan, a Baylor graduate student at the time, worked with me to get copies of relevant materials from the collection. The Halls provided me with additional documents and pictures that were invaluable.

Dr. T. Bradford Willis read an early draft of the Waco chapter, provided visuals, and made many suggestions for where additional information could be found. In the midst of the COVID pandemic, he even ventured past warning signs to take photographs for me. Dr. Willis also put me in touch with Jacob Mangum at the University of North Texas Libraries' Portal to Texas History, who graciously provided me with many visuals and secured the permissions needed to reproduce them. Suzanne Spain of Bryn Mawr College read an early draft of the courthouse chapters. Randall Miller of St. Joseph's University read a later draft of the biographical sections and offered suggestions that were immensely helpful in adding context to Wesley's story. Dan Utley and Bob Brinkman of the Texas Historical Commission critiqued the architecture chapters. Ron Maxfield of Marlow, Oklahoma, led me to the discovery of the Odd Fellows Widows' and Orphans' Home, and Paolo Musto of Columbia University helped secure needed research materials.

I received particularly helpful assistance finding valuable materials in courthouse and church records from Myrce'Tez Gowan at the McLennan County Courthouse, Sherry Lawrence at the Coryell Genealogical Society, Susan Smith of the Young County Historical Commission, and Pam Corder at the Kaufman County Courthouse, all of whom went out of their way to identify information that might be of use to me. Boyce Cabaniss, Peggy Wolff, Sherry Boultinghouse, and Amy McDaniel at the Lampasas County Museum and Historical Commission; Kathleen Cholley and John Dulaney of the Hill County Genealogical Society; Elvis Allen and Suzanne Bass at the Van Zandt County Historical Commission; Nancy Gregory at the Wichita County Courthouse; Kay Hardin at the Young County Courthouse; Donna McCauley at the Parker County Historical Commission; and Sarah Martin at St. Paul's Episcopal Church in Waco all provided me with invaluable information.

Others who volunteered their time to help me were: Cheryl Doran at the Palestine First Presbyterian Church; Kirsten Misciagno at the Anderson County Courthouse; Kenneth Hafertepe at Baylor University; Lila Deakle and Karol Slates at the Parker County Courthouse; Tasha Bates at the Lampasas County Courthouse; Laura Robinson and Sherry Zindars at the Fannin County Courthouse; Bryce Blair at the Wichita County Archives; Kathryn Frost at the Hood County Courthouse; Rhonda Mohler at the Coryell County Museum and Historical Center; Gwen Womack at the Houston County Courthouse; Pam Beam at the Mason County Courthouse; and Robert Chadwick, Cathy Harman, and Frank Reeves at the Swisher County Archives and Museum.

Assistance locating and getting permission to use visuals came from many sources. They include Leonard Lane of 254 Texas Courthouses; Keith Vincent at courthousehistory.com; Amy Oliver and Geoff Hunt at the Texas Collection; David Chase, Anne Stimmel, and Jay Firsching at Architexas; Larry Standlee of the Fannin County Historical Commission; Dorman Holub at the Young County Historical Commission; Christine Rogers at the Leyland Museum in Cleburne, Texas; Kim Cupit at the Denton County Museum; Dr. Valerie Burnes at the Sumter County Historical Society; Judge Bob McGregor at the Hill County Historical Commission; Teresa Cave of the Edward Cave Collection; Dave Fulp of texascourthousetrail.com; Joyce Walden at the Allen County Historical Society in Kentucky; Terry Phillips of the George A. Smathers Libraries at the University of Florida; Bryan Collars of the South Carolina Department of Archives and History; Anton Duplessis of the Cushing Memorial Library at Texas A&M University; Brenda Light at the Lee Lockwood Library and Museum; Carol Kennedy at the Texas Historical Commission; Anne Cook of the Texas Department of Transportation; Sheila Bickle at Texas Woman's University Libraries; Hal Jespersen of cwmaps.com; Jeffrey D. Goldberg of the United States Military Academy; Nathan Shapard at shapardhistory.blogspot.com; Charles Reeves; Jim McNamara; Wayne Wendel; Jordan M. McAlister; Stephen Michaels; Jim Bell; Dave Benbennick; Dreanna L. Belden; Stephen Pence; Mary Shearer; and Diane Gravlee.

I want to particularly acknowledge the help of my brother Rhett Dodson, who was an early researcher on this project and who encouraged me to continue working. Without the help of my daughter, Carolyn Kahn-Hall, who critiqued my work, offered constructive suggestions, and spent countless hours helping with the manuscript, this book would never have been completed. Finally, I wish to thank Bill Musto, who, for more than two years, sacrificed my company while I worked and then listened patiently as all I talked about was the book.

# The Architecture of **Wesley Clark Dodson**

# Introduction
## "Memoirs of W. C. Dodson"

In 1913, eighty-four-year-old Wesley Clark Dodson sat in the comfortable home he had designed on Ethel Avenue in Waco's Sanger Heights. The home was the last of seven he had built for his family since settling in Waco in 1876. He was trying to write his memoirs, but the pain in his hip and leg, an ever-present reminder of a Civil War injury, surely made it hard for him to concentrate. His health was declining, and he had recently stopped going to his architectural office downtown. He longed to go for a buggy ride and enjoy some of "nature's loveliness," as he referred to the beauty of the natural world. But since he no longer had a horse and buggy, he sat in his front parlor and wrote on the yellow legal pads he always used to capture his thoughts. In documenting his life's story, he had three goals in mind:

First, he wanted his children to understand something about his childhood and how he acquired the principles and values by which he lived his life. He wanted them to see how those principles served him when, later on, he faced a series of challenges and misfortunes. "As I am now past my eighty-fourth year," he wrote, "and have witnessed many important changes and events in the political, moral and scientific world, and have passed through many scenes of danger and of strife; and through many vicissitudes of fortune, I think it well for my children to know something of my life more than they have seen."

Second, he wanted his children to know "something of my ancestors," who had lived on the American frontier. They valued family, took responsibility for one another, and, at the edge of the wilderness, attempted to create a civilized society. His ancestors also fought in the American Revolution and the War of 1812 to protect the rights and freedoms that he worried his children enjoyed but perhaps took for granted.

Finally, he wished "to record the mercies and providential care of our heavenly Father who has been my shield in every danger from infancy down to this day." As Wesley wrote about events throughout his life, he would always conclude with an expression of gratitude to God that He had chosen to bless him and his life. Wesley believed that whatever happened was God's will, and even if he did not understand it, he would accept it since God had done it.

Sensing his life was in its final chapter, he felt it was "a time to remember all these things; . . . for it is only by keeping the past in mind that we can avoid the errors and have faith to meet the requirements of the present and the uncertainties of the future."

He stopped his writing abruptly, as if he intended to resume again later, with the comment "enough of this for the present." Either he never resumed his memoirs, or whatever else he wrote has been lost. But, because Wesley wrote these brief memoirs, we are able to glean much more about this peaceful man of great faith and integrity than we would have otherwise.[1]

Today, most of what people think about the South comes from watching movies such as *Gone with the Wind*, *Roots*, or *Mississippi Burning*. Most Americans know little about what happened to the Southern middle class during the Civil War era. This book tells the story of how the war destroyed the lives of the Southern middle class, and how one man dealt with it. Wesley gave up a comfortable, secure life to fight for the South, despite having no interest in protecting the Southern slaveocracy. Following the war, having lost everything, he faced the daunting task of starting over.

This book explores the difficulties Wesley encountered as he took his family to Texas after the war. He faced military rule, a depressed economy, rampant lawlessness, and a lack of the usual social constraints that held society together. But, determined to help build the institutions needed for Texas to become an orderly, civilized society, Wesley persevered through the turbulent times and launched a career building courthouses, jails, schools, and churches—the institutions he believed Texas needed in order to become a "good society."

In Texas, Wesley transitioned from master builder to post–Civil War architect, assuming a leading role in establishing his craft as a recognized and highly regarded profession. He eventually oversaw the construction of eighteen magnificent courthouses, often referred to as "cathedrals of justice." The seven that survive today, as well as several other public buildings he designed, are all in the National Register of Historic Places, a testament to the significance of his work.

This book is the first to bring together in one place all of Wesley's known public buildings. It is the first to document the life of one of the foremost architects of Texas' golden age of courthouse construction. This carefully researched account of Wesley's life draws heavily from his letters and memoirs, which allows the telling of much of his story in his own words and from his point of view. The titles to chapters 1–6 are taken from Wesley's memoirs.

# "My Childhood"

One day in 1832, when Wesley was about three years old, his mother, Elizabeth Dodson, brought Wesley and his baby sister Juliett to spend the day visiting at a family friend's farm. Elizabeth's husband, Elisha Jefferson Dodson, a Methodist minister, was probably away, as he often was, covering the circuit to which he was assigned, and she longed for some company. The women were sitting in the Alabama farmyard working on their mending as they chatted. As Wesley played with the Stone's children, he noticed the family's pet bear chained to a hogshead, which was turned on its side to make a den for the bear. Absorbed in his play, Wesley forgot about the bear and eventually drifted too close to him. Without warning, the bear snatched Wesley, dragged him to the back of the hogshead, then lay down in front of him and wouldn't let the frightened mothers get him out. Hearing the women's cries, Mr. Stone ran from the field, lured the bear out, perhaps with a tasty morsel, and retrieved the child.[1]

Elizabeth was thoroughly shaken by the realization of how close she had come to losing her third and only surviving son—the first two had died as infants. Wesley would later say that this was his first intimation that God would protect him; he believed God had saved him that day because He had a purpose for him and his life. What that purpose would be, he did not know, but he would later resolve to live his life being useful to his friends, his family, and his community.

Wesley's views of God's saving grace and His call for a purposeful, useful life were strongly influenced by his father's teachings and the example he provided. Eleven years earlier, on September 6, 1821, Elisha had presented his credentials as a Methodist preacher to the Madison County Court, in the new state of Alabama, prepared to devote his life to the religious movement.[2] The Methodist Episcopal Church was the first American branch of the Methodist movement, founded in England in the late eighteenth century by John Wesley, an Anglican minister. The Methodists were mostly middle-class people: shopkeepers, merchants, and small farmers. The early Methodist message condemned the lifestyle of the slaveholding upper-class gentry and preached an ascetic life without card playing, alcohol, or much frivolity but with a duty to serve mankind and God.[3]

Elisha had not attended any theological school,[4] but both his father and grandfather had been Baptist ministers. From his grandfather, the Reverend Joshua Dodson, and his father, the Reverend Charles Dodson, Elisha gained a thorough understanding of the Bible and how to preach and minister to others. For the next ten years, he served in Alabama, ministering to settlers in an area recently taken from the Cherokee, and perhaps evangelizing the Cherokee themselves, seeking converts among them.[5]

Riding the circuit. Credit: Edward Eggleston (Wikimedia Commons).

In the fall of 1832, shortly after Wesley encountered the bear, the Methodist bishops appointed Elisha to a circuit in the Tennessee Conference, and the family moved to Williamson County, Tennessee. As a married man, Elisha was paid $200 annually, with a small housing and expense allowance. He bought a farm about four miles north of Franklin, on the Davidson County line. There, Elisha began his circuit. He rode on horseback, carrying his rifle and everything else he needed in his saddlebags, covering a route that would take him five or six weeks to complete. He traveled through the wilderness inhabited by Native Americans to reach distant farms and villages. Along the way, he faced the constant threat of animal attacks, unfriendly encounters, illness, and exhaustion. He would stop almost daily to preach in courthouses, cabins, and open fields—wherever he encountered people. He baptized children, conducted marriage ceremonies, and said prayers for the departed. He sought to secure converts and organize new congregations. He was a voice in the wilderness, laying a foundation for a civilized, God-fearing society on the American frontier.[6]

While his father was away, Wesley had a second encounter with the saving grace of God: "At our home near Franklin, we had a beautiful place with a spring about thirty yards from the house. It was several feet down to the water and the water was five or six feet deep, with stone steps from the top of the ground to the water. One day I was down on the steps and fell in the spring, and in spite of all my exertions to get out, I failed, and when I was strangled and about given up hope, a presentment came to me that I wouldn't drown—that God had a use for me in the future, and just as I was sinking the third time sister Angeline came for water and got me out. I record this incident exactly as it occurred—for it is as fresh in my mind as if it had occurred today, and I mention it in gratitude to God who spared my life then, and has been my shield in all the days of battle, and in all the dangers through which I have passed."[7]

In the summer of 1833, when Wesley was only four, he was introduced to the camp meeting, an important social and religious event that evangelicals, particularly the Methodists, used to maintain and expand their membership. Up until the Civil War, these religious revivals took place every summer for about a week. Campgrounds were built all over the South, generally spaced about ten or fifteen miles apart from each other. The meetings were scheduled each year so that none interfered with another. People attended as many as they were able to, and ministers attended all those held in their districts. Campgrounds were generally built on high ground in treed areas to keep them cool in the summer heat. Each site had a large square, around which individual campers built log cabins that they would stay in each summer.

A Methodist camp meeting. Credit: Engraving by Jacques Gérard Milbert (1819) (Wikimedia Commons).

At one end of the square was a raised shelter with a pulpit and space to seat about twelve preachers. In front of the shelter were enough seats for two to three thousand worshipers to gather. The Methodist ministers, like the Baptists, did not read long, dry sermons dealing with abstruse, arcane religious dogma. Instead, they tried to connect with people spiritually and emotionally and connect them with both a moral life and a belief in the saving grace of God.

At the end of a typical revival service, the preachers would leave the pulpit area and go down to pray for the penitents who had come forward to confess their sins and profess their faith. The preacher's move was the signal, as Wesley remembered, for little boys like himself to scamper onto the pulpit platform and watch what was going on below. "It was a scene both solemn and joyous, singing, praying and shouting, and sometimes amusing—to me, as small as I was."[8] Wesley was too young to be interested in the preaching of the various ministers or to mull over their call for people to repent and submit to God's will. But later on, Wesley would seek out opportunities to hear ministers expound on the theological differences among the various Protestant denominations.

While living in Williamson County, Wesley witnessed a spectacular meteor shower, a celestial phenomenon that people of the time referred to as "the stars falling." In November 1833, the comet Tempel-Tuttle, which returns every thirty-three years, made its closest approach ever to the earth and sun. All across North America, the meteor shower was unusually prolific, and it became one of the most spectacular astronomical sights ever seen. The moon had set, so the sky was dark, and the display was even more spectacular. As Wesley recalled, "It was the most beautiful sight I ever saw . . . The air was cold and crisp, and . . . filled with meteors like blazing fireballs. It was in the night between 12 o'clock and daylight, and made everything as light as would thousands of electric lights burning. It looked as if the whole ethereal heavens were on fire."[9]

While Wesley viewed the event as a "display of grandeur," a revelation of God's glory, which he watched with delight and astonishment, many others feared, as he remembered, "that the Day of Judgment had come and knew that they were not prepared for it." There were reports of one frightened woman grabbing her minister by the collar and threatening to kill him if he did not pray for her. At the time of the meteor shower, Elisha was sick in bed, but he was awakened by the light and the noise of the neighbors milling about his yard. All had come, as Wesley recalled, "praying and shouting and confessing their sins," but all left having been reassured by their trusted minister that they were only witnessing an anticipated meteor shower. The world was not coming to an end.[10]

In the winter of 1833, Elisha moved his family to a farm that he had bought about halfway between Franklin and Nashville. Wesley described it as "another beautiful place with a red clover pasture and a creek made up of never failing springs, running through it. . . . It was a delightful neighborhood too—with little boys for me to play with."[11] There, Wesley had yet another incident that demonstrated God was his protector.

*The Night the Stars Fell.* Credit: Engraving by Adolf Vollmy (1889) (Wikimedia Commons).

Elisha Jefferson Dodson's farms in Tennessee: Williamson County (1832–33), Davidson County (1833–36), and Marshall County (1836–45). His last circuit was in Bedford County. Credit: Map courtesy of Charles A. Reeves Jr.

One day he was visiting the McCrory farm with his mother and sisters, as the family often did. While their mothers talked and did handwork, six-year-old Wesley and young Tommy McCrory played in the horse corral, chasing one another under the troughs. A few moments after Wesley wriggled out from under one, Tommy went under on his back. The heavy trough fell on him, crushing his breast bone and killing him immediately. "I was spared and he was taken. Young as I was, it made such an impression on my mind of God's providential care that it is with me this hour."[12]

In the fall of 1836, the Methodist bishops appointed Elisha to a new circuit in Bedford County, Tennessee. Elisha sold his place between Nashville and Franklin and moved to a farm he bought in Marshall County, near the line with Bedford, Williamson, and Rutherford Counties. Wesley wrote about the beauty of his new home in a description that probably reveals as much about his appreciation of the natural world being God's creation as it does about the farm:

"It was a lovely farm, lying in a valley with a long mountain range on the North, and a short and abrupt mountain on the east. The land was generally level and rich. It had seven never failing springs on it, which united and formed a creek, which ran diagonally through the middle of it. There was an elevation on the farm with its foot at the creek and ascending to the South East with a gentle slope to the height of about three hundred feet, with an abrupt rock termination on the East. This ascension lent a charm to the landscape which, taken together with the surroundings, made the scene exquisitely beautiful."[13]

At the top of the hill, a peach orchard of about six acres covered a plateau. An apple orchard of ten or twelve acres formed the western edge of the property. More apple trees grew in the farmyard, and cherry, apple, peach, and plum trees were scattered over the property. All produced bushels of fruit annually that, when stored in the two-story spring house, lasted the entire year. Elisha made cider from the apples every year but never made hard cider, as the Methodists disapproved of drinking. To prevent the cider from fermenting, he boiled some of it, then put tallow and some of the boiled cider in each barrel.

On some of the farm's acreage, Wesley's family grew corn, wheat, and oats, with a few acres of cotton for home use. They kept other acreage as pastureland for grazing the stock, with still more acreage rented to others to cultivate. A forest of oaks, ash, hickory, maples, chestnuts, buckeyes, and black walnut trees covered the rest of the farm, with foliage so full that Wesley ascribed to it "a majestic appearance." Because the woods were clear of underbrush, it was possible in the spring to see the dogwoods, redbuds, and red and black haw trees all in bloom, which, Wesley remembered "lent an enchantment to the scene indescribable."[14]

As Wesley wrote, "With father's and mother's teaching me that God made all things it was in such scenes that I first learned to adore Him in His works, and to love nature, and that love has grown with my growth, and has increased with my years until the works of men appear so trifling in contrast that I care little for the so-called grandeur of the works of men. It was in such environments as the mountains and valleys, the running brooks and resistless torrents and the vast forests with their variegated beauties mingled with the songs of the birds that I first felt the love and all-pervading presence of God. What landscape is complete without the Majestic woods, and what more elevates the thought and inspires the souls than to contemplate the handiwork of God?"[15]

Wesley's family lived a self-sufficient life that wanted for very little. "We had horses and cattle, sheep and hogs, turkeys and chickens, geese and ducks—the geese and ducks for their feathers, the horses to work and to ride, the cattle for milk and butter and for their hides to make leather, and the sheep for their wool, and the hogs for their meat, and for bacon to sell, as bacon was about the only thing that could be sold—for every family had their own, in abundance, of what he had."[16] They sold the bacon to large slaveholders, who preferred to keep their acreage in cotton production rather than using it to raise their own meat.[17]

Elisha Jefferson Dodson. Credit: Photograph by author.

Wesley's early schooling was at home with his mother and father and was based on religious and moral principles. He took delight, as he remembered, in "the Bible histories of the men who were illustrious in the annals of the church" and learned them by heart. He also read a great deal of history and the "biographies of our great men," including Washington and Jefferson. To prepare their children for "a life of usefulness," Wesley's parents taught "correct deportment and respect for others . . . daily, both by precept and example."[18]

Jane Elizabeth Blackwell Dodson. Credit: Photograph by author.

Wesley held both his mother and father in high esteem. His mother, Elizabeth Blackwell, was born in Halifax County, Virginia, in 1788, just as Virginia was ratifying the United States Constitution. She took pride in the fact that she was a native of Virginia, home of patriots such as Patrick Henry, and that her father had served with the Continental troops and was with General Washington when the British surrendered at Yorktown.[19] Her father died when she was thirteen, but as a war veteran, he had been given land grants for his service, which passed to his heirs. Sometime after 1805, Elizabeth moved with her brothers and mother to Warren County, Kentucky, where they claimed land newly opened to settlement.

Wesley always looked to his mother for advice and support. He remembered her wearing a lace-bordered dress and the old-fashioned style of cap, under which she tucked her long dark hair. Her stern appearance reflected her strictness and her expectation of orderliness and timely fulfillment of duties. She hated hypocrisy and sham. Her hazel-blue eyes revealed her kindness and her willingness to help the poor and suffering.[20]

Wesley's father, Elisha Dodson, was born in Stokes County, North Carolina, in 1788. His father, the Reverend Charles Dodson, was a Revolutionary War soldier who had fought at the battles of Brandywine Creek and Germantown and had wintered with General Washington at Valley Forge. When Elisha was two, his family migrated to South Carolina's Pendleton District, newly created from former Cherokee land. There, on the Keowee River, Elisha's father, Charles, served a small Baptist church.[21] Elisha's grandfather, the Reverend Joshua Dodson, moved with the family and served a Baptist Church on the west side of the Keowee River in Georgia.

In the early 1800s, at about the same time that the Blackwells arrived in Kentucky, Charles Dodson used his Revolutionary War land grants to claim land there. His children and their families moved with him, settling near one another in Allen County, Kentucky.[22] At the Treaty of Paris, the British ceded all the land east of the Mississippi River, including the Northwest Territory, and agreed to evacuate the forts they held there. But following the war, they refused to abide by the terms of the treaty. They remained in the forts and continued supplying arms to the Native Americans who inhabited the areas all along the frontier, helping them resist the expansion of Americans into their territory. Elisha's uncle, Elijah Joel Dodson, was killed by a Native American as he cleared a field in Lincoln County, Tennessee, on land he had obtained with a land grant. With British arms, the Native Americans constantly raided American settlements, raising the anger of American frontiersmen, who then clamored for war with Britain.

When the War of 1812 broke out, Elisha enlisted in the Kentucky militia to fight the British and their Native American allies. Elisha was a sturdy man of five feet, nine inches and one hundred ninety pounds. He had black hair, was always clean-shaven, and had brown eyes "as keen as a hawk's" that to Wesley "seemed to pierce through you when he was talking." He was a kind and gentle man who Wesley knew "despised an act that was mean and dishonorable and debasing and rebuked it with Christian forbearance." He was also an intelligent man with a mind "as active as an electric current," who "seemed to grasp and comprehend a subject by intuition."

Following the war, Elisha married Elizabeth Blackwell and embarked on his life's work as a Methodist minister. Wesley remembered that his father "was a student all his life, and the Bible, with Church History, and the sermons and writings of eminent divines and the English Classics, were his daily companions."[23] Wesley admired his father as a man who never sought political or civil office, "esteeming the office that he held as a Minister of the Gospel of Christ greater than any that man could confer."

Elisha was a highly respected leader in his community, as were most ministers during this period of United States history. He was trusted to assist people with their wills and legal filings, often attesting to legal papers. He was well-read, well-spoken, and knowledgeable about religion, philosophy, and the ideas undergirding the state and federal constitutions. Because of his travels, he knew what was happening in the community, such as where there were problems with lawlessness or disorder, and he knew what issues settlers were concerned about. Religious and political leaders of Tennessee often visited the farm, riding miles to confer with Elisha.

In his memoirs, Wesley recalled how whenever these men arrived, Wesley would pull himself away from the play of the neighborhood boys and go to where the men talked with his father. Wesley, a serious, somber boy, was eager to listen as the men talked about church or state affairs. What he did not understand he would get his father to explain to him afterward. These sessions sparked Wesley's lifelong commitment to serving as a leader of his church and community. Standing silently in the doorway, listening to the conversations of his father and influential community leaders, he learned "far more," he later wrote, "than could be learned in any school or college."[24]

All in all, Wesley had a very happy boyhood. When he was nine, he went to an old-field school, so named because it was built on worn-out or rocky land not suitable for farming. The school was taught by his uncle, James Blackwell. Wesley enjoyed vying with the boys and girls in reading and spelling and playing games of marbles and baseball, including "cat" or "bull-pin," with the boys. On Saturdays, the boys shot squirrels and partridges in the woods, and, at night, they hunted raccoons and possums with their dogs.[25]

In 1842, Elisha and his brother Armstead went to Kentucky to visit their brother Dillingham, who was living about a hundred miles north in Allen County. There they discussed the proposed marriage of Wesley's sister Caroline to Dillingham's godson, William J. Thacker. Shortly after their return, Elisha developed a fever and died. At his death, the Methodist Tennessee Conference reported that Elisha "was an able minister of the New Testament; filled many important appointments in North Alabama and Tennessee, and finally closed his useful life on the Bedford Circuit July 29, 1842, in the fifty-fourth year of his age." The Reverend John McFerrin, Elisha's close friend, was with him when he died. He recorded the last words of a man at peace with everything: "Good is the will of the Lord, for I am prepared to live or die; for me to live is Christ, to die is gain; let the will of God be done."[26]

A few months later, Caroline was married to William and returned to Kentucky with him. Wesley, his mother, and his remaining sisters, ten-year-old Juliett and eighteen-year-old Mary, tried running the family farm themselves. But the task was overwhelming, particularly since Elizabeth really wanted Wesley to go to school. Elizabeth asked William and Caroline to come live with them and take over running the farm. That arrangement worked well until Caroline died in childbirth the following winter. William then returned to Kentucky. This series of events, Wesley later wrote, "cast a gloom of trouble over a quiet and happy home, and from here began a change that altered the course of my life."[27]

# "A New Existence"
## Gainesville

In the fall of 1845, a horse-drawn wagon carried Wesley, his mother Elizabeth, and his two youngest sisters, Mary and Juliett, with all their belongings on the arduous trip along the dirt roads from Marshall County, Tennessee, to Gainesville, Alabama. Elizabeth had reluctantly concluded that since they were not able to operate the Tennessee farm, they had no choice but to sell it and move back to Alabama. There they would live with her daughter Angeline and her husband, Chapin Frost, who had offered them shelter. Wesley's other married sisters, Elizabeth Seely and Matilda Tureman, were also living in Gainesville. The plan, as Wesley later related, was that the family members would "all be together and our interests looked after." What Wesley did not know was that the 250-mile trip would end in a totally new world, completely alien to what he had known before.[1]

The town of Gainesville was a humming commercial mart with a population of about two thousand. It was a new town that had been established in Sumter County in 1832, only thirteen years earlier. Gainesville was situated on the Tombigbee River, just east of Alabama's border with Mississippi, in an area that was part of the Choctaws' traditional territory. Following the Treaty of Dancing Rabbit Creek in 1830, the federal government removed most of the Choctaw to Indian Territory, in present-day Oklahoma.[2] At that time, white settlers began flooding into the area and established the town of Gainesville.

Wesley had never lived in a town before. He was awed by the many beautiful residences with lawns and yards and, as he later said, "everything betokening refinement and taste." Gainesville had two hotels, one of which was a large, four-story building. It had a sawmill that provided the lumber that the town and surrounding areas required. A flour mill ran day and night to fill the area's needs. From Gainesville, a steamboat ran to Mobile, and since there were not yet any railroads, Gainesville served as a commercial center for all of middle-east Mississippi as well as the surrounding Alabama counties. Immense cotton sheds and warehouses lined the river. Loads of cotton were shipped down to Mobile, with goods shipped back to Gainesville, then taken by wagon to the surrounding areas.

All the men in town were in some kind of business. Wesley's brother-in-law Zachariah Tureman ran a blacksmith shop, his brother-in-law Chapin Frost a wagon shop, and his brother-in-law Amariah Seely a carpenter shop. Doctors, lawyers, ministers, and merchants had offices or stores in the town. As Wesley characterized them: "The population was made up of Virginians, North Carolinians and Yankees, the Yankees being the principal merchants and capitalists; the Carolinians were the doctors, lawyers and speculators;

and the Virginians—with a few exceptions—were the gentlemanly loafing class."[3]

What Wesley was describing, and what he would later elaborate on in relating his pre–Civil War life in Alabama, was the developing Southern middle class, distinct from the planter class, the yeoman farmers, and the slaves. Some had migrated from the North and retained their Northern values; most connected to Northern culture in ways that included magazine and newspaper subscriptions. As a group, they believed in the importance of education as a necessary avenue to advancement and were largely responsible for Alabama's new public education system. They participated in cultural organizations, such as literary and debating societies, and in the reform movements of the day, seeking, for example, to outlaw dueling. While still accepting the institution of slavery, they did not share the large slaveholders' ideology of patriarchy and honor but had values more in line with the Northern middle class. Wesley and his family members represented this emerging middle class.[4]

The people of Gainesville greatly perplexed Wesley. They were all strangers to him but, more importantly, as he said, "their ways and manners were stranger than their faces." These, he wrote, were "about as different from those that I had been used to as are the people and manner of Texas to those of France." In Tennessee, people grew or made everything they ate or wore and had an unpretentious lifestyle, helping their neighbors whenever needed. "Work was honorable and idleness was dishonorable," he explained.[5] Although most farmers in Tennessee held a few slaves, the owners and their sons all worked, as did their wives and daughters. Wesley asserted, "A man's standing and importance was not in the ratio of the slaves that he had. . . . White women did not think it beneath their importance to cook and to do any other household work that needed their attention."[6]

Wesley's family had had at least one slave, a black woman Wesley referred to as "Aunt Nancy." Aunt Nancy worked with his mother and sisters preparing food in the kitchen or carding—spinning and weaving cotton and wool—and making clothing. Wesley considered Aunt Nancy a member of the family, a person he treated with the respect due to an older woman. Perhaps because Nancy was the family's only slave, he easily saw her humanity and did not regard her merely as part of the "labor force." He referred to her death in 1835 as "a death in the family."

As loved as she might have been, Nancy was, nonetheless, a slave who had no say in her situation. Wesley never seemed to question the institution of slavery or to see the moral issue in owning another person, regardless of how well the person was treated or included in the family. He knew that his ancestors were "upper middle class" people who had held slaves and yet had considered themselves to be "liberty loving and life defending people."[7] He did not see the contradiction between a belief in liberty and the practice of keeping people in bondage. Wesley shared this moral blindness with his ancestors and with most of the South at the time.

Later dubbed the Black Belt, the Gainesville area was fertile farmland covered with many large cotton plantations. The plantations were worked by gangs of slaves, numbering anywhere from fifteen to fifteen hundred, and operated by overseers who ran the farm business for the plantation owners. The plantation owners' only interest, as far as Wesley could see, was "to buy more negroes, with which to raise more cotton, with which they could buy more negroes, for the number of negroes a man owned was a large factor in his importance; and what was true about Gainesville was the same from Virginia to Louisiana, in all of the rich cotton producing lands, Tennessee and Kentucky excepted, and continued such until the Civil War."[8]

The black slaves who worked the plantations outnumbered the white residents about twenty to one and lived in small villages of crude cabins. The plantation owners and their families lived on the plantations themselves in what Wesley noted were "large and fine dwellings and grounds . . . with fine carriages and matched horses, with every convenience and luxury; and a pack of trained hounds for they loved the chase of fox and wild-cat and deer and it was their chief sport."[9] They sent their daughters to be educated at the best female colleges and their sons to the universities. Their sons, according to Wesley, usually became "the lawyers or loafers of the towns, and were politicians, and were generally our law makers in Legislature and Congress. Their political views were the echoes of the politics of their fathers and of their communities, for the planters controlled the country in laws and government."

Wesley found the large slave owners to be "a pretentious aristocracy" that "considered themselves a 'caste' above all others, and regarded manual labor as servile and degrading." They treated the local townspeople, such as Wesley's brothers-in-law, all men who worked with their hands, as "poor white trash." Their "deportment toward those who worked was lordly and dictatorial, or patronizing and they expected and demanded, entire obedience—from this class to their views of government, and to the color of their political opinions . . . and even the negroes were so much affected with the feelings of their masters that they denominated all who didn't own a gang of negroes as 'Poor White Trash.'"[10]

Alabama, as Wesley described it, was "a new existence. . . . I had never been used to seeing idlers, men or women, boys or girls, dependent upon servants to do everything; but here the town and country was full of young and old men who disdained work as unbecoming to a gentleman." Wesley felt the planters had a contempt for the towns, seeing them only "as a place to meet and talk politics, and arrange their plans for filling political offices."[11]

With Elisha's death, Wesley's family members had lost the respected position accorded them in Tennessee as the family of the beloved and admired minister. They had also lost their secure financial situation. Wesley's uncle, Thomas Blackwell, who owned property near the family's Tennessee farm, had taken over the sale of the farm and eventually found a buyer. But a financial panic had wracked the country in 1837, and as late as the mid-1840s, land prices, wages, and profits were still down. Thomas sold the land for much less than Wesley's father, Elisha, had paid for it, but it was apparently all it would command during that economically depressed time. A dismayed Elizabeth told her brother that although she and Elisha had worked hard all their lives, they had "squandered their money and their hard work."[12]

Elizabeth did not immediately receive the money from the buyer, Mr. Holt, and she worried how to go about getting it. She did not want to send sixteen-year-old Wesley back on what would be a hard and expensive trip. Yet she worried that Mr. Holt did not intend to get the money to her. Finally, a Methodist minister colleague of Elisha's offered to bring Elizabeth the money on his way to the annual Methodist conference in Memphis. After this, her only income came from the Methodist Conference, which was obligated to pay Elizabeth a dower, or pension, every year until she died.[13]

Elizabeth enrolled fourteen-year-old Juliett in the Female Academy in Gainesville, a school for twenty girls that had opened in 1844, the previous fall. It was partly supported by public money, and Elizabeth paid an annual subscription of about $7.50. Public schools were just being established in Alabama at the time.[14] Elizabeth wanted Wesley to go to the public school for the year and a half left before he aged out at eighteen and would no longer qualify for the free education.

Wesley enjoyed his time in the high school for boys and had many fond memories of it. Initially, he felt at a disadvantage to the other boys, for they had benefited from what he perceived to be the best schools and teachers while he had been homeschooled and taught the old-field-school curriculum. But he found, as he later wrote, that his "strict home training" and "the thorough work done and required in the Old Field Schools" held him in good stead: "I not only held my own as an equal but in several instances went before any of them in honors." And, not surprisingly, in an age when the teachers used the switch freely to maintain discipline, he never got a whipping. "This I attribute to the teachers never seeing me idle, and that I always knew my lessons, I was so particular about this that I would not join play until I knew my lesson—the first that would come up after playtime; nor did I use profane or vulgar language, for I had been taught better at home; nor was I ever seen in 'fusses' or quarrels with other boys, and the consequence was that I had many friends and few enemies."[15]

Wesley joined a debating society that the older high school boys and the town's young men were just forming. This was an opportunity, he thought, to gain knowledge of the subjects being debated, develop his thinking and reasoning skills, and improve his public speaking. The society held weekly meetings to debate questions of importance. Once a month they held a formal debate, which was well attended by the public, especially by the town's lawyers, doctors, and ministers. As Wesley later recalled, "It was stimulant that incited in me a thirst for knowledge of everything that enters in the making of politics, morals and civil life, and I used everything that I could get hold of that would be a means of getting such knowledge."[16] He gained a reputation for being an excellent speaker and debater, one who, with a strong, deep voice, used logic and thoughtful arguments, rather than flowery speech or emotional appeals, to make his points.

While going to school, Wesley worked with his brothers-in-law whenever possible, helping Chapin to build and repair wagons or assisting Amariah with carpentry work. Their businesses were struggling in the depressed economy, and Chapin was giving some thought to selling out and going to the newly annexed state of Texas. Both men eventually decided to move their businesses to the nearby town of Livingston, the county seat, hoping to fare better. Elizabeth and Juliett moved with them, leaving sixteen-year-old Wesley, as he said, "bereft of mother's advice and encouragement." But he did not want to interrupt his schooling, so he remained in Gainesville. He had particularly enjoyed the construction work he had done with Amariah and concluded that he had a natural talent for designing and building. After finishing high school, he approached a highly regarded architect in town, Evan Allen, and asked to be taken on as an apprentice.[17]

In those days, before the Civil War, most architects were also contractors and were called "master builders." They would have an office where they did architectural drawings and design work, and a carpenter shop where they employed the workmen who carried out the designs developed for clients. Many builders relied on pattern books, such as the ones published by New England architect Benjamin Asher. His books included drawings of plans for houses, churches, and even courthouses, with examples of fireplace mantels, moldings, cornices, and window and door trims. His book *The Architect or Practical House Carpenter*, published in 1830, helped facilitate the shift away from building in the Federalist style, popular in the early nineteenth century, to the Greek Revival style that came to dominate pre–Civil War architecture.[18]

Allen already had an apprentice working and learning carpentry, but Wesley wanted to be taught designing and drawing as well as construction. He convinced Allen to place him in the office where he could learn everything. Wesley would work, as he recalled later, "for three years at six dollars a month for the first year, twelve the second and eighteen the third—he to board and lodge me and to have my washing done. . . . His wife was a southern woman, and was as kind to me as she could have been to a brother."[19]

The apprenticeship was a perfect situation for Wesley. Allen, Wesley noted, "was from Boston, was skilled and posted in his profession and in all public matters, was well educated and cultured with an air of refinement in all he said or did, and had the respect and confidence of all who knew him." For the three years Wesley worked for him, he felt Allen did all he had promised and helped him gain the technical and mathematical knowledge needed for a successful career. Allen taught him how to draw plans and write clear specifications, how to estimate the cost of construction, how to run an office, how to hire and manage carpenters, and how to deal with clients. He also helped Wesley develop his artistic abilities with an eye for the beautiful. Wesley stayed with Allen an extra year to gain additional skills. When he left Gainesville in 1851, he was confident that he was prepared for the responsibility of designing and constructing quality buildings. He was ready to go out into the world and hang up his shingle as a master builder.[20]

# "Setting up in Business"

## Livingston

In November 1851, Wesley left Gainesville and went to nearby Livingston, planning to set himself up in business and begin his career as a master builder. Like Gainesville, Livingston was a town situated in traditional Choctaw territory, taken from the Native Americans with the Treaty of Dancing Rabbit Creek. In 1833, a commission formed to organize Sumter County designated Livingston the county seat and named it after then Secretary of State Edward Livingston. When Wesley arrived, it was a small, picturesque village of about seven hundred people, with well-kept homes, picket fences, and stone-paved streets. Set in a predominantly rural area, Livingston lacked the commercial interests that dominated Gainesville. The town also lacked the involvement of plantation owners in its civic affairs, as the planters did not do business in Livingston. The few black slaves in town either worked at various trades in the shops or were servants in homes. The town had several newspapers and four schools, including the Presbyterian-supported Livingston Female Academy. The town had also just replaced its first courthouse, which was built of logs, with a frame Federalist building.

Wesley had a joyful reunion with his mother and his sisters Juliett, Angeline, and Elizabeth. With all his older sisters now married, including Mary, who had recently wed a prominent Gainesville merchant, his mother and Juliett were the two remaining women he felt an obligation to look after. Juliett was a student at the Livingston Female Academy, which offered both secondary education and teacher training.[1]

Wesley was only in Livingston a short time before he was introduced to Sarah Moffitt, a friend of Juliett's who also attended the academy. Sarah seemed to be a perfect match for Wesley. The pretty young woman was studying English literature at a time when Romanticism was sweeping across the country, replacing Enlightenment classicism in literature, music, art, and architecture. The Romantic movement emphasized an appreciation of the natural world, both as a reflection of the Divine and as being more desirable than the emerging urban industrial society. In contrast to the Enlightenment's focus on reason, Romanticism embraced emotion as an authentic source of aesthetic experience.

In one of her college classes, Sarah wrote a short paper titled "Country Life," in which she extolled, with the great enthusiasm of a college sophomore, the ideals of Romanticism:

"God is seen in brooks and trees,
Is heard in wind and sighing breeze."

"As the result of the above, is it not natural that the country, where such things are seen and heard, should be the home for the soul; the weary-hearted and careworn find refuge from the chimneys and smoke and crowded streets of the city." The country represented peaceful serenity. In contrast, she wrote, "The great wicked city has to answer for many a broken-hearted mother, who has seen her son, once so pure and care-free, gradually descend the devil's winding stair until he stands on the very brink of an awful precipice." Reflecting the ideals of the Romantic poets William Wordsworth, William Blake, and John Keats, Sarah argued that while the "haughty citizens" of the city might be able to go hear operatic singing, of which they could "scarcely understand a word," they would "never know what it is to hear the warbling of a bird which even to the cultivated ear is the most perfect music in the world."[2]

Sarah was completely and thoroughly a Romantic. She wrote poetry and verse about the beauty of the countryside. She enjoyed reading, analyzing, and discussing literature. Wesley was equally a Romantic, loving poetry and unafraid of expressing his emotions. Throughout his life, he often included small bits of poetry in his letters, mostly impromptu poems with imperfect rhyme and meter but with poetic thoughts that appealed to his ear and heart. He seems to have found pleasure in reading and listening to others speak, seeing how they crafted their ideas and how they used words to effectively deliver their messages.

Sarah and Wesley frequently discussed books and articles. Both had read *The Tower of London*, a novel by William Harrison Ainsworth serially published in 1840. The book is a historical romance that follows Lady Jane Grey from her reign as Queen of England to her execution in the Tower of London. Sarah wrote to Wesley, "I have read the 'Tower of London' and like it very much. At some portions of it I laughed outright but at others was almost affected to tears. The author confined himself pretty closely to facts but I think he cast a lighter shade upon Mary's character and a darker one upon Elizabeth's than historians generally have done. His description of Lady Jane Gray corresponds nearly exactly with that of all other writers with whom I am acquainted."[3] Such correspondence, exchanging ideas about differing literary interpretations of British royalty, was probably unusual for young lovers in the 1850s.

For a Christmas gift, Wesley gave Sarah a subscription to *Peterson's Magazine*, a periodical consisting of short literary pieces that began publication in the early 1840s. "It has some beautiful pieces," he told Sarah. "'May among the Mountains' is truly beautiful. Peterson's descriptions are very natural and his feelings exhibit the true lover of nature."[4] The magazine delighted Sarah, who read all the stories and found them "most excellent."[5] Sarah even wrote several short stories of the type found in *Peterson's*: "The Transplanting of

Bluegrass" and "The Least of These."[6] Whether Sarah ever submitted any of her stories for publication is not known.

Wesley and Sarah's relationship very quickly became serious. On Christmas Day 1851, they took a carriage to Gainesville to celebrate the holiday with his family there.[7] Before long, Wesley had, as he later said, "expressed his sentiments" to her and she had reciprocated them. After graduating with first honors in 1852, Sarah made plans to return home to Memphis. Her parents, Dr. L. H. Moffitt and Mary Hunt, were natives of North Carolina but had moved to Memphis, where her father practiced medicine. Wesley decided to accompany her on the stagecoach both to provide protection for her on the journey and to meet her family. It was a long trip, about 250 miles, over roads in varying, mostly poor condition.

The visit in Memphis was cordial. Wesley was undoubtedly nervous meeting Sarah's family, which included her sister, Bet, and her brothers Romulus and Zan, or Alexander—both popular names during this period of the Greek Revival. Bet later confided to Sarah that she found Wesley to be "the gravest, saddest, and most melancholy looking man" she ever saw. Despite Bet's evaluation, the family was favorably impressed with Wesley, and, as Sarah later related to him, "Ma and Bet speak of you every day and in the most flattering manner."[8] Indeed, the sparks between Wesley and Sarah were so obvious that Bet and her mother "guessed the whole truth" the day Wesley left. Sarah did not deny it.[9]

When Wesley left Memphis to return to Livingston, he stopped at his Uncle Armstead's farm in Marshall County, Mississippi, where he was an admittedly poor, uncommunicative guest. At Uncle Armstead's, he wrote Sarah that he did "not feel like engaging in conversation with anyone, but rather muse with my own thoughts as it is more pleasant to me to look at those places that are eloquent with your memory than to enjoy the company of the world."[10]

Wesley was desperately in love with Sarah. "Never upon earth did I attempt to write with such mixed feelings of joy and sorrow, pleasure and pain: joy—that I have the strength and inclination to write to you, and pleasure to have the privilege, but sorrow to have to substitute a letter for presence. I have parted with many friends in my life, old ones and tried long, but never in the world did I experience the same feelings, upon any occasion whatever, that I did when I bid you farewell. Sarah it may be unmanly to weep, if so I cannot help it—for I wept—like a child, and am only glad that I love you well enough for it to convulse the fountain of my feelings when I part with you."[11]

When Wesley arrived back in Livingston, he still wanted to be with his thoughts of Sarah, who was constantly on his mind, and in those places that were alive with her memory. The evening he returned, as he told Sarah, he walked to a place on the river where he had sat with her, "the spot that will always be hallowed to me, and lingered at least two hours, spellbound, wrapt in my own sad thoughts. . . . I remembered those promenades we used to delight in so much; your own merry voice—it still rings in my ears, and sat down pensive and lonely." The following evening, he strolled to a spot on the river where they had climbed up the steep banks to look out over the water and enjoy the exquisite scenery beyond. That night, as Wesley related: "The broad faced moon rode high, and lent a new lustre to the scene, its mild beams played with sylph-like modesty upon the water, and the evening star—constancy, shone with its original beauty above the horizon, until the whole vision before me seemed an enchantment." Wesley confessed, "Sarah my destiny is fixed—with you I am happy, away from you I am wretched, beyond the power of words to tell, you are my only hope, my only care. Your likeness is now before, and I gaze upon it with new delight—'tis my only solace. . . . In love, and until I see you, I remain in anguish your own devoted Wesley."[12]

A letter from Sarah did not arrive for almost seven weeks. Wesley wrote her another letter, then a third. A letter from Sarah arrived for Angeline and another for Wesley's niece Mary Tureman.[13] Wesley was almost beside himself with anxiety. "I can neither think of my business nor pursue my studies, but pass silently along with all thought, and sense, feeling and affection turned towards you . . . for you know, or if you do not, let me assure you, that you are my life, my vital breath, that one line from you is more to me than the flattering smile of all the world. . . . The same sentiments that I expressed to you five months ago, I still retain. . . , and what would I not sacrifice to see you; 'I miss your merry voice, I miss your pleasant smile.' I miss you at noon and at evening, those hours that have been so dear to me. I miss you every where and whatever I gaze upon seems but the monument of my desolation." He concluded: "Sarah read this letter carefully and closely, for it contains my sentiments faintly expressed, and remember they are from your own lonely and pensive Wesley."[14] One can only hope he was not serious about calling his words a "faint expression."

Three weeks later, when he received two letters from Sarah, Wesley joyfully concluded that the heavy rains and resulting muddy roads had caused the delayed letters, not a change of heart. "I was extremely gratified to receive them, and hear once more from my Sarah. I read them and reread them a hundred times, because they expressed a sentiment that is dearer to me than life, and from one that is more to me than all earth besides."[15] Sarah told him that apparently two of her letters had been lost. In them, she had relayed that he had been well received by all members of her family. Her mother and sister had even wept at his departure. Her father had no objections to Sarah receiving and answering letters from Wesley. "You know that in thought and sentiment I am still the same."[16]

Wesley had made plans to take college classes in the winter of 1852 but before long told Sarah that, regrettably, it was not going to be possible. The college would not deviate from its policy of having students begin in September, not in midyear.[17] He remained upset about it for some time. He may have thought he was not good enough for her without attaining the same level of education that she had; perhaps he thought her parents might object to a marriage because of it. Or, more likely, he saw college as an opportunity to improve his mind and acquaint himself with new ideas. "I have no doubt but my failure in going to college this winter did disappoint you. I know it did, for it disappointed me, and when I learned for certain that I could not go, it gave me anguish of spirit to inform you of it."[18]

Numerous festive parties were held in Livingston that winter, but a melancholy Wesley chose to stay in, reading, studying, and writing to Sarah. He was reading the classics and had finished *Cicero's Orations*, a Latin text then read in college classes "and reading it," he said, "with all of the facility of a true Latin." He told Sarah, "The memory of thee makes labour sweet, and study a pleasure."[19] He declined invitations to the weddings of three friends, not expecting "any pleasure or enjoyment" from them without Sarah.[20] He preferred to walk and visit those places that he and Sarah had frequented together, constantly lost in his thoughts of her.

Wesley's mother noticed her son's pensiveness and questioned him several times.[21] At first he evaded her questions. He knew she had some reservations about Sarah since the Dodsons were Methodist and Sarah's family was Irish Catholic.[22] Then she took him by the hand and asked him to "tell her as an only son" if he and Sarah were engaged to be married. As Wesley relayed to Sarah, he "candidly told her all and asked what she thought of it. She said she had nothing to say against it and if I thought it was for the best, she was perfectly reconciled as my happiness would afford her pleasure."[23]

In Memphis, Sarah also avoided the festive gatherings and was even sorry when guests came to the house. She had "not the slightest inclination" to visit with them,[24] preferring to be alone with her thoughts about Wesley. Her greatest pleasure came from talking to her mother and Bet about him, "a subject always interesting" to Sarah. With them, she relived all of the wonderful times she and Wesley had spent together and contemplated what their future might hold. She had told her father of Wesley's intentions and gained his approval for another visit "as soon as it suits your convenience."[25]

In late February, Sarah relayed to Wesley the startling news that on the first of May the Moffitts were leaving Memphis and migrating to Texas. "Pa says he can never make anything here and is determined to leave and ma and Bet say the same." The family had "two pretty good teams" of horses and planned to pack up their belongings and "travel the whole distance overland." Nothing would delay the departure date unless it was impossible to cross the swampy areas at that time of year. Sarah knew a trip to Memphis would be expensive and inconvenient for Wesley. Nonetheless, she asked if he could come and spend three weeks with her before she left for Texas.[26]

The receipt of Sarah's letter left Wesley "troubled, restless, uneasy, and perplexed at the thought" of her moving further away. "Nothing that I can do," he wrote, "will relieve the anxieties of my mind." He implored Sarah, "If you know how well I love you, I know that you will give me your hand without hesitation, rather than we should part again. . . . Tell me that when we meet it shall be not to part again, and make your devoted Wesley the happiest man upon earth will you!"[27] After three long weeks of what he deemed "unuterable suspense,"[28] Wesley heard from Sarah. Written hastily so that it would reach Wesley before he left Livingston, her short reply said, "I wish that I could reply to it as you desire but I cannot. I can tell you nothing more until I see you. . . . Come."[29]

Although Wesley had lots of work and was doing it as fast as possible, he had to go to Sarah.[30] He abandoned whatever construction projects he had under contract, perhaps trusting his brother-in-law Amariah to oversee his workers, or perhaps leaving dismayed clients awaiting their completed designs. Four long days of riding in a stagecoach over bumpy, poorly maintained roads, "the worst road you ever saw or imagined of,"[31] brought Wesley to Holly Springs, Mississippi, not far from his Uncle Armstead's farm. He stopped to see his uncle, which he felt obliged to do, and probably appeared once again as a morose young man. From Holly Springs, he caught what he called "the train of cars" to Memphis. He was anxious about the visit and confessed to not having "one moments peace of mind" since receiving Sarah's letter.[32] Wesley could not bear for Sarah to go so far away. Because of his responsibility for his mother and sister Juliett in Livingston, Wesley was not in a position to go with the Moffitts to Texas.

Whatever kept Sarah from accepting Wesley's initial marriage proposal is unknown, but two weeks after he arrived in Memphis, on April 19, 1853, he and Sarah were married. A few of his family were present at his wedding. His cousin Dillingham, Uncle Armstead's son, was there.[33] At the time, Dillingham was living in Collierville, Tennessee, about thirty miles from Memphis. Wesley's Uncle Armstead and his wife, Nancy Creel, were probably there, for

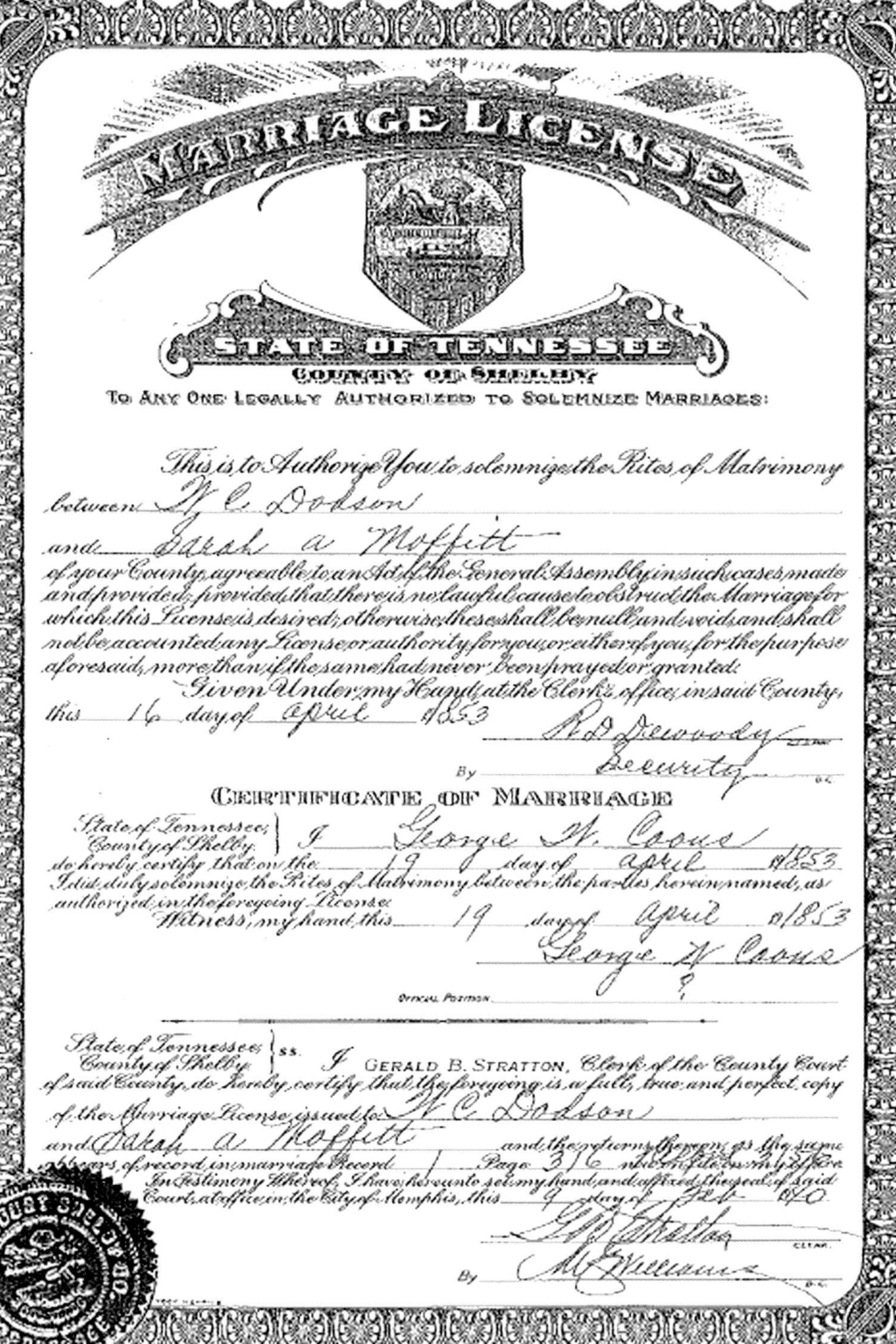
MARRIAGE LICENSE

STATE OF TENNESSEE

COUNTY OF SHELBY

TO ANY ONE LEGALLY AUTHORIZED TO SOLEMNIZE MARRIAGES:

This is to Authorize You to solemnize the Rites of Matrimony between W C Dodson and Sarah A Moffitt of your County, agreeable to an Act of the General Assembly in such cases made and provided; provided that there is no lawful cause to obstruct the Marriage for which this License is desired; otherwise these shall be null and void, and shall not be accounted any License or authority for you or either of you, for the purpose aforesaid, more than if the same had never been prayed or granted.

Given Under my Hand at the Clerk's office, in said County, this 16 day of April 1853

R D Dewoody

By Security

CERTIFICATE OF MARRIAGE

State of Tennessee,
County of Shelby.

I George W. Coons do hereby certify that on the 19 day of April 1853 I did duly solemnize the Rites of Matrimony between the parties herein named, as authorized in the foregoing License.

Witness, my hand, this 19 day of April 1853

George W Coons

Official Position

State of Tennessee,
County of Shelby. ss.

I GERALD B. STRATTON, Clerk of the County Court of said County, do hereby certify that the foregoing is a full, true and perfect copy of the Marriage License issued to W C Dodson and Sarah A Moffitt and the returns thereon as the same appears of record in marriage Record 1 Page 316 now on file in my office.

In Testimony Whereof, I have hereunto set my hand, and affixed the seal of said Court, at office in the City of Memphis, this 9 day of Feb 1940

G B Stratton
Clerk

By M Williams
D.C.

The marriage license granted to W. C. Dodson and Sarah A. Moffitt. Credit: The family of Mary Alice Hall.

Wesley Clark Dodson in his wedding attire, 1853. Credit: Courtesy of the Texas Collection, Baylor University.

Sarah Moffit. Credit: The family of Mary Alice Hall.

Armstead regularly traveled to Memphis from his farm in nearby Marshall County, Mississippi.[34]

After their wedding, Wesley and Sarah returned to Livingston. Wesley was, as he later wrote, "about as happy as a young man could be." He built himself a house next door to his brother-in-law Amariah, where Wesley's mother and his sister Juliett also lived.[35] Wesley and Sarah began attending the Presbyterian church in Livingston. Sarah taught at the Livingston Female Academy, and as Wesley proudly noted, she "had an aptitude for imparting instruction that I have never known surpassed."[36] Soon she was appointed assistant to the principal of the academy, a position she held for the next twelve years.

**THE MASTER BUILDER**

Before his marriage, Wesley had already opened a carpenter's shop, hired help, and begun working as a master builder. At first, it was hard to get business in Livingston. As he later recalled, he had to overcome numerous obstacles. For one, the wealthy townsmen felt that manual work done by white men had minimal value since slaves could do the same work, an attitude that clearly irritated Wesley. Such men generally thought that "about a dollar and a half (per day) for a carpenter, or other skilled labor, was as much as one was worth." Wesley had seen Evan Allen face the same attitude in Gainesville and had learned how best to counter it. He could "beat the proprietor at intelligent estimating" and "usually get about what the work was worth."

Another obstacle was the established Livingston architect, who Wesley described as "an old Yankee architect and contractor—not much architect—who disparaged me all he could with the idea that no one raised in the south knew anything about building, especially a young fledgling without experience." Wesley was twenty-two. His competitor was a Methodist with strong connections to that community. He had been working in the town for about ten years and had built the courthouse and jail, done all the county work, and become well-established in the community. He did his building with a crew of three or four black slaves that he had inherited, and he "did work at prices that would ruin a man who had to hire men."[37]

But Wesley felt he had an edge over the competition. For one, he had a talent for drawing the "plans of the buildings contemplated, with descriptive specifications, all so plain, which he [the Yankee contractor] could not do intelligently."[38] Wesley's ability to show a prospective client what his finished building would look like gave him an advantage.

Second, Wesley's interest in politics helped him. Americans in this period had a healthy interest in government and politics. Citizens participated in the political process, became loyal to their political party, and voted in record numbers. They attended weekly or monthly gatherings where people engaged in heated debates on issues such as American nationalism, political representation, and industrial modernization. The debates were both a form of entertainment and an opportunity for intellectual engagement. Wesley enjoyed participating in such debates. As he later wrote: "I would make speeches for my party. I had studied elocution, and if I had nothing interesting to say, I would make it interesting by the manner in which I presented it. My voice—then—was as clear as a bell, was strong and penetrating, and my enunciation perfect and I could control its modulations at will, so that I could hold my own with able men."

The Spence-Moon house, built for planter James Spence.
Credit: RuralSWAlabama.org.

Third, Wesley's interest in what he called the "public welfare of the town" and its "improvements and betterments" led to his being elected an alderman. At that time, the town's citizens were considering drilling an artesian well, and Wesley promised to complete this project.[39] Beginning in 1854, an old blind mule was hitched up to pull an auger, day in and day out, boring down until it reached an artesian aquifer in 1857. The flowing mineral water was perceived to have medicinal value. Because of the well, Livingston gained a reputation as a health spa,[40] and Wesley became known by all the town's influential people.

In the early 1850s, the Whigs held the presidency with Zachary Taylor and his successor Millard Fillmore. At the time, the two major parties, the Whigs and the Democrats, competed on relatively equal footing in most parts of the country. In Sumter County, however, the Democrats controlled power. The cotton interests were solidly Democratic because of the party's position on supporting the aggressive expansion of slavery and its opposition to reformers, especially anti-slavery advocates, who sought to use government to effect moral reform. The middle class, with its businessmen and professionals, was more likely to align with the Whig Party, which sought government involvement in promoting the economy, expanding banking, easing credit, undertaking internal improvements, and finding funding for public education. While Whigs were willing to seek legislation to outlaw the practice of dueling, which they saw as barbaric, they were not anxious to promote any anti-slavery legislation. Many of them were small slaveholders themselves. Wesley identified more with the Whigs' positions, especially on moral betterment and internal improvements, although, as he said, he stood primarily in opposition to what he saw as "incompetence and stupidity."[41]

The country increasingly was dividing along sectional lines, especially regarding the issue of the expansion of slavery into the territories. New parties such as the Free-Soilers, the anti-slavery Republicans, and the Know-Nothings appeared. The Know-Nothings, formally the American Party, were a primarily anti-Catholic, anti-immigrant, and xenophobic nativist movement. When the Know-Nothings organized in 1854, they offered the first real opposition to the Democrats in Sumter County. Wesley observed their candidates running as Independents and generally trouncing the entrenched Democratic incumbents. "These were lively times," Wesley recalled, "and created much fun for everybody except the democrats, who looked as foolish as a duck hit on the head and didn't know what did it. . . .The political troubles which terminated in our Civil War were getting warmer every day, and entered largely into every political campaign since 1850, and added much to the intensity of excitement."[42]

Wesley worked hard at his business and before long could claim to have all the new work contracts in Livingston.[43] Although there are no records of his designs from this period, he probably built in the Greek Revival style. The style's symmetrical buildings featured Doric columns, pediments, and architectural details that recalled the glory of ancient Greek democracy and appealed to Southerners in the era of Jacksonian democracy.[44]

By 1860, Wesley was a master builder, designing and constructing houses and employing four young carpenters, all of whom boarded at his house. Wesley was prosperous, well-respected, and actively involved in contributing to his church and community. By this time, Sarah and Wesley had a five-year-old son, Frank Moffitt, who was born in 1855. Another son, Robert Wesley, was born in 1857 but died in 1859. Wesley and Sarah's daughter, Mary Elizabeth, or Mollie Bet, was born in 1860. The family had two house slaves, an eighteen-year-old boy and a twenty-seven-year-old woman, who helped care for the children and the house.[45] Wesley was still looking after his mother and Juliett, who lived next door with his sister Elizabeth and her husband, Amariah.[46]

The sectional issues that had been tearing the country apart came to a head during the presidential election of 1860, with the candidates of four parties contending. Lincoln was elected with 180 electoral votes but without a single Southern electoral vote. The South's secession from the Union soon followed, bringing with it the start of the Civil War and an end to Wesley's happy life in Livingston.

# "Scenes of Strife"
## The Civil War

The outbreak of the war forced Wesley to abandon his career in architecture. On March 27, 1862, almost a year into the war, Wesley joined a company of soldiers being organized in Sumter County.[1] Most of the talk in Livingston then was that the war would be short and that the Rebels would soundly and swiftly defeat the Yankees. When he enlisted, Wesley could not have imagined that the war would keep him away from home for over three years. He could not have anticipated that the war would destroy the life he had built for himself nor that he and his family would become refugees fleeing the devastation of the war-torn South. Neither could he have foreseen that the war would leave him partly crippled, facing the daunting task of starting completely over.

Wesley never spelled out his reasons for enlisting. Clearly he had no interest in protecting what he called the "gentlemanly loafing class" of slaveholders, who disdainfully regarded middle-class people such as himself as doing "servile and degrading" manual labor.[2] Given his gentle temperament, it is unlikely Wesley was caught up in the thrill of going into battle to drive out the Yankees. He could have been caught up in the rhetoric that compared the looming struggle to the American colonists' fight against the British. The secessionists argued that the South was fighting for its rights and liberties against the tyrannical North and for the principles of constitutional liberty and self-government. Wesley may have believed that the Southern states had the right to secede from the Union that had come to be dominated by the Northern states. Or he may have opposed secession, as many of the Southern middle class did, but felt pressured to do what everyone else was doing, lest his manliness be called into question. Regardless of Wesley's feelings prior to enlisting, once the war began, his sense of honor and duty—the same duty that called on him to protect his mother and his sisters—led him to protect his homeland and, once in the military, to support his comrades in battle.[3]

Soon after he enlisted, his company was ordered to a military camp about five miles from Mobile, Alabama, at the Dog River Factory village. In its earlier life, the Dog River Factory had been a textile mill. The factory had burned in 1861, and the abandoned village transformed into a basic training facility for soldiers. The enlisted men found comfortable quarters in the factory workers' cottages while the officers were quartered in the former superintendent's house.[4] For several months, the men organized, drilled, and prepared for battle.

Wesley was with the company for less than three months when he received news from Sarah that their infant son Ernest Clark, a child he had held only once before leaving for Dog River, had died of a fever.[5] Wesley consoled his wife saying: "It was our Heavenly Father's will and it should be our daily

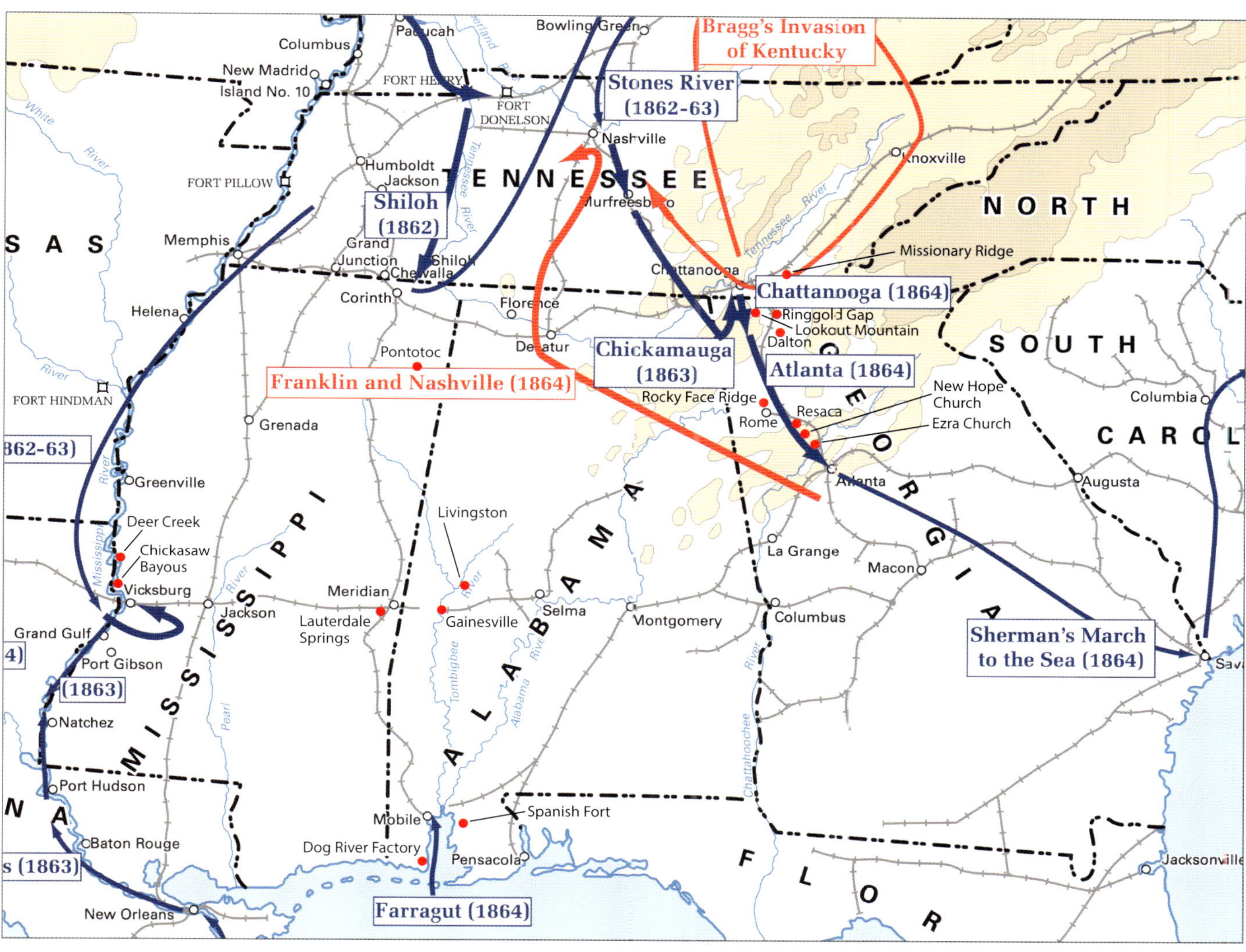


Civil War campaigns. Red dots indicate Wesley's locations during the war. Credit: Courtesy of the United States Military Academy, Department of History.

prayer: 'Thy will be done.' . . . Yes, I grieve more on your account than on little Ernest's: for he is saved, *eternally* Saved—freed from a life of sorrow and trouble. God has blessed him by taking him unto himself. We now have another tie to bind us to God and Heaven and another friend to welcome us when the Lord, through the riches of his grace, shall call us away and take us to himself. Do not dear wife lay it to heart but let your loss be blessed with the recollection that it is his eternal gain. And although we cannot see it—yet we know it is best—for God did it."[6] A week later, Sarah wrote: "Mrs. Jones has just been here with her little babe. I have nursed it for her since Ernest's death."[7] It may have been a custom of the time, and Sarah might have found solace in helping another child to survive, but such a practice must have been difficult for a grieving mother.

In December 1862, Wesley's company was mustered in, ready to fight as Company C, 40th Alabama Regiment, Infantry. Wesley entered with the rank of private but soon became a commissary sergeant, responsible for procuring supplies for the company. This regiment became part of Gen. John C. Moore's brigade (later becoming Baker's Brigade) in Mississippi.[8]

### VICKSBURG CAMPAIGN

At the outbreak of the war, the Confederate forces controlled the Mississippi River. They held Vicksburg, a fortress city high above the Mississippi. From there, they could train their guns on any Union boats that tried to bring supplies up the river to Union forces. The Confederates could also stop Northern commerce heading south, attempting to reach the Gulf of Mexico.

During the week of Christmas 1862, Union Gen. William Tecumseh Sherman came down the Mississippi with about twenty thousand soldiers and a number of gunboats to Chickasaw Bayou, about five miles north of Vicksburg. There, as Wesley later wrote in a tribute to Confederate Gen. Stephen D. Lee, Sherman "turned up into the Yazoo and landed his army on the peninsula formed by the two rivers with the idea of turning our fortification at Vicksburg and capturing the city. . . . Lee—who was then a brigadier—was in command of the small force we had, some four or five thousand, to meet and repel the federal army, and this, under the command of Lee, we certainly did in three days' fighting, killing and wounding hundreds and taking nearly five hundred prisoners, and so thoroughly convincing Sherman of the serious mistake he had made that he got on his transports and left."[9]

In March 1863, Wesley's division spotted Union forces on Deer Creek about fifteen miles below Rolling Fork. Before his cavalry could engage them, Colonel Samuel W. Ferguson, commander of the 40th Alabama forces, learned that five Union gunboats had entered Deer Creek from Black Bayou and were rapidly making their way to Rolling Fork. He sent cavalry to fell trees across the river to block the advancing gunboats. Colonel Ferguson's men drove the retreating Union forces back, with his sharpshooters pressing them on the right bank and Wesley's 40th Alabama Regiment pressuring them on the left bank. By then, Confederate Gen. Winfield S. Featherston had arrived with two regiments and agreed to attack from the Union's rear. But no attack came all day. He promised to attack the next morning but again failed to do so. He even moved away from the Union forces. On the third day of fighting, when the Union forces discovered that General Featherston was behind them, "they halted in an open field," as Colonel Ferguson reported,

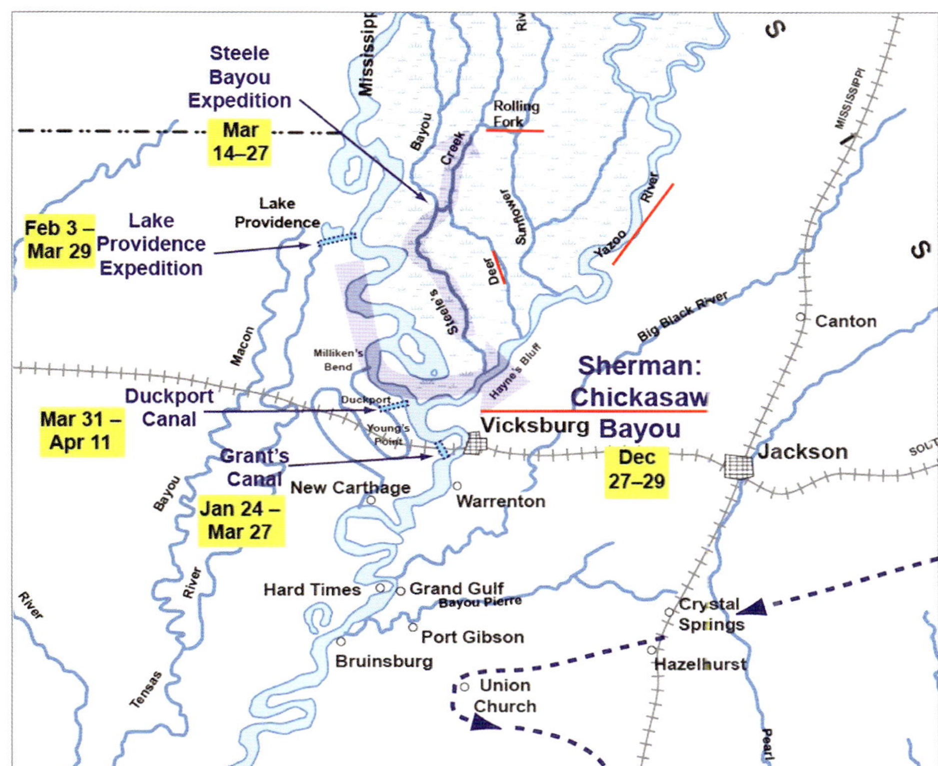


The Battles of Chickasaw Bayou and Deer Creek. Credit: Hal Jespersen.

"and fired furiously at everything which could be seen."[10] In the skirmish, Wesley was hit in the leg.

The Confederate forces had prevailed, successfully repulsing the Union. They captured nine boats and destroyed a large coal barge, but for Colonel Ferguson it wasn't enough. He believed "that all the boats should have been captured or destroyed by a vigorous attack and the infantry reinforcements destroyed in detail as they came up,"[11] and he blamed General Featherston for failing to attack as promised. This was the first battle in which Wesley witnessed inept Confederate generals failing to capitalize on their opportunities.

At this point in the campaign, seven companies under General Moore's brigade moved from Deer Creek to Vicksburg to help in its defense. Meanwhile, Union Gen. Ulysses S. Grant maneuvered his forces and surrounded the city. Throughout May and June, the Union bombarded Vicksburg, launching repeated attacks that were beaten back by the Confederates. By late June, however, the trapped Confederate forces faced two bad alternatives, as Wesley explained later: "surrender or attempt to cut out through the Federal Army . . . The condition of our army was such, caused by insufficient rations, sickness and loss of physical endurance, cramped up in the trenches with no exercise, with nervous strength exhausted from continual alarms and loss of sleep . . . [that] the men were too weak to undertake to attempt such a hazard." And so, on July 4, 1863, the Confederate forces surrendered and were taken prisoner.[12] Vicksburg was lost, and the Union forces gained control of the Mississippi. In doing so, the Union gained a supply line for their forces, reopened the Mississippi for Northern commerce to reach the Gulf of Mexico, and cut Texas and Arkansas off from the rest of the Confederacy.

Because Wesley's wounds from Deer Creek made him unfit for battle, he was detached from his regiment, assigned to now Brigadier General Ferguson's staff, and promoted to captain. During the fighting around Vicksburg, Wesley remained with Ferguson and three of Moore's companies. When Vicksburg was taken, Wesley, Ferguson, and his men escaped capture, swimming across rivers, lagoons, and backwaters and wading through the swamps until they reached Confederate Gen. Joseph E. Johnston's forces. In the last week of June 1863, Wesley accompanied Ferguson and his staff to Pontotoc in northern Mississippi, where they had orders to organize a cavalry brigade.[13]

### BATTLE OF CHICKAMAUGA

In the first week of September 1863, having recovered from his wounds, Wesley should have returned to his old brigade. But his company was still in the custody of the Union forces at Demopolis, Alabama. Since rejoining his own brigade was impossible, Wesley joined Gen. Mathew D. Ector's forces, which included the three companies of General Moore's brigade that had avoided capture. The troops boarded trains carrying them with Gen. William H.T. Walker's division toward Chickamauga in northwest Georgia, near the border of Tennessee. There the troops would join Gen. Braxton Bragg.[14]

At that time, General Bragg and his forces had been driven out of Chattanooga, Tennessee, and had fled south about fifteen miles into Georgia. The Confederate War Department was desperate for General Bragg to stop retreating and to assume the offensive. As Wesley later wrote, "Chattanooga was the strategic point in the Confederacy. If the enemy occupied and held it, it gave them middle and East Tennessee and North Alabama, and secured to them Kentucky as a permanent possession; and was the gateway to Atlanta and on through Georgia to the Atlantic, severing the Confederacy East and West from the Mississippi river to Savannah, and isolating the Southern tier of States from the middle and Northern tiers, and from Richmond, and severing the army of Northern Virginia and the army of Tennessee, the two pillars upon which rested the arch of the Confederacy."[15]

The Confederates knew how desperate the situation was. General Bragg ordered Gen. S. B. Buckner and all of his troops in East Tennessee to come south to Chickamauga. Gen. Joseph E. Johnston sent Gen. John C. Breckinridge's division back from Mississippi. General Lee sent Gen. James Longstreet and his two divisions from the Army of Northern Virginia. Confederate President Jefferson Davis sent Gen. D. H. Hill from Virginia, and General Walker and General Ector approached from the South with their troops. Now that General Bragg had over sixty-five thousand troops, commanded by twenty-four generals—an advantage over the sixty thousand Union forces—he seemed willing to advance.[16]

The site of the battle was the rolling, wooded land along Chickamauga Creek. The huge armies were spread out along the river. Wesley's company was assigned to fight under Generals Ector and Walker with the forces on the right wing. On September 18, the Confederate army received orders to cross West Chickamauga Creek at four points. Wesley's unit tried to cross at Alexander's Bridge but encountered Union cavalry armed with Spencer repeating rifles as well as four large guns. The brigade in front of Wesley's suffered over one hundred casualties against that firepower. Rather than continue their attempt to cross there, General Walker and his men withdrew, walked downstream a mile to the unguarded Lambert's Ford, and crossed Chickamauga Creek in the dark. They came up behind Confederate Gen. Bushrod Johnson's forces, which had crossed at Reed's Bridge another mile downstream, and spent the night there.[17]

The next morning, the Union forces attacked. Fighting broke out along the entire front. On the right, Confederate Gen. Nathan Bedford Forrest's troops came under heavy fire, and he called for reinforcements. Ector's brigade, including Wesley's company, responded but was unable to drive the Union forces from their position.[18] The battle raged all day. By the end, General Walker's forces, which included Ector's brigade, lost over 20 percent of their men, while other divisions lost even more.

The fighting was difficult for numerous reasons. For one, the wooded terrain was such that no general could see all of his command at the same time. As the fighting raged, the various brigades shifted their positions as they moved to support beleaguered units, and they could not clearly see where either neighboring Confederate or Union forces were. Communication between the forces was difficult, and misunderstandings occurred. The overlap of forces prevented some troops from advancing when directed. Added to all of those factors, several generals had such poor regard for Bragg from earlier battle losses that they were reluctant to obey his orders. In fact, Lt. Gen. Leonidas Polk openly disregarded Bragg's orders to attack.

Some of the generals criticized Bragg soundly for failing to take advantage of several opportunities. He might have sent heavier reinforcements to Walker and attempted to break through the left side of the Union lines. He might

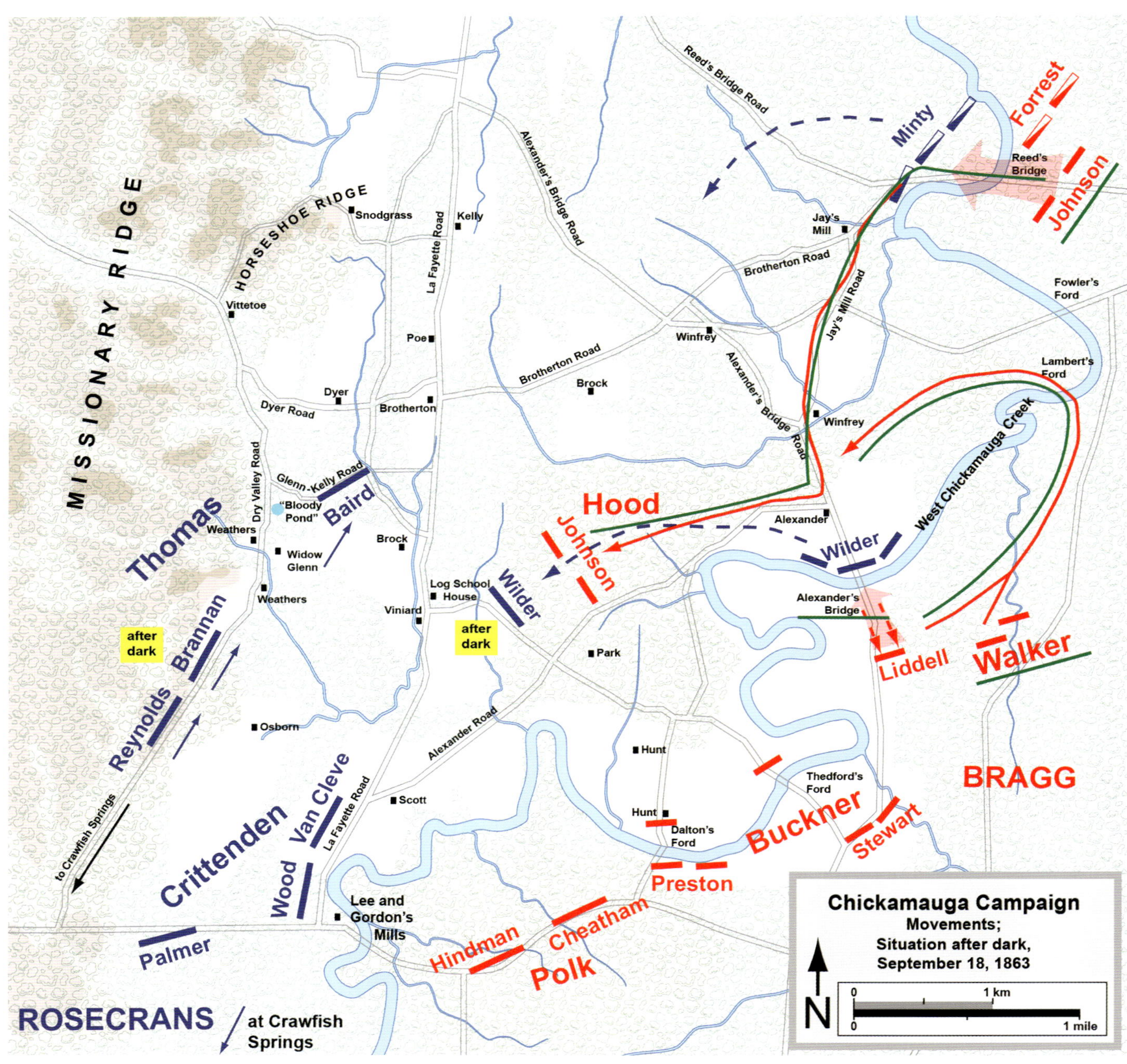


Troop movements during the Chickamauga campaign. Credit: Hal Jespersen.

have attacked the Union center where he knew troops were moving away to the left. Unable to decide on either, Bragg tried to do both, wasting his men in sporadic assaults. At the end of the day's fighting, his army was crippled and in no better position than it had been in that morning. Gone, too, was any hope for the advantage of a surprise attack against the Union forces.[19] One historian later concluded, "Taken as a whole, the performance of the Confederate right wing this morning had been one of the most appalling exhibitions of command incompetence of the entire Civil War."[20]

The next morning, Bragg ordered the attack to start at dawn. But the courier sent to tell Gen. D. H. Hill to initiate the firing could not locate him. The courier returned but failed to tell Bragg his message had not been delivered. Because of this communication error, Hill's attack started four hours late. By then the Union forces were prepared for the assault, and the line encountered heavy fire. Once again, some of Walker's corps were called in to reinforce the line.

The Union forces were having similar communication problems. Misunderstanding their orders, commanders pulled their forces from the center of the lines to reinforce their flank. As they did so, Confederate General Longstreet launched an attack at precisely that vacated point. His forces pushed through the line and soon had the entire Union army in a rout. The victory was theirs.

But Bragg did not pursue the Union forces when he had the opportunity to destroy them. Instead of crushing them, he let them withdraw. Generals Longstreet, Hill, and Forrest were eager for Bragg to order a pursuit, and, as Wesley later wrote, they "went in search of him, and when they found him at 10 o'clock at night several miles in the rear, they urged him to order the pursuit at once, and to not allow the enemy to recover from their panic and re-occupy Chattanooga. . . . All pleadings failed to move Bragg, and Bragg's failure to move lost Chattanooga and dug the grave of the Confederacy."[21] Bragg let the Union forces escape back to Chattanooga, where they had a strong defensive position and could await reinforcements.

Wesley's criticism of Bragg was biting: "Think of it? The earth strewn with 16,000 confederates, who had given their lives and their blood on that field that the enemy might be beaten and their army destroyed; and the living begging that the promise to destroy the Federal army should be kept, were all in vain—they had to lie inactive and see the fruits of the grandest victory we had achieved . . . lost by the iron obstinacy of the Commander."[22] The troops had suffered the highest losses of any battle in the western theater during the war, all to no avail.[23]

**LOOKOUT MOUNTAIN AND MISSIONARY RIDGE**

Following the Battle of Chickamauga, Bragg sent away many of the generals whose troops had supported him. General Ector's brigade returned to Mississippi, and the three Alabama companies that had been under Ector now rejoined General Moore. Also rejoining Moore were the seven Alabama companies that had been captured at Deer Creek and exchanged for Union forces.

Bragg's remaining forces marched to Chattanooga to lay siege to the city. They occupied the surrounding heights on Lookout Mountain and Missionary Ridge where, from their vantage point, they could see the river and roads leading to Chattanooga. They launched attacks on any supply wagons that approached the city. For two months they held the city under siege. Then, in November, General Grant's army arrived, prepared to reinforce the beleaguered Union forces and to force a change in the momentum.

In late November, Grant's forces began an assault on Lookout Mountain. Wesley was with Moore's forces, situated toward the base of the mountain along the east bank of Lookout Creek. In a letter to Sarah, Wesley described the disastrous battle: "I will now give you a succinct statement of our misfortunes in the last ten days; and will state here, that we have lost more in that time than we will gain during the war.

> On Monday evening the 23rd, the enemy made a furious assault on *our* extreme right, next to Chicamauga station, which was intended to deceive, and had the desired effect to a charm, for that night Genl Bragg took nearly all his forces from Look Out Mountain and sent to our right, expecting them to renew the attack at the same place on Tuesday morning, and thus left only about one Division to defend the mountain, which was the key to our whole position around Chattanooga.[24]
>
> The morning of the 24th opened with a slow, chilly rain, and the valleys covered with a mist that shut from sight all that was in them; and as the day advanced it increased, until the mountain was wrapped in a fog, so impenetrable that men could not be seen a hundred yards, and the rain still falling. . . . The ground was difficult to move across, being rough and in chasms, and covered with rock and fallen timber.[25]
>
> Early on Tuesday morning the 24th, they made the attack on us on the mountain, with at least ten to our one, and so admirably was the movement made, that the first intimation we had of them they were *above* us, and had possession of our own trenches, completely cutting off and capturing all of our Pickets. Our Brigade went into it about 11 o'clock, and from that time to midnight the roar of artillery and the rattle

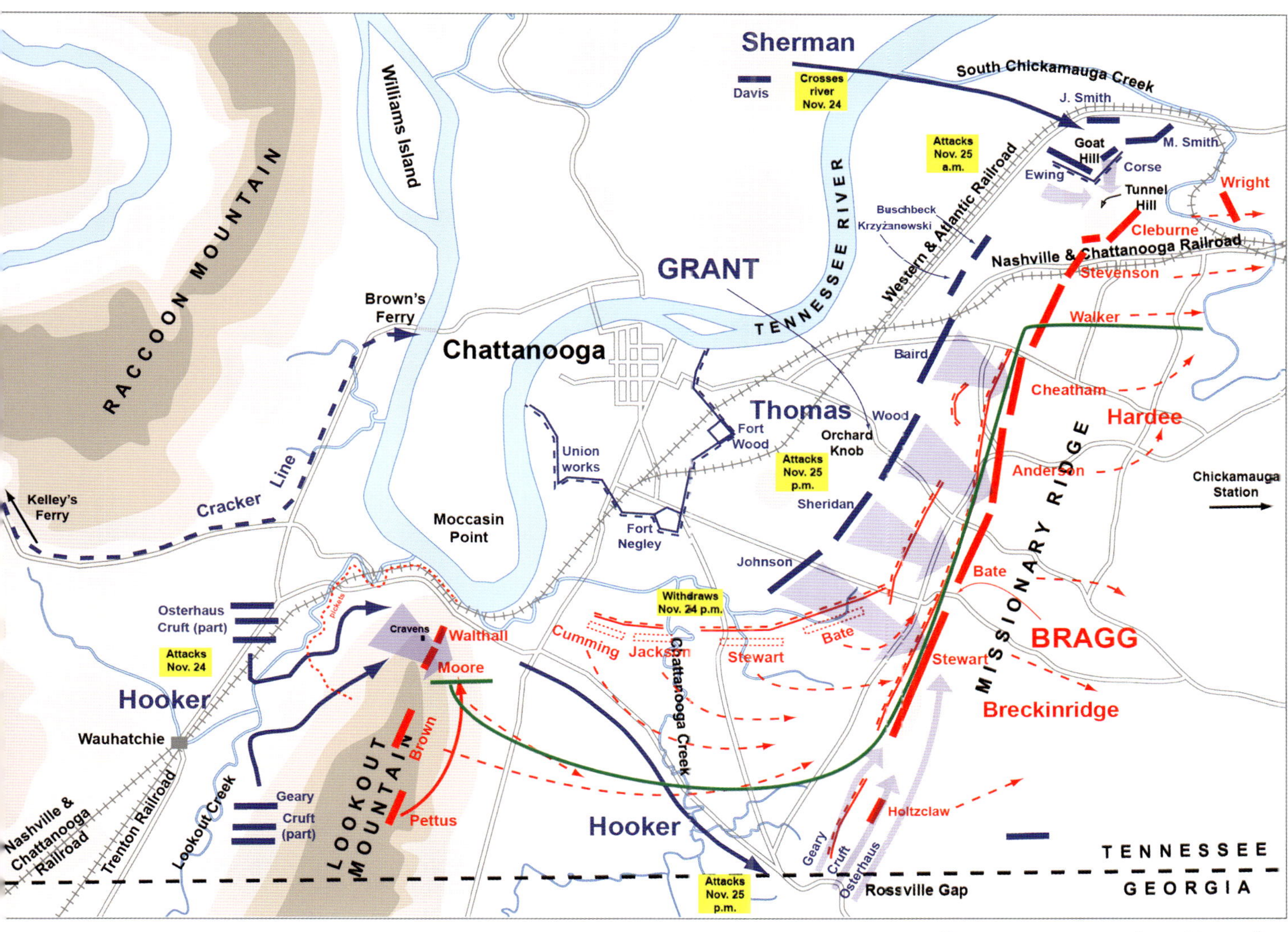


Chattanooga campaign, November 24–25, 1863. Credit: Map by Hal Jespersen.

of musketry was deafening. During the evening, I was at our camp right at the foot of the mountain, and the noise of battle was so intense, that one could hardly hear a man talk. The worst storm of wind and rain, accompanied by incessant lightning and thunder with all the elements of war, is but a *faint* description of the uproar. The shells shrieked through the air, with a sound that reminded me more of lost spirits than anything you can imagine.

That night, about dark we got orders to move the wagons and everything to Chicamauga station, and we started with all the wagon trains, traveled all night, went about 7 miles, and camped a little after

> sunrise. Our troops abandoned Look Out Mountain about 4 o'clock that morning, and fell back to Missionary Ridge.
>
> At daylight they [the troops] found the enemy had followed them, and were ready to finish the work. At 9 o'clock they advanced to the assault all along our lines, and in a little time the battle became general, and raged without intermission till dark, they having swept our left as with a broom, our right alone holding its position, and saving our army from total destruction.[26]

Wesley's 40th Alabama Regiment, fighting on the right, held their position until all had left the mountain, giving the others a chance to evacuate the wounded and escape.[27]

> Thus ended the fight of the 25th, and in hard down fighting and generalship, has never been surpassed on this continent, although it was achieved by our enemy. To say that it is disgraceful is a mild term, for we were out-generaled so badly, that it discouraged the troops, and many of them threw down their arms and fled without firing a gun. Our brigade did nobly, and done some of the hardest fighting both days that was done. Our Regt lost six killed, forty three wounded, that we know of, and one hundred and fourteen missing, many of whom it is supposed are killed and wounded, as the most of them were left in the hands of the enemy. Bennett Harris and Tad Monette are both missing, and it is feared are killed, as the last that was seen of them they were completely enveloped in a fire of musketry.
>
> As soon as night came on, on the 25th, our army began the retreat, and the wagons again started to Ringold, and so crowded were the roads, and so great the confusion, that in *six hours* we got *one mile* with them. We got to Ringold the next evening, and stoped a while, then pushed on to Dalton and reached here Friday night—stoped about an hour—got orders to hitch up and go on—traveled all night, and stoped Saturday morning, and stayed till Sunday morning. This was the first rest I got from Monday night to Saturday, and traveling all the while through the rain, and cold, and as cold as you have ever seen it in Alabama, with my feet blistered, and every muscle and bone in me sore. All this is what is called the pomp and glory of war, but may the Lord deliver me from all such glory! The yankees followed on our rear nearly to Dalton, where they got a good whipping and turned back. We lost a great many wagons, and things with them, and about half our artillery, and take it all together, we are ten times as badly whipped as they were at Chicamauga.[28]

A crucial battle in the Civil War was over. The concentrated Confederate forces had lost an opportunity to destroy the Army of the Cumberland. Had Bragg's forces routed the Union forces, they would have removed the threat to Atlanta. As it was, the way was opened for Gen. William T. Sherman to move south toward Atlanta and undertake his destructive campaign through Georgia. A sound Union defeat before the upcoming presidential election would have undermined Lincoln's chances for reelection. Some conjectured that had the Democratic nominee George B. McClellan won the election, the federal government would have ceased its effort to bring the South back into the Union.[29] Wesley's assessment was similar: "Now as to the effect of our defeat, it is awful to think about. We have recvd a blow that we will never recover from, and I think will have the effect to shorten the war, for our Government will have to come down from its high demands, in order to save anything. We will soon be out of provisions, and when we are, we had as well be out of men, for they will not fight and get nothing to eat."[30]

In December, Braxton Bragg was relieved of his command, replaced by Gen. Joseph E. Johnston. "Well was it for the country that Bragg resigned when he did," Wesley told Sarah, "for had he remained here the army would have been broken up before now;—he couldn't have held it together; he hasn't the moral influence."[31]

The surviving Confederate soldiers retreated to Dalton, Georgia, where they camped from December 1863 to April 1864. They badly needed the time to recover, as so many had been wounded and all were weary. The men were thin and worn from inadequate rations and constant fighting and marching, and all were mentally exhausted and discouraged about the prospects for victory. "The army is demoralized," Wesley told Sarah, "and will have to be reorganized before it can do anything." He was glad to have been reunited with his Company C compatriots, as they were all from Sumter County, and most were people Wesley had known before entering the forces, including his nephew Perry Tureman, son of his sister Matilda,[32] and his Livingston neighbor Joseph Lake, the captain of Company C.

While they were camped in Dalton, many suffered from illnesses that spread through the company. Six Company C soldiers "died this winter and spring," Wesley wrote Sarah, "four of them being original members of it. Elias Sanders, . . . Alex Dean, Wm Bobbit, and Shiren. 'Bolly' Bevill, grandson to the old man Phares is dead also. Jack Parker was sent off some time ago to the Hospital, but has not been heard from. We fear he is dead also." Wesley himself had suffered and recovered from two illnesses, which he referred to as "chills." In the postscript to this letter, Wesley added: "Mr. Thoas Johnston, from near Bellmonte, an original member of Co 'C,' died last night, after an illness of 24 hours, with congestion of lungs and bowels. He leaves a large family to the public. May God protect them!"[33]

Thankfully, the camp had some lighter moments. Wesley noted that he disliked being "batchelorized," in a camp with "no women—no children, no tender ties, no endearing relations, no sweet affections, nor love. . . . I think old bachelors, or hen-pecked husbands first started war to have a barrier against women, and destroy men. The Devil started it, and men keep it up. Who ever saw a man happy at home, who was in favor of war! I never."[34]

Because one of Captain Lake's sons went home to Livingston on furlough and his other son came down with the measles, the camp was without a cook. Wesley took over doing most of the cooking, baking cornbread, frying meat, and making coffee from acorns and chicory. Although he did not enjoy sweating over the fires, he was willing, if occasion required it, to cook for his company. He was pleased when Captain Lake's wife, Sally, came from Livingston: "She makes a good soldier, puts up with bad fare and inconveniences, better than most of the men." And, apparently, she was prepared to cook for the men.[35]

News in the camp was scarce and unreliable. Wesley heard all kinds of rumors and reports about battles in Louisiana, West Tennessee, and Virginia. "The 'victory' in Virginia I spoke of in my last letter," he told Sarah, "all turns out to be nothing but the report of a drunken officer." He had also heard that General Forrest "is just letting down on them in West Tennessee, teaching them what it is to 'occupy and hold' a country against its will." But, as Wesley wrote Sarah, "the news [reports] are conflicting and unsatisfactory."[36]

And then on April 24, 1864, he wrote: "On our front here, the enemy are making formidable preparations, and an early advance on their part is expected. [Gen. Joseph E.] Johnston has stopped *all* furloughs, and is making every preparation for them. In fact, he is pretty well prepared for defence, or attack, and has the army in better condition than it was ever before."[37] Shortly after Wesley wrote this letter, Company C broke camp and moved a few miles west to Rocky Face Ridge. The Atlanta Campaign was about to begin.

### ROCKY FACE RIDGE

On high ground along the steep Rocky Face Ridge, the Confederate forces dug in for a strong defensive stand against an impending attack. Led by General Sherman, the Union army had marched from its victories at Lookout Mountain and Missionary Ridge and invaded Georgia unopposed. As the Union army approached Rocky Face Ridge, Sherman engaged these strong Confederate positions with two columns of his forces and maneuvered the rest of his forces around on their flank, planning to hit the railroad at nearby

Bronze memorial plaque at the Rocky Face Ridge pocket park, built in the 1930s by the WPA in Dalton, Georgia. Wesley was severely injured fighting at Dug Gap. Credit: John Foxe (Wikimedia Commons).

Resaca. When Johnston saw that his forces were being outflanked, he evacuated his strong position, came down off the ridge, and moved south toward Resaca. Wesley was positioned at Dug Gap on the left flank. There, he was hit by shrapnel in his hip and leg and severely wounded.

The next day saw several skirmishes, and Johnston was forced to withdraw again.[38] At one skirmish, a Presbyterian clergyman, the Reverend J. P. McMullen, was killed. He had been with Wesley's division while it was wintering in Dalton and had won the men's confidence and respect by his unselfish ministering to them, comforting the sick and the dying. At the Battle of Resaca, when the brigade charged, Reverend McMullen refused the entreaties of the commander to stay back. Instead, he advanced with the men, saying, as Wesley later recalled, that he "would not forsake them in the hour of trial but would go with them into the gates of death. He went in front, waving his hat and cheering the men until he was struck down."[39]

At another skirmish at Resaca, the color-bearer, Sergeant P. S. Gilder, was killed while leading the charge. When the order to retreat was given, the flag remained on the field. The flag was important to the men because Sergeant Gilder had already saved it from dishonor once—when they surrendered at Vicksburg, Gilder cut the flag from the staff, wrapped it around his body, and smuggled it out. After the skirmish at Resaca, three men, Adjutant Ellerbee, Lieutenant Peteet, and Lieutenant Knighton, volunteered to retrieve the flag. All three went, facing heavy fire and risking their lives, "the determination," Wesley remembered, "being to recover the colors at all hazards."[40]

Although severely wounded, Wesley remained with Company C as it fought in battles at New Hope Church and Ezra Church, both futile attempts to prevent General Sherman from taking Atlanta. In July, Gen. Stephen D. Lee arrived to assume command. On the day following his arrival, he ordered an attack on the Union army at Ezra Church. His forces, Wesley noted, "were defeated with fearful loss."[41]

### THE LAST MONTHS OF THE WAR

In August 1864, the remains of Wesley's brigade were ordered to leave Atlanta and proceed to Spanish Fort, Alabama, on Mobile Bay.[42] While the battle for Atlanta was raging in the east, Forts Morgan and Gaines, on the western shore of Mobile Bay, had been captured by Union forces. Spanish Fort, on the eastern shore of Mobile Bay and across from the city of Mobile, was still in Confederate hands. It was the only fort left from which the Confederates might repel the Union forces, block them from capturing Mobile, and maintain control of the railroad line to Montgomery. At Spanish Fort, the Confederate troops built massive fortifications on the bluffs and prepared to fire down on the Union gunboats.[43]

For housing, Wesley's brigade settled in on the eastern shore, where they found a number of vacant summer cottages owned by wealthy Mobile residents stretched out for ten or fifteen miles along the bay from Mobile. "Some of them," Wesley wrote Sarah, "are desirable beyond any thing you ever saw. They are just upon the first rise of ground on the beach, with . . . bathhouses on the water, and wharves running out from two to eight hundred yards in the Bay. The grounds are beautifully laid out, and are covered with Holly, Magnolia, and other sweet southern flowers." Wesley was enjoying the warm Gulf waters and the "delicious sea breeze." The situation would have been perfect if it were not for the Union gun boats nearby that might fire on them any time they chose.[44]

In late November 1864, the winter weather set in. Wesley's health, weakened by his wounds, deteriorated so badly that he was sent to the hospital in Mobile. Sometime later, he was sent by train to the "disabled camp" at Lauderdale Springs, Mississippi. Because its natural sulfur springs were thought to have recuperative powers, Lauderdale Springs had been a popular health resort before the war. The Confederate forces turned the resort into a hospital, and the trains that had once brought vacationers now brought wounded soldiers. Eleven hundred Confederate soldiers died and were buried there. Fortunately, Wesley began to recover from his wounds. Before Christmas 1864, he was considered well enough to be transferred to post duty at Gainesville, Alabama.[45]

Throughout the war, Wesley and Sarah tried to remain connected. She wrote weekly and occasionally sent socks that she had knitted. She sent letters through the mail but found many of them never reached Wesley. She sent others with soldiers from Livingston returning to their unit, such as Booker Lockard and Lieutenant Monette, and then with Sally Lake when she joined the troops at the camp in Dalton. Wesley found a number of his letters to Sarah also never arrived. This caused both of them great frustration. "If you are all well and doing well, I want to know it, and I want to hear from you any how... I miss you so much, and the prattle of those dear children. I miss your society, your affection, your presence."[46]

Although conditions were bleak, Sarah seemed to keep the household operating. She continued to work at the Livingston Female Academy during the war; the house slaves cared for the children and the house while Sarah was at school. She had somehow obtained wheat, which she sent to the flour mill for grinding. "My wheat yielded 223 lbs. of flour, about 40 lbs. of seconds, and 3½ bushels of bran," she told Wesley.[47] Where the wheat came from is unclear, but it was the first wheat Sarah had ever had ground. Perhaps Livingston had reverted to a barter economy, and the school or a group of students had paid her in wheat.

In late December 1863, a cold spell hit Livingston. Sarah found she was so cold she couldn't finish the letter she had intended to post for Wesley. "I never suffered so much with cold in my life, as I did New Year's night; my feet were like ice all night, and I scarcely slept a particle." In the same cold spell, one of her favorite students, Viony Arrington, died of a "congestive chill." The wife of a friend, Robert Beck, also died, and Sarah told Wesley that Beck had "broken up housekeeping and given his children to their relations."[48]

Sarah and the children were surviving, but the separation and the anxiety of war were hard on everyone. Their loneliness, their fears, and their desperate desire to see each other weighed heavily on them. Frank and Mollie Bet particularly missed their father during the Christmas holidays, which they found gloomy and dreary without him.[49] In his letters home, Wesley tried to offer parental advice. "Tell Frank," he wrote to Sarah, "to gallant the girls until he will be looked upon as a necessity, and enjoyed as a pleasure. Tell Mollie she must not forget pa, and to be a good little girl when she goes to church so that she can go with ma and pa when he goes home."[50] Upon hearing that Frank had acted charitably in a situation, Wesley urged Sarah to "cultivate the feeling, and let him get in the habit of doing good. Give him some little change to put in the charity box at church and advise him of worthy and unworthy objects."[51]

In December 1864, from his post in Gainesville, Wesley wrote a Christmas Day letter to Sarah, reflecting on all that had transpired: "It is three years since I have had the pleasure of spending a Christmas with you and our dear little children; and how many changes there have been since that time.

> Thousands have fallen far away from home, torn and mangled, and died, thinking of wife and children whom they should never see again. Others who have been spared from death have lost a dear wife, or some loved one while they were unable to get to them, and take the last farewell. In those years I have been in the midst of death and carnage, trials and sufferings, and have been preserved from them all by Him Who ever watcheth over, and preserveth me. And while thousands of homes have been draped in the habiliments of wo, my dear ones have been kept from all evil. When I think on these things, it fills me with humility, that one so unworthy has been surrounded with such rich blessings, and yet it makes my heart to rejoice, and go up with gratitude, and praises to God who doeth all things for me.[52]

Wesley focused on his many gratitudes. He did not focus on the loss of his son Ernest and his brother-in-law Zachariah Tureman, both of whom had died in his absence. He did not focus on the dreadful battles in which he was wounded, he was not bitter about the inept generals under whom he had served, and he did not bemoan his broken health and crippled condition that would leave him deaf in one ear and dragging one leg for the rest of his life.[53] He must have had concerns about how he would be able to carry on his business and support his family in his weakened condition, but his faith was so strong that it carried him through the war and enabled him to be grateful for that which he had not lost.

"Yes, it is Christmas day, and I am within twenty-four miles of home, yet I can't get there; but how much better is my condition than to be far away on the battle-field, the cold ground for my bed, and the angry heavens for my covering, with the deadly missile eternally seeking my life. Such reflections reconcile me to my lot, and make me lean on God, Who has promised to uphold all who put their trust in Him."[54] Wesley did not know when he would be able to return home. He promised to do so as soon as he could "honorably." Sarah and Wesley both knew the situation was bleak. "I think our prospects for peace are anything but flattering," Sarah wrote, "but I shall not yield to despondency, as long as there is the least thing to hang a hope on."[55] "The future is as dark as ever," Wesley agreed, "and impenetrable gloom curtains it from sight."[56]

On April 9, 1865, Gen. Robert E. Lee surrendered to Gen. Ulysses S. Grant at Appomattox Court House in Virginia. Two days later, Gen. Joseph E. Johnston surrendered to Gen. William T. Sherman at Bennett Place near Durham, North Carolina. News of the surrenders traveled slowly, and knowing nothing of them, Wesley's company, under Gen. Richard Taylor, continued the fight at Spanish Fort. Greatly outnumbered with only a few thousand men, they held off over thirty thousand Union troops for ten to twelve days. When the Union troops finally broke through their defenses, the 40th Alabama Regiment evacuated Spanish Fort. Only then did news of the surrenders and of the capture of Jefferson Davis in Georgia reach General Taylor. He abandoned the fighting and surrendered to Union Gen. E. R. S. Canby at what became known as the Surrender Oak in Citronelle, Alabama.[57]

General Canby offered terms, as General Taylor later wrote in his memoirs, "consistent with the honor of our arms." The Confederate soldiers were paroled, or given passes for safe conduct back to their homes with the assurance they would not be rounded up as prisoners of war. Men with horses were allowed to keep them. Officers with sidearms also kept them, and Taylor kept control of the railways and steamships long enough to get his men back to their homes. The surviving Company C men with whom Wesley had fought finally returned to Sumter County. Wesley was paroled from his Gainesville post on May 16, 1865, having sacrificed three years to the war effort. He returned home preparing to face whatever the future had in store for him and his family.[58]

# 5 "The Vicissitudes of Fortune"

## Post–Civil War

*The war came on. I was in it to the close, got home a cripple and everything lost but my wife . . . and our two Children and honor, all was gone.* —Wesley to his cousin Dillingham[1]

The war left the South totally devastated, with no possibility of a swift recovery. The abolition of slavery threw the cotton economy into chaos. The railroads that had carried products to market could not operate because of irreparable damage sustained by the tracks, engines, and cars. Most farm machinery had been ruined. Money was scarce, and credit for people seeking it was nonexistent. Farmers who were unable to pay their debts or taxes lost their land to foreclosure. In his memoirs, General Richard Taylor of the 40th Alabama summarized the situation: "Bank stocks, bonds, all personal property, all accumulated wealth had disappeared. Thousands of houses, farm buildings, work animals, flocks and herds had been wantonly burned, killed or carried off. The land was filled with widows and orphans crying for aid, which the universal destitution prevented them from receiving."[2]

Wesley made it home to Livingston in May 1865 to find Sarah still teaching and assisting the principal at the college. For months, the weak and haggard Wesley continued recuperating from the wounds to his hip and leg, navigating with crutches and slowly regaining his strength. He also basked in the nearness of his wife and the children that he had missed so desperately during the war. It was a time spent reestablishing the close bonds with his family that he cherished.

In the winter, when Wesley was finally strong enough to look for work, he could find nothing. No one was building anything. Needing to support his family in any way possible, he secured a position seventy-five miles away in Selma, Alabama, working for Baker Brothers.[3] It was a long, cold ride from Livingston to Selma. Wesley located a place to stay but regretted that he was once again away from his family. His major comfort then, as throughout his life, came from attending church. From Selma, he wrote Sarah about the excellent sermon he heard one Sunday and how he looked forward to the next Sunday, which he characterized as a "sacramental occasion," adding "I hope and pray it will be a time of refreshing from the Lord."[4]

Given the economic and political outlook in Alabama, Wesley and Sarah began to consider leaving the South. Many Southerners had already fled to Texas. Wesley's sister Angeline and her husband, Chapin, had gone there before the war, settling in Bryan, near the Brazos River. Sarah's family had moved to Texas in 1853, settling in Leon County, about sixty miles northeast of Bryan. Wesley's mother had died in 1861, so he no longer needed to remain in Livingston to support her. Although it was hard to abandon their home, Wesley and Sarah decided their best hopes for future happiness lay in migrating to Texas and starting over. He told his sister Juliett that as soon as they were settled, she could come and live with them.[5] They left Livingston in February 1866, planning to go be near Sarah's family.

Friends and family soon sent news confirming the wisdom of their decision to leave. In November 1866, Wesley's sister Eliza Seeley wrote that she did not know where they would live next year or what her husband would be doing as there was no carpentry work in Livingston.[6] A year later, a group of their former neighbors who had just left Livingston told Wesley he would no longer recognize Sumter County. Many of the middle class—the merchants, teachers, lawyers, and small farmers—had gone bankrupt, lost everything they had, and left their homes. The minister, Mr. Bingham, had departed the area, and their Presbyterian church stood abandoned.[7] A friend from Selma gave Wesley a similar account of the dire situation in that area too.[8]

A wagon took Wesley, Sarah, Frank, and Mollie Bet to Demopolis, Alabama, on the Tombigbee River, where they expected to catch the steamer *St. Nicholas* at noon for Mobile. However, the *St. Nicholas* had passed by early the night before, and they had missed it. They were fortunate not to have been on the *St. Nicholas* for it sank, and the wet, bedraggled passengers were brought back to Demopolis. Feeling truly grateful, the family caught the steamer *Virginia*, which according to Sarah was "a nice little boat with good accommodations."[9]

Five-year-old Mollie, the only child onboard except for her brother, engaged with the passengers and soon became a universal pet. One day Wesley introduced Mollie to a Mr. Goin. Later, when the man saw the child again, he asked Mollie what his name was.

"'Walkin,' she replied.

"'No.'

"'Runnin.'

"'No, but that is most it.'

"'Goin.'

"'Oh! Yes, Goin, Goin all the time.'"

The child's answer brought forth a roar of laughter. Mollie had remembered that the man's name expressed motion, but she had forgotten what kind. The man then entered into play with Mollie, asking her what the ship was carrying. Every answer had to begin with the same letter, such as "corn, cotton, calico." Sarah beamed with pride as the bright little girl played for some time following the signals and answering every question quickly, without making any mistakes.[10]

When the family arrived in Mobile, they caught the steamer *Frances* to New Orleans. They stopped there long enough to spend a day shopping and admiring the distinctive French architecture in the city. They visited Jackson Square, dedicated to President Andrew Jackson, and the historic St. Louis Cathedral with its triple steeples. They also enjoyed more good food than they had had in many years.[11]

The SS *Morgan*, the paddle wheeler built in 1865 that Wesley and Sarah took to Galveston. Credit: Photo courtesy of Captain Jim McNamara.

In New Orleans, they boarded the steamer *Morgan*, a brand-new ship that was headed to Galveston, Texas. They delighted in the Mississippi River scenery as they steamed past a number of beautiful residences. Orange groves and sugar plantations stretched out for miles and miles. When they entered the Gulf of Mexico, Sarah was really excited and relayed to a friend how they all soaked in the "'wild waste of waters' and the 'glorious sunset' with a zest unknown to common observers."[12] Soon they disembarked in Galveston.

Sarah's enthusiasm began to wane when they boarded the riverboat *Rob Roy* for Houston. The boat took them into the Buffalo Bayou, which Sarah characterized as a "narrow, shallow, dirty, sluggish stream" that "did not give me a very favorable impression of Texas." Houston did not excite her either, "for that place is small, ugly and muddy."[13]

From Houston, a train took the family north to Navasota, where they spent the night "at a very indifferent hotel" before hiring a carriage to take them on to Leon County. The first day traveling was beautiful, and Sarah delighted in seeing the rolling countryside, which she characterized poetically as "diversified by hill and dale." They spent the night at a mediocre boarding house, where, according to Sarah, "a few feathers on some dried cow hides formed our beds!" The next morning, the February weather turned cold when a "terrible Norther" blew in, making travel uncomfortable. It was dark before they reached the house of Sarah's sister, Bet, "nearly frozen to death." But Sarah was so anxious to see her parents that, instead of spending the night, she borrowed a blanket to keep the children warm in the bottom of the carriage and went on the last two miles to the Moffitt home. A delighted Sarah exclaimed, "Home, 'sweet home' gained at last! I was almost crazy with excitement!"[14]

In the time Sarah's family had been in Texas, they had done very well, having established a ranch and begun raising cattle. Dr. Moffitt was also practicing medicine. Sarah did not think her parents had aged at all in the thirteen years since she had seen them. Her father rode every day, sitting straight in the saddle. Her mother frequently walked two miles to Bet's home and back. Sarah was glad to see her brothers and sister, and Bet's husband and three strong boys. The Moffitts were anxious to give Wesley and Sarah land and stock to help them get settled.[15]

Initially, Sarah and Wesley were delighted to be in Leon County and planned to settle there. But within a few months, they became discontented. They considered the area to be unhealthy, as they all suffered from coughs and colds, fevers and chills, and sores and boils. Sarah was constantly ill, and in six months, she lost twenty-seven pounds. The presence of cholera in the area worried them.[16]

The society they found there was even more concerning. When the neighbors began to visit, Sarah learned that she had nothing in common with any of them. She told her friend Fanny: "I soon found out from their conversation and manners that I was indeed 'in a strange land among strangers.' No congeniality between us at all. Subjects most dear to my heart, they took no interest in at all."[17] Probably none of them shared Sarah's interest in literature and poetry. Even more importantly, none shared the values and morals that Wesley and Sarah were trying to instill in their children. As she told her friend Addie, "We felt that it would be criminal in us to bring up our children in such a place, not a church in the neighborhood, and but one in the county! Drinking, swearing, Sabbath breaking, and every other vice is practiced by the majority of the people and the others smile at it instead of frowning it down. The children where I have been grow up like weeds without a particle of culture of any kind! . . . We could not reconcile it to our consciences, for 'what is a man profited, if he shall gain the whole world and lose his own soul?'"[18]

The farming opportunities in Leon County were less than ideal. The land was not as rich and fertile as in Alabama. All the low-lying lands were subject to flooding, and the uplands were so poor they scarcely yielded a crop. Wesley must have wondered if he would ever regain the physical strength and stamina needed to pursue farming. While they had fantasized about living a bucolic farm life in Texas, Wesley and Sarah decided that it would be better to go somewhere where they could resume their old occupations, Sarah teaching and Wesley designing and building.[19] Opportunities for an architect were few in Leon County, but in Bryan, about sixty miles away, Wesley soon had a contract to build a storehouse and a dwelling for a merchant. In September 1866, he went to Bryan alone to start work and to find suitable living arrangements for his family.[20]

### BRYAN

In 1866, Bryan was a new town just starting up as a stop on the Houston and Texas Central Railway. When Wesley arrived, the railroad wasn't even there yet; it reached Bryan the following year. The town was situated between the Brazos and Navasota Rivers in scenic rolling countryside. It had been designated the county seat for Brazos County, and the post office would soon move from Boonville to Bryan. The town consisted of one or two dusty dirt streets, lined with crudely built board buildings, a mill, a grocery or a saloon, a blacksmith, a few boarding houses, and a few other businesses. Some small residences had been built, but many people were living in tents. Fewer than three hundred people lived in town. Among them were Wesley's sister Angeline and her husband, Chapin, the wagon maker, who had settled in Bryan about ten years earlier.

Wesley had difficulty finding a place suitable for his family. The houses, or shanties, were all too small for people to take in boarders as they had in Alabama. The boarding houses were such that Wesley had trouble locating one that he would be willing for his family to live in. "The society here is bad," he reported to Sarah, "and I have not met with a religious man in the place. Their drunkenness and profaneness is the reason I would not board with them." He considered the possibilities of getting land and building a shanty on it, but he could not yet manage it financially. With the railroad not yet running to Bryan, lumber was very expensive. Besides, as he wrote Sarah, he was already "having second thoughts about Bryan, nor do I think you will like the place any more than I do." The town had no church and no school worth mentioning. Wesley recognized the one teacher in town as T. Kemp Eads, someone who had killed a man in another town, run away, and changed his name to Crittenden.[21] He was a drunk who would fail to show up to teach for a week at a time.[22] Later that winter, he fell asleep outside in the cold one night when he was drunk, and died of pneumonia.[23]

Despite his considerable misgivings, Wesley found space in a boarding house run by a Mr. Stevens for fifty dollars per month. The family could stay there while he finished the storehouse and dwelling he had contracted to

The main street of Bryan. Credit: Cushing Memorial Library and Archives, Texas A&M University.

design and construct. Like the other buildings in Bryan, the boarding house was hastily and poorly built, with spaces between the boards and no insulation. The wind and rain blew through the cracks, and the rooms were cold and difficult to heat.

Sarah and the children came by wagon from her parents’ home in Leon County. Sarah’s first impression was that Brazos County was superior to Leon County in some ways, but, as she wrote to a friend in Livingston, “the moral atmosphere is bad here. Stores are kept open on the Sabbath, country people come in and buy the same as on other days; wagons loaded with cotton and goods are passing and re passing all the time; drinking, gambling, stealing, shooting, and horse racing fill up the picture."[24] Worse yet, someone had doused a drunk found sleeping outside with turpentine and set him on fire.[25] "But I hope a better day is dawning, for last Sabbath, a Baptist church was organized here, and sixteen members united with it. If we had churches, schools, and good society, Bryan would be a very pleasant little village; for it is situated in the edge of a beautiful, high, rolling prairie, dotted here and there with clumps of trees, and abounding with cattle, horses, sheep, and goats as far as the eye can reach. Occasionally, a mule-eared rabbit crosses your path, and a bird of paradise, a wild goose, or blue crane flies over your head. At every step, curious pebbles and pieces of petrified wood meet your gaze."[26]

Despite its natural beauty, Wesley and Sarah soon agreed that Bryan was not where they wanted to live. Instead, as soon as Wesley finished the buildings he had under contract, they would move on to Waco, eighty miles away. There they hoped they would find what they were looking for: "good churches, good schools, and as good society as is to be found in the State."[27]

But things did not go as they planned.

### GALVESTON

When Wesley finished constructing those two buildings in Bryan, he did not go to Waco. It wasn't that work opportunities still existed in Bryan; they did not. But Wesley got word from James Webb, a Livingston friend now living in Galveston, that some men there wanted to have buildings constructed. Feeling a "sense of duty" to find work to support his family,[28] Wesley took the train to Galveston in February 1867 to investigate the situation.[29]

Wesley arrived just as Congress wrested control of Reconstruction away from President Andrew Johnson and initiated new, harsher policies for readmitting the conquered Southern states into the Union. After the war, Congress had divided the South into five districts and put them under military rule. Texas and Louisiana comprised the Fifth Military District. In March 1867, Gen. Philip Sheridan was appointed to head this district. Sheridan started his rule by sending troops to all the port cities of Texas, including Galveston—a large commercial port and the biggest city in Texas at the time. Sheridan administered with strict, punitive policies. He severely limited voter registration for former Confederates and ruled that only registered voters, including black men, were eligible to serve on juries.[30]

A discouraged Wesley wrote Sarah: "But the way things are going I fear that we will not live here, nor hardly any where else." Under Sheridan's military rule, "the lives, liberty, and property of every one is at his disposal, and he responsible to no one for his acts. What they will next do cannot be told, but what they have already done is depressing business sensibly, and I fear will prostrate all the energies of the Southern people. All business stops unless capitalists advance money, and capitalists fear to invest when they will only hold tenure at the caprice of a military ruler." Wesley cautioned Sarah to be careful with their money: "Keep every dime of specie that we can get, and spend it for nothing, for business men all believe that the president will be impeached within the next month, and then green-backs will be worthless."[31]

The political situation had a devastating effect on Wesley's job prospects. When he met with men who were planning to build and needed designs, including those he had originally come to Galveston to see, he found they had all decided to defer building and await developments. "I am afraid that at the present prospect," he told Sarah, "I shall not be getting much drafting to do. . . . They say that things will brighten after a little, but I do not wish to cherish false hopes, nor induce others to do so, and if what has been done, so disarranges finances, the future will completely prostrate it, for we are only at 'the beginning of the end.'"[32]

Wesley found a room on Tremont Street at Captain Munion's, a boarding house that catered to mechanics and served meals at times that fit their schedules. Board and lodging was ten dollars per week, paid in advance. Captain Munion's was so close to the Gulf of Mexico that Wesley was able to walk along the beach in the evening, picking up pretty shells for Mollie Bet. From inside his room, Wesley could hear the crashing waves. He enjoyed hearing the tumultuous roaring of the water, which he felt was "fit emblem of God's majesty and power."[33]

In Galveston, Wesley immediately sought out the churches, his main source of solace. "Church privileges are so much better in the city than the country," he wrote Sarah. One Sunday, he attended a Presbyterian Sunday school that he found to be "a fine school and well conducted." There, he became acquainted with several of the people, good moral people who afforded the companionship for which he yearned. He attended church services there, and one Sunday, "heard a good sermon" from Mr. McNair, "a plain and sensible and sound preacher," who, he thought, "would bear acquaintance." When McNair was out of town the next Sunday, Wesley went to the Methodist church, where he heard "a good sermon from 3rd chapter of Gal., 24th verse. And the subject was very well handled." He probably would have loved to discuss the sermon with Sarah, the way he loved discussing literature with her, but he had to satisfy himself with pointing out the biblical verses on which the sermon was based. She could, at least, read those in her Bible.[34]

Two Sundays later, back at the Presbyterian church, Wesley was pleased to hear "one of the most impressive sermons I ever listened to." The Reverend Dr. Reed of Richmond, Virginia, preached "from the words 'All power is given to me in heaven, and in earth' etc. See the passage," he told Sarah, "from the latter clause of the 18th verse to the close of the 28th chapter of Matthew." Wesley went to hear him again at the evening service. His preaching style, not shouting, not exhorting, reminded him of his father's manner of preaching. While "dignified and commanding," his tone was conversational.[35] Wesley always wrote Sarah on Sundays. Perhaps that is why he closed so many of his letters with words that sounded as if they were benedictions: "And to you, my own precious wife, I send all my love, and sympathy, and with the prayer for God's grace to be with, and sustain you, and may His mercies keep you all in perfect peace. Your fond and affectionate husband, Wesley."[36]

In Galveston, Wesley found a construction job paying five dollars per day and was initially optimistic that if times remained good, he could make some money. By now he was off crutches and needed only a cane to steady himself as he walked.[37] He was, however, far from well. During his first month in Galveston, Wesley was not able to work much. Some days, particularly when it was damp and foggy, as it was much of the time in Galveston, he suffered from debilitating rheumatism that made working impossible. Other days, bad weather shut down all construction work. One week, a discouraged Wesley told Sarah he had worked less than half the time. Nonetheless, he said, "I know I had better be here if I make only my board, than there doing nothing."[38]

Back in Bryan, where Sarah was trying to teach school at the boarding house, nothing was going well. The weather that winter was dreadful. As Sarah indicated, it was "the worst weather I ever saw any where in March." One day while she was teaching, it began to sleet. The sleet came down so fast, blowing through the cracks in the boards, that in just minutes, it covered her bed and the floor. She and her class retreated into Mrs. Stevens's room. The sleet continued all day, covering everything in her room. The house was cold. Mr. Stevens was out of town and not available to replenish the dwindling pile of firewood. The next several days were so cold Sarah canceled her class. Finally, the weather moderated and the sleet melted, but Sarah was left with a soggy bed and wet floors. The next night, a heavy frost covered the ground followed by strong winds from the north that blew right through the boarding house walls.[39] Not surprisingly, everyone became sick.

Frank had chills, Mollie Bet had a cold, and Sarah had a cold and a sore throat that would not go away.

Even Sarah's teaching was going badly. She wrote Wesley that of all the children she had ever taught, these were "the dullest intellects I ever worked on." Sarah worked harder than she had ever found necessary, repeating herself to the students "over and over till I can talk no longer." Because the Stevens children were in the class, she tried especially hard to help them do well, but it was all to no avail—the class gave her the most trouble she had ever had. The children were poorly mannered, and they whispered and passed notes rather than applying themselves to their work. Probably less patient and more short-tempered than usual because her throat hurt so badly, Sarah whipped a student nearly every day, even the girls. The Mulkins pulled their daughters, Mollie and Laura, out of the school after they were whipped "for misconduct." Then the Zelvertons withdrew their daughters after Ada was whipped "for whispering and idleness."[40] This brought the class down to twenty, in addition to Frank and Mollie. "I think by the time the session ends, my health, strength, and patience will be all, entirely gone. If I live I shall never take charge of another school except from the direst necessity."[41]

Sarah worried about the influence of these unruly children on the manners and morals of her own children. Frank and Mollie were "growing so wild and rude" that Sarah was "at times, almost ashamed of them."[42] Most of Frank and Mollie's classmates were under no restraint whatsoever. When Sarah looked at the children's parents, she understood why. Even those who were church members lacked the deportment she would have expected. Then again, Sarah's idea of a suitable way for the children to celebrate May Day was a bucolic picnic in the woods—not, as did happen, a daylong dance party at the local hotel.[43]

Wesley had had reservations about Sarah teaching in Bryan as he felt that Texas children were "like mustangs and teaching the one as about as easy as breaking the other."[44] While he sympathized with Sarah's wish for the children to have suitable friends, he warned Sarah there were none to be found in Galveston either. He himself "had seen no good children anywhere, except isolated cases, for they and their parents appear to have all run wild." In the post–Civil War world, all of the social constraints and societal expectations that had existed before the war and that had held society together had come loose, just as law and order and respect for property were gone.[45]

From afar, Wesley tried to exert some influence over his children and their behavior. In one letter, he wrote, "Give my love to my dear little children and tell them that I am in hopes they will not be rude, and become like these Texas children but be gentle, kind, and obedient, and obey their mother."[46]

In another letter, he asked Sarah to "give my love to my dear children . . . and tell them to do as Ma wishes, and not as others wish them to do. God says for children to obey their parents, but tells them also, not to go with the multitude to do evil; that is, to do as father and mother wishes them to do, and not to do as others wish them to do, nor even follow their own wills."[47]

In her letters to Wesley, Sarah often enclosed notes written by Mollie Bet and Frank to their father. Wesley usually replied directly to them. In one letter, he told Mollie Bet: "Be a good girl, and mind Ma, and learn your books. . . . Kiss Ma and brother for me and do all you can to make them happy."[48] In another, he complimented her on "getting along so well in school and getting so many tickets"[49] and told her to "be a good little girl and learn a great deal, and not give dear Ma any trouble."[50] Mollie Bet wrote back, "How glad I was, the other morning, to get a nice little letter from you, with my own name on it."[51] In his own letter, Frank told his father that he wished to see him very much and, probably drawing a chuckle from Wesley, said he hoped "we will meet again some time."[52]

Despite her concerns, Sarah was still proud of her children. Six-year-old Mollie Bet was a bright child, very much like her mother. "She has recently learned a very pretty piece of poetry, of her own accord, about the 'Modest Violet.' She learns all the verses on her 'tickets' also. You would be surprised to hear how well she recites her 'definitions.' Better than any other child in school under twelve years of age!"[53]

The young Mollie was enterprising. She made ten cents, her first money, by gathering a bouquet of Indian blankets for a Bryan store clerk who wanted to take flowers to a young lady he was seeing that evening. When they were staying with the Moffitts, Sarah and Mollie Bet had regularly gathered wildflowers—the bright yellow buttercups, the wild purple violets, and the blue bonnets of Texas. Years later Mollie wrote: "As a child I tramped the woods and fields with my mother who loved them and taught me to love all nature. On a long day in the woods in order to have our flowers fresh when we got home (for no flower wilts as quickly as a wild flower) she would carry a pan or bowl with us and fill it with wet sand taken from the spring branch, then carefully arrange the flowers in stars and different shapes; . . . these were all buried in the sand until only the flower showed, and how proud I was to help carry them home to show to grandmother where they would be placed in a cool window and keep fresh and bright for days."[54]

Sarah was also proud of the industriousness of thirteen-year-old Frank. He regularly got up early before school and carried buckets of water to the merchants in town for ten cents a bucket or sometimes for ammunition or candy. He wouldn't, however, carry water for "stingy" Mr. Wilson, who refused Frank's offer of five cents per bucket and offered only three and a third cents. Carrying water, Frank earned $3.30 as well as "powder and shot and caps" that he used to shoot birds to earn more money.[55] The last birds he shot were sold to Mr. Lyons at the restaurant. "I feel greatly encouraged by seeing him show so much energy," Sarah wrote, "and think he will make his way in the world, if he has half a chance."[56]

Sarah was desperate for the family to be together again and was open to any possibility. Galveston, if Wesley found a good situation there, would be all right. After all, the city would afford them the churches and schools they sought and would be better for the children. Or maybe it would be better for Sarah and Wesley to be in the country. In Bryan, Wesley's brother-in-law Chapin had bought some acreage and had offered them a half-acre lot if they wanted to build on it.[57] Sarah had found that with the arrival of the railroad, lumber prices had fallen. For $125, they could buy the lumber needed to build a small one-room house with a shed on the back. There, they could make do for a while if they could support themselves in Bryan. Whatever Wesley decided would be fine; she would willingly defer the decision to him. Anywhere. Just together.[58]

Almost every letter from Sarah to Wesley during this period contained the same hope:

"I hope you will soon get into profitable business, so that by fall, we may be able to go to housekeeping. . . . I don't suffer myself to dwell upon our separation, for I hope it is for the best. Take care of your health and means, and perhaps we may be happy together some day."[59]

"If we all live, let us endeavor by every means in our power to go to housekeeping next fall."[60]

"Do the best you can, and leave the rest to Providence. If it is the Lord's will, I would like a home somewhere by next fall, and hope we may be able to get it; but if not, I hope He will give us grace to bear our disappointment without complaint. . . . I want to see you very much, but cannot expect to have the wish gratified while business here is so dull."[61]

"I wish we could arrange matters so as to be together, and make money at the same time. . . . I try to be contented in the present, and let the future alone. I know our destiny is in the hands of a Higher Power Who doeth all things well, but though the spirit is willing, my flesh is weak, and I find myself cumbered with many cares. May the Lord preserve me, and keep me from being utterly lost!"[62]

Wesley also felt the pain of separation, admitting to Sarah, "I think about you, and dream about you, study about you, and worry about you." He was missing her and the children so badly, he told Sarah, that "it almost makes me sick."[63] Wesley was trying to plan for the future, investigating the possibility of moving his family to Galveston and weighing this option against remaining in Bryan. Clearly, he preferred to live in the country, but he did not think he had any chance of making a living in Bryan. Wesley knew from his contacts in Bryan "that a workman can't get a job in the place." As he told Sarah, "I am not going to beg their work and then do it for nothing."[64] In Galveston, at least, he was finding work. Wesley was now a foreman, supervising a crew of workers for six dollars a day.[65] His health was holding up, and, although his war wounds were bothering him, he had been able to work four straight weeks without having to miss a day.[66]

Wesley liked Galveston in many respects and thought Sarah would also be pleased with the city. He found "the dark, blue, illimitable waters" and the beautiful beaches "enrapturing beyond description." Galveston was "much cooler than up country, and it has a great many advantages." He thought Sarah would like the availability of churches and the beginnings of what he would call "society." A number of Livingston acquaintances were planning to settle there soon. Dr. Robert Webb, leader of the Livingston Female Academy during the Civil War, was coming in October to accept a professorship at the nearby medical college. Dr. Webb's brothers James and John and John's father-in-law were discussing settling there as well. Wesley told Sarah that these friends, especially the women, "will be a great comfort to you in a social point of view." With good acquaintances and all the advantages in Galveston, he wrote, "I think it will appear more like home to you than any other place in Texas."[67]

Wesley was looking for places to bring his family, preferably close to the church. He found no affordable places to rent; even small, two-room houses with no conveniences were beyond his means. Those places he might afford were about a mile from the church, too far away to easily attend services. And, even though he was lonely and anxious to have Sarah and the children with him, Wesley felt Galveston was not safe for them until the fall. In the summer months, cholera or yellow fever was always threatening. Every time it rained, mosquitoes multiplied, and Wesley admitted, "I dread to think about them, they will be so bad." Cholera had already broken out in Pensacola, Florida, and fearing yellow fever, the federal authorities had mandated the use of disinfectants, ordering people to bathe and clean their premises daily. "I suppose they have some grounds for their fears, or they would not be so rigid about it," Wesley reflected to Sarah.[68]

While in Galveston, Wesley studied the city's buildings. He was confident, as he told Sarah, that his designs would "at least come up to the best, and excel the most."[69] He decided the time was right to advertise himself as an architect, "assured by many" that he "would get a good deal of business."[70] He rented a store from a Mr. Barkley, hung out a sign, and opened his establishment.[71] Wanting to look respectable when dealing with potential clients, Wesley bought himself "a nice frock coat, pants, and gaiter shoes" and said he felt more like himself than he had for years. Giving in to a rare moment of vanity, he wrote Sarah, "I wish you could see me this morning, I think you would give me a kiss. . . . I think I really look nice."[72]

Having saved a little money, Wesley also bought clothing and books for the children, including a gray flannel coat and pants that Frank, a growing boy, needed and a Bible for Mollie's birthday. He had about one hundred dollars that he wanted to send to Sarah, but he dared not risk it in the unreliable mail system; indeed, the one letter to Sarah in which he had contemplated sending money went astray. It was safer to take the clothing and money with him when he returned to Bryan.[73]

Before long, Wesley had clients who wanted buildings designed and built. What he lacked, however, was capital.[74] Without access to financing, he had to ask clients for payment up front and many declined. "If I had only had a few hundred dollars to pay hands with," he lamented, "I could now have had several large houses on hand, and which would have paid, but so it is, and I will bide my time."[75] Eventually, he got a few contracts, and he was hopeful that as he gained a reputation, he would get more. "The better I am known, the more confidence I will command."[76]

Wesley had one good fortune that he attributed to the "good providence of God." He had worried that his rented room had no key for him to lock the door, so one night after work, he cut a stick to prop the door shut. That same night, someone broke into the boarding house. The owner "raised the alarm, and found that <u>every boarder who had not fastened their doors was robbed</u>. One man lost $115.00 and another $240.00. Now what do you think of that? <u>Just in time</u> I was caused to fasten my door, or every cent that I have worked so hard for, would have been gone. God alone watched over me, and secured me. To Him be all praise."[77]

Wesley usually wrote on Sundays, after his spirits had been lifted by his attendance at church services. But some Sundays his pessimism emerged. He worried about the lawlessness and the breakdown of decency and order.[78] He worried about how a white ex-Confederate would "not wish to be tried before a military tribunal, or a negro jury."[79] He was concerned that the race riots that had broken out in New Orleans, encouraged by "bad men . . . determined to keep up as much disturbance between the whites and blacks as possible, might soon spread to Galveston."[80] And he worried about economic conditions while the country remained under arbitrary military rule. Most

Sarah was buried in the Bryan cemetery. Her marker reads: “Sarah A, wife of W. C. Dodson, Died June 6, 1867.” Credit: Courtesy of Mary H. Shearer.

of all, he was concerned about Sarah. "I want to see you very much, and long for the time to come around when we can get settled, and stay together the remainder of our lives, but I fear that just as that begins, one of us will be removed. God pardon us and help us to be ready when our time comes."[81]

In late April, Wesley wrote Sarah that as long as the two of them were well and he was working, he would not return to Bryan until July.[82] But in Bryan, Sarah was not well. "I have had a cold, cough, and sore throat for nearly two months; and Monday there blew up a terrible norther, and I have been worse ever since. . . . I manage to teach still, but go to bed as soon as school hours are over, noon and evening. I never expect to enjoy anymore good health, these Texas winds are killing me, 'slowly but surely.' . . . I know not what to do, I am so completely used up." A lonely Sarah wrote, "I have no one here to give me an encouraging word, or a particle of comfort, under any circumstances, except aunt [Angeline, Wesley's sister]; and her health is so bad [with neuralgia] she cannot come to see me often."[83] Sarah was desperate for a letter from Wesley to cheer her up. "I don't think I can wait till the '1st of July' to see you, but I will try if you think it best." Then she begged him not to take another job in Galveston and to come home.[84]

In May, Wesley finished up one job and bid on another that would pay well but keep him in Galveston until at least June 15.[85] He did not get that job, as he told Sarah, "because I would not wait for the money and I shall be up as soon as possible to see you."[86] Since neither wrote again, Wesley probably arrived in Bryan before Sunday, May 26, a day he would have written another letter. If so, he arrived in time to see Sarah before his "precious Tay," as he called her, died of pneumonia on June 6, 1867.[87] She was a casualty of the cold and wet Texas winter, and of the drafty boarding house she was forced to inhabit, but foremost she was a casualty of the Civil War and its aftermath.

A brokenhearted Wesley buried his "precious, darling wife," "the centre of all [his] earthly love and affection," the woman "never out of [his] mind."[88] She was only thirty-six years old. Wesley and Sarah had been married for fourteen years but had spent almost five years apart—first when Wesley was fighting in the war and later when he was working in Selma and then Galveston. Mollie Bet was only seven years old at the time of her mother's death. Frank was thirteen.

## WHEELOCK

Not much is known about Wesley in the decade following Sarah's death. Wesley probably did not return to Galveston except to retrieve his tools and any belongings he had left at the boarding house.[89] Although he had begun establishing himself in Galveston, he did not want to take the children and go back there. The danger of yellow fever and cholera in the summer would have been too great.[90] In any event, he couldn't possibly take care of the children and work. It seems unlikely that Wesley was willing to abandon his children. He had told Sarah once that he "believed it was never intended for a man and his family to be apart and satisfied."[91] Another time he had told her, "All that I live for is my family, and to live away from them without an actual necessity, I cannot do."[92]

Wesley and Frank may have continued living in the Bryan boarding house for a while, but he could not care for Mollie Bet there. He had to resort to what was the custom of the time: accepting the offer of his sister Angeline, who was in poor health herself, to take Mollie Bet into the Frost household. Chapin had planned to build a house on the edge of Bryan, but when the well dug for him in April 1867 came up dry,[93] he apparently gave up on the Bryan location and decided to build in nearby Wheelock. In any event, Chapin was living in Wheelock, Robertson County, about fifteen miles from Bryan, with Angeline and Mollie Bet in 1870.[94]

Also living in Wheelock at that time was the Watson family. James A. Watson, his wife Eliza Ellis, and their seven children had left Boligee, Greene County, Alabama, the county adjoining Sumter, just before the outbreak of the Civil War. The Watsons had only traveled about one hundred miles when James took ill and died in Hines County, Mississippi. His body was returned to Alabama for burial, but having sold everything there, Eliza and her children continued on to Wheelock with the party of family and friends. After arriving in 1860, Eliza found a farm to rent. She hired sixteen-year-old John Young, the son of an Alabama neighbor, to work as a farm laborer. Twenty-one-year-old Bessie Watson, the oldest child, found work as a seamstress. But the Watsons had a rough time in Wheelock: before the year was out, both nine-year-old Margaret and six-year-old James had died.[95]

In 1867, after returning to Bryan, thirty-eight-year-old Wesley met then twenty-eight-year-old Bessie, and on November 14, five months after Sarah died, they were married. It is difficult to believe that Wesley had grieved and was ready to move on with his life. More likely, he was so distraught from losing the woman he deeply loved that he found a situation to numb his pain. To Wesley, Sarah's death was God's will, and he could not question it. He had to accept it. As he had told Sarah fifteen years earlier, "It is my intention after this to take the world as I find it, but never to be driven from my highest design, that of making myself useful to my friends and my country."[96]

After their marriage, Wesley and Bessie probably lived with the Watsons. If so, Frank probably lived with them, too, and worked on the farm. In June 1869, Bessie's mother, Eliza, died, leaving twenty-year-old Leticia, seventeen-year-old Mary Ann, fourteen-year-old Laura, and thirteen-year-old William without a home. If they were not already living together on the Wheelock farm, Wesley must have taken all of them into his home at that time. He probably did not even contemplate alternatives; that was simply what he did. He felt an obligation to help people in such a situation.

In the Civil War, the South lost over three hundred thousand men, leaving many young women without potential marriage partners. Mary Ann never married but lived in Wesley's household for the rest of her life. Years later, Wesley wrote his daughter Mollie Bet about a recently orphaned girl named Nancy. His letter helps explain why he took Bessie's sisters in: Young women and girls need "a home and a protector," he wrote. "They cannot safely be on their own. Tell her to go [to her cousin's home], and to be thankful that God has put it in their heart to offer her a home."[97]

Wesley and Bessie attended the Presbyterian church in Wheelock, the church where Wesley was most comfortable theologically. The Presbyterians preached the Calvinist doctrine that a person's destiny had been "predetermined" by God and that He had chosen who was among his "elect" and who was not.

"I am asked," Wesley wrote later, "'how came you to be a Calvinist?' My answer is 'I was born one,' and the event at the spring [in Tennessee where his sister saved him from drowning] was the first intimation that I had of the fact, and it has grown with my years, and has given me strength in my weakness and courage in days of trial and ever and anon that same presentment has flashed in my mind, 'You are safe, I have a use for you.' What that use is, may be, in part, the life I have used in trying to benefit others, and being the means of saving some soul for whom Christ died; and further, to be a help and comfort to my mother and sisters after father was called to his reward, and yet another—that I, as the only son to bear his name, might live to raise up boys to perpetuate it—and to give His honor through coming ages—but whatever it was will be revealed in eternity."[98]

Wesley was actively involved in the Wheelock Presbyterian church. In 1869, he was elected to serve as one of the ruling elders who, in court of sessions, governed the local congregation. He was chosen to accompany the minister to meetings of the Presbytery of Brazos, the district organization, and to the synod, the statewide governing organization. Synod meetings were held for about four days, during which ministers gave sermons and keynote addresses, administrative issues were discussed and decided, and new ministers and congregations were admitted to the Presbytery. About fifty-five ministers attended, representing all of the Presbyterian churches then functioning in Texas. At these meetings, Wesley became acquainted

Grave marker of Wesley Troy, son of F. M. and Emma Dodson. Credit: Courtesy of T. Bradford Willis.

with the state's ministers and elders, including Samuel A. King, the minister of the First Presbyterian Church of Waco.[99]

Wesley probably enjoyed going to synod as much as he had enjoyed attending the camp meetings of his childhood. He was in the company of men of good character who talked about spiritual matters that interested him. Always wanting to make himself useful, Wesley served as the clerk and kept the minutes when given the opportunity to do so.[100] In 1874, he was the Wheelock church's only representative to the synod held in Jefferson.[101] In 1875, he attended the synod held in Austin. One purpose of that meeting was to secure a permanent location and building funds for Austin College. The school of higher education, founded by a Princeton-educated Presbyterian missionary in 1849, was struggling at its location in Huntsville. The following year, the synod agreed to relocate Austin College to the town of Sherman, construct a new building there, and secure additional funding for the faculty.[102]

Meanwhile, Wesley's family continued to grow. From 1868 to 1876, Wesley and Bessie had six children: Anna Letitia, Lee Jefferson, Cavitt Watson, James William, Martha Juliett, and Bessie A.[103] In 1877, Bessie's brother William died, and her sister Leticia married William Moss and moved out of Wesley's home. Mollie Bet moved back from the Frosts and lived in the home he had built on Pitts Bridge Road until June 1877, when she married Albert Gallatin Board.[104] She would live in Bryan the rest of her life.

Wesley's son Frank married Emma Frazier in Wheelock on February 8, 1877, and then moved to Waco. Not much is known about Frank after that. In 1878, he and Emma buried their five-month-old son Wesley Troy in Waco. They had another son, Albert, born in 1879. In 1880, at age twenty-five, Frank worked as a farm laborer in Milam County, just south of Waco. In 1893, he sold property in Bruceville, also south of Waco. Where he lived and what he did after that is unknown. He died sometime between 1896 and 1912.[105]

In Wheelock, Wesley continued working as an architect, overseeing the construction of local stores and houses, but little evidence of what he built in the Bryan area exists today.[106] In 1876, Wesley secured a contract to build a new church for a Methodist congregation in Waco, eighty miles northwest from Wheelock. How he secured the commission is unknown. The early records of Waco's Methodist Episcopal Church South have not been preserved nor has any notice to architects been found in the Texas newspapers. Perhaps Samuel A. King, the minister of Waco's Presbyterian Church, was instrumental in connecting Wesley with the Methodist church building committee. From the Presbyterian synods, King knew Wesley to be an honorable man, and he would likely have recommended him to church committee members searching for a reputable architect. In any event, the church adopted the plans and specifications developed by Wesley, conducting business as W. C. Dodson, to construct the Fifth Street Methodist Church in Waco. The award of this project was the beginning of a thirty-year career building churches, courthouses, schools, and other public buildings in Texas.

Mollie Bet Dodson. Credit: Courtesy of the Texas Collection, Baylor University.

Albert Gallatin Board. Credit: Courtesy of the family of Mary Alice Hall.

Wesley Clark Dodson. Credit: Courtesy of the Texas Collection, Baylor University.

# "The Good Society"
## Waco

Built on the site of a former Waco Indian village, Waco was a mere settlement in 1850. In 1866, a group of Waco citizens formed a company to build a suspension bridge across the wide Brazos River, which transects the town. At that time, the bridge would be the longest single-span suspension bridge ever built. The group contracted with the John Roebling Company in Trenton, New Jersey, the company that later built the Brooklyn and Golden Gate Bridges, to provide the cables and steelwork. Completed in 1870, the Waco Suspension Bridge provided a safe crossing for covered wagons moving west and easy access for farmers bringing their crops into town. With the bridge open, farm production increased dramatically. The Chisholm Trail, over which cowboys drove herds of Texas cattle to the railhead, crossed the Brazos at Waco. While some cowboys continued to swim their herds across the river, others chose to pay the toll and drive their cattle across the bridge. Once the bridge opened, Waco grew rapidly.[1]

Wesley arrived in Waco in 1876 to supervise the building of the new Methodist Episcopal Church South. The congregation, numbering almost four hundred members, started in 1850 when Joseph P. Sneed preached in Waco. Sneed was a Methodist missionary of the Tennessee Conference, the conference of Wesley's father, Elisha Jefferson Dodson. W. C. Dodson drew plans for the new Fifth Street Methodist Church to be built from brick in the Gothic Revival style, a style many Texas architects employed at this time. The building plans called for the sides of the sanctuary to have tall, narrow stained-glass windows with pointed arches and for the front of the sanctuary to have a large grouping of stained-glass windows, all of which would draw worshipers' eyes upward. The plans also called for a soaring 130-foot steeple reaching heavenward with a bell to call the congregation to services. On May 5, 1876, the church began advertising for builders to bid on its project. Then on June 1, the church accepted a contractor's low bid of $20,000. Until the building was completed in 1878, the church, under the Reverend M. H. Wells, held services in the Waco Female College.[2]

While construction proceeded, Wesley investigated Waco to see if it was a suitable place to bring his family. What he found pleased him. By the late 1870s, the town had grown to about fifteen thousand people. Churches in town, including Catholic, Episcopal, and Lutheran as well as several Baptist, Methodist, and Presbyterian, were flourishing with sizable congregations. The Jewish townspeople had established Temple Roddef Sholom. A number of benevolent societies, including the Masons, the Knights of Honor, and the United Friends of Temperance, were actively involved in the community. Private schools, including Waco Female College and Paul Quinn College—the

(Top) Waco Suspension Bridge. Credit: Georgi Petrov (Wikimedia Commons, CC BY-SA 2.5).

(Bottom) Waco Suspension Bridge and Bridge Street, 1876. Credit: Courtesy of the Lee Lockwood Library and Museum, Waco, Texas.

The Fifth Street Methodist Church, Waco, Texas. Credit: Courtesy of the Texas Collection, Baylor University.

first black college west of the Mississippi—had already been established. Two newspapers were operating.[3] Wesley must have decided that Waco promised the good society he had been trying to find because, in January 1877, he moved his family there, to a home on South Eighth Street near Waco Creek.[4] At that time, Wesley and Bessie's household consisted of their six children and Bessie's sisters, Mary Ann and Laura. Their last two children, Samuel Byars and Laura Angeline, were born in 1878 and 1880.

### CIVIC INVOLVEMENT

Wesley immediately became engaged in the civic life of Waco. As had been his practice in Livingston and Wheelock, he attended and participated in the public meetings. In 1877, Waco bought an old race track and fairgrounds as a site for a cemetery. Although he was still new in town, Wesley volunteered to design the cemetery. He laid out the roads, walkways, and burial plots through the fifty acres and called for tree plantings to line the roads, creating a dignified and peaceful space. His efforts brought his name to the attention of the Waco officials and helped establish his reputation as a civic-minded architect.[5]

Years later, Wesley was still engaged in civic endeavors. In 1889, Texas staged the Karporama of Texas at the Spring Palace in Houston. The event was a presentation of the natural products found in Texas, showcasing what the state had to offer manufacturers. Agricultural and livestock products were on display, including birds, flowers, and fruits, as were all kinds of natural resources. Wesley volunteered to serve as general manager of the department of building stone and timber. In that role, he called for "specimens of all kinds of timber, stone, rock, limestone, clay and material for cement" to be displayed at the event.[6]

When he first came to Waco, Wesley began attending the First Presbyterian Church. Founded in 1855, the church had grown from an initial membership of seventeen to about one hundred five.[7] When his family arrived, Wesley and Bessie transferred their memberships from the Wheelock Presbyterian Church. On February 4, 1877, a week after he became a member, Wesley was elected as a ruling elder, both because he had been ordained a ruling elder while in Wheelock and because he had already gained the respect of the Waco congregation.[8] That fall, he accompanied the minister, the Reverend Samuel A. King, to the Presbyterian synod in Marshall, where over 130 churches were represented.[9] Wesley attended almost every synod held over the next twenty years.[10]

At the 1893 meeting, held in Waco, the synod proposed establishing a Pres-

The Waco streetcar ended at the gates to the Oakwood Cemetery. Credit: Courtesy of the Texas Collection, Baylor University.

byterian university in Texas. Wesley, a staunch supporter of higher education, was one of two elders appointed to the eight-person committee charged with considering possible steps forward. The committee recommended that the synod secure a charter for a Presbyterian university combining Austin College at Sherman, the Austin School of Theology at Austin, and the Female College at Gainesville. Like Austin College, the other two schools both had Presbyterian connections: the Austin School of Theology was founded in 1884 by Presbyterian ministers R. K. Smoot and R. L. Dabney,[11] and the Female College was established by the synod in 1891.[12]

The committee recommended that, for the time being, the three schools remain at their present locations, with provisions for the future establishment of schools of law and medicine. They also recommended that the curriculum be designed to prepare graduates for "the professional courses which they may intend to pursue in the several schools of the university." Finally, the

Wesley at the meeting of the synod in Tyler, Texas, 1888. Credit: Courtesy of First Presbyterian Church of Waco and the Portal to Texas History, University of North Texas Libraries.

committee urged the appointment of a financial agent to solicit funds for the endowment of the schools' chairs.[13]

The synod adopted the committee's recommendations. Unfortunately, the United States suffered an economic collapse later in 1893, and the economy remained depressed for the remainder of the decade. While Austin College survived the depression, the Female College closed in 1893, and the Austin School of Theology closed in 1895. In 1899, the synod decided to use the theology school's remaining resources to establish the Austin Presbyterian Theological Seminary in Austin. That school opened its doors in 1902.[14]

When the Waco Presbyterian congregation resolved in 1882 to build a larger church in a more convenient location for its members, Elder W. C.

The First Presbyterian Church of Waco as it appeared with its tall, graceful spire. Credit: Courtesy of First Presbyterian Church of Waco and the Portal to Texas History, University of North Texas Libraries.

Dodson volunteered to design the new building. The church sold its building at Jackson and Second to the St. Paul's AME Church and bought property at 812 Austin Avenue.[15] Dodson designed a Gothic brick structure with striking stained-glass windows and a towering spire. The church records summarized the construction: "Our present building was commenced in 1883; the lecture room occupied by the congregation in spring of 1884, and soon the new building was completed, furnished and occupied free of debt. The membership then numbered only 157."[16]

The First Presbyterian Church of Waco, 812 Austin Avenue. The spire was damaged and replaced with the shorter "temporary" tower. Credit: Courtesy of the Texas Collection, Baylor University.

Wesley attended church in that building until a new structure was built in 1912. By that time, Waco had grown to about thirty-five thousand people. The church then had over three hundred members and over two hundred children in the Sunday School. Wesley's son James William (J. W.) was an elder, and Wesley's son Cavitt Watson (C. W.) was going to synod with the minister. According to the church history, "The church was composed of the best culture of the state, men and women of education, much travel, refinement and true spirituality. Men attended church in silk hats, long coats, gloves, and bore canes." Austin Avenue "was paved with wooden blocks, and through it ran a little street car. There were only two or three automobiles in Waco."[17]

**WACO ARCHITECTURAL CAREER**

When he arrived in Waco in 1876, Wesley needed to quickly establish himself as a respected architect. His Methodist church building had been well received, and he subsequently was hired to build a new county courthouse.[18] In 1878, the *Waco Daily Examiner* ran an article lauding Dodson as "one of the best architects in the South" and vouching for his honesty, fairness, and integrity.[19]

That fall, Wesley ran a series of ads in the paper offering his services as W. C. Dodson, the professional name he used in his architectural business.[20] In the 1878–79 City Directory, where he ran an advertisement on the back cover, he was the only architect listed in Waco, with an office at the new courthouse on Franklin and South Second Street.[21] Dodson was still operating as a master builder, both designing and constructing buildings. The city directory referred to him as an "architect and builder."[22] Although Wesley's injuries prevented him from fully participating physically in construction, he was capable of supervising workers and ensuring the job was done correctly.

In November 1878, Dodson signed a contract to build a new residence for a real estate agent, John Walton. The *Waco Daily Examiner* concluded that Walton's ten-room home would "be one of the handsomest and most convenient residences in the city."[23] Over the next thirty years, Dodson built a number of homes. He developed a pattern of buying two or three lots in the city, then building a home for his family on one lot and building homes on the others, either for clients or as speculative homes. When those were sold, he would buy two or three more lots, or even a whole block, and continue the process. In the late 1890s, his grown sons began to buy half interest in the lots with him. Three of his sons went into real estate and bought a number of lots on their own.[24] Wesley moved his family within Waco seven times over a period of twenty-five years. One of his last homes, built in 1896 in the Queen Anne style, is still standing and occupied today.[25]

In 1884, with his office still at the courthouse, Dodson formed a partnership with W. W. Dudley, a local architect who had just finished building a Second Empire courthouse for Coleman County. Dudley was born in Missouri in 1842. A carpenter's son, he was educated in the Missouri public schools until he was seventeen, at which time he became a farmhand. When the Civil War broke out, Dudley enlisted in the 16th Missouri Infantry and served for four years. At the end of the war, he was paroled in Shreveport, Louisiana. He taught school in Louisiana and Arkansas for eighteen months before returning to Missouri to take up carpentry. In 1870, Dudley went to Texas, where he worked as a carpenter in Paris and Gainesville before moving to Waco in 1882. There, although he had no training, he began practicing architecture.

The First District Public School on North Fourth Street. Credit: Courtesy of the Lee Lockwood Library and Museum, Waco, Texas.

Dudley was a member of the Methodist Episcopal Church South and the Masonic Temple.[26] Little more is known about Dudley's work other than, like Dodson, he seemed to prefer designing in the Second Empire style.

Dodson and Dudley worked together for about five years.[27] What role Dudley played in their partnership is not entirely clear. After the partnership was dissolved, Dudley continued to be listed as an architect in *Morrison & Fourmy's Directory of the City of Waco*. In the 1910 Census, he was listed as a "house builder."

Dodson probably wanted a partner because by 1884 he had more work than he could manage unassisted. When he formed the partnership, he had already built five courthouses, was engaged in supervising the construction of another courthouse, and was intending to seek commissions for four additional courthouses. Supervising the construction of public buildings meant Dodson was frequently away from home, traveling sometimes by stagecoach and, once the railroad lines began operating, by train. The *Waco Daily Ex-*

The Second District Public School on the corner of Columbus Avenue and North Eleventh Street. Credit: Courtesy of the Lee Lockwood Library and Museum, Waco, Texas.

*aminer*, which covered the comings and goings of its citizens, reported in 1885: "Mr. W. C. Dodson, the architect, returned from Weatherford yesterday, where he has been engaged on the [Parker County] court-house and will leave next week for Palestine to attend to that [Anderson County] courthouse."[28]

Dodson was also interested in work opportunities in Waco, making it important that he or a partner be in town. He wanted to continue building homes and commercial and public buildings. In 1884, Dodson and Dudley won a commission to design three new public schools for the city of Waco. The city awarded the contract to build the schools for $20,300 to John H. McNeil, whom Dodson would work with several more times as the years went on. For their work, Dodson and Dudley were paid $304.50, or 1.5 percent of the contract.[29]

The townspeople were proud of their new buildings. A decade earlier, Waco had had no public schools. In an 1882 election, the citizens authorized the imposition of a tax to support free public education. With the three new

The Third District Public School at 920 South Eighth Street. Credit: Courtesy of the Lee Lockwood Library and Museum, Waco, Texas.

The cornerstone of the Austin Avenue Methodist Church was laid in 1901, but the building was not dedicated until 1906 when all of the debts had been paid off. Credit: Private Collection of T. B. Willis, the Portal to Texas History, University of North Texas Libraries.

The minister greeting his parishioners in front of the parish house to the left of the church, 1913. Credit: Courtesy of the Texas Collection, Baylor University.

schools, the *Waco Daily Examiner* reported, it is "broadly acknowledged" that Waco has "the very best local system of public schools in the state." Waco also boasted about its Academy of the Sacred Heart and its schools of higher education, including Waco University and Waco Female College, all of which combined "to make Waco what we claim for her, the educational center of Texas and we don't consider the claim a forced one either, in any respect."[30]

In 1894, after the partnership with Dudley had been liquidated, the former partners divided a new commission: Dodson designed an addition to the Columbus Avenue School, and Dudley designed an addition to the South Eighth Street School.[31]

In December 1900, the Fifth Street Methodist Church decided to divide its large and still-growing congregation and erect another church building. The Reverend John R. Nelson, who had been the minister at the Fifth Street Methodist Church since 1898, was named the pastor of the new church. The building committee purchased three lots on Austin Avenue. Dodson was one of five architects to submit drawings. His design was not chosen, but he was hired to assess the plans and specifications submitted by W. A. Cann, the St. Louis architect preferred by the church, and to supervise the construction.[32] The building became the Austin Avenue Methodist Church, which held its first services on December 29, 1901, with eighty-one charter members.

In 1906, Waco's St. Paul's Episcopal Church hired Dodson to supervise the construction of a parish house next to its church building on Columbus and North Fifth Street. The cornerstone of the Gothic church had been laid in 1878. An addition to the frame building, made to accommodate a growing congregation, had been carried out in 1897.[33] The committee asked seventy-seven-year-old Dodson, in what was probably his last public project, to supervise R. M. Ligon's construction of the building according to the plans and specifications of the Philadelphia architect George Nattress. The parish house more than doubled the size of the existing church facility, adding space for clergy and staff offices as well as a chapel for children's services, Sunday school classrooms, a children's choir rehearsal room, meeting rooms, and a great hall.[34]

## ESTABLISHING ARCHITECTURE AS A PROFESSION

In 1885, Dodson became a fellow of the professional society known as the Western Association of Architects (WAA).[35] The association had been founded the year before by a group of non–East Coast architects who felt disrespected by the members of the elite American Institute of Architects (AIA). The WAA included the influential Chicago architect Louis Sullivan, known as "the father of the skyscraper." Dodson and seven other WAA fellows felt

Texas needed a recognized professional association that would uphold high standards of integrity and professionalism in the practice of architecture. In 1886, they joined together in Austin to found the Texas State Association of Architects (TSAA) under the umbrella of the WAA. Among the charter members were Oscar Ruffini, E. T. Heiner, Alfred Giles, W. W. Larmour, J. N. Preston, S. A. J. Preston, James Wahrenberger, Nathaniel Tobey, Nicholas J. Clayton, and J. J. Kane, all of whom were leading architects of the time.[36]

For several years, Dodson headed the TSAA's executive committee, which drafted a constitution and bylaws for the organization, set membership requirements, and established rules of practice. The executive committee established a schedule of usual and proper charges, drew up uniform contracts for architects to use with clients, and agreed on other regulations so that all architects in good standing would practice under a uniform code.[37]

Since the end of the Civil War, architects had been working to gain recognition as a respected profession rather than a trade. In doing so, they faced a number of problems. For one, clients often did not value their design work or appreciate their construction knowledge and skills. During design competitions, builders, contractors, and architects themselves sometimes disparaged the work of others, trying to undermine the reputation of their competitors in order to gain an advantage for themselves. Some architects were known to approach other architects' clients to take away already contracted work. When numerous architects submitted proposals, as was typical for public buildings, the commissioners tasked with choosing the most meritorious plan often lacked the qualifications to do so and based their decisions on political considerations. In dealing with the counties' commissioners courts, bribery and kickbacks were not unheard of.[38]

The architects also had to deal with what they viewed as unqualified people competing for contracts. Anyone could call themself an architect, even someone who lacked the training and knowledge to design buildings with pleasing proportions and lines, with the functionality required, and, most importantly, with proper construction so as to be safe for habitation. To address this problem, the TSAA executive committee prepared for submission to the state legislature an Act to Regulate the Practice of Architecture in the State of Texas. The committee sought passage of a law that would institute a licensing examination and effectively bar unqualified individuals from practicing.[39]

Dodson was elected president of the TSAA in 1888 and was reelected in 1889. In his address to the Fourth Annual Meeting of the Association held in Waco on January 15, 1889, Dodson stressed the importance of getting a licensing law passed for the protection of the people. He also urged the association to lobby the state to provide for a school of architecture, arguing that such a school was needed as much as schools of law or medicine, which the state already supported. "This subject [schools of architecture] is intimately blended with the bill for regulation of the practice of architecture which we are preparing to present to the legislature; it is blended with it, because a profession of significant importance to require a license for the protection of the people before it can be practiced should require suitable proficiency to be made in the science and knowledge attaching to that profession, and ample means should be made to attain that proficiency. Graduation and license are linked together. . . . I do insist that men should be examined and licensed by competent authority before they are allowed to practice."[40]

The state legislature was not eager to enact regulations on the practice of architecture. The bill proposed by the TSAA in 1889 would have been the first in the nation,[41] and business interests pressured legislators to oppose such a bill. The legislature failed to pass the licensing bill and also failed to establish schools for the rigorous training of architects. Architects continued to press their concerns. In 1905, Texas A&M began an architecture program, the first in Texas. In 1910, the University of Texas at Austin began offering a professional degree in architecture. Eventually, but not until 1937, the state set up the Board of Architectural Examiners to license qualified practitioners.[42] It took a long time, but Dodson's efforts, as well as those of other Texas architects, helped to further the establishment of architecture as a profession.

In 1889, the WAA merged with the AIA. Under the terms of the merger, all fellows of the WAA became fellows of the AIA; thus, Dodson and seven other founding members of the TSAA who had been WAA members automatically became AIA fellows.[43] Led by the San Antonio architect J. Riely Gordon, a number of TSAA members who had not belonged to the WAA lobbied the AIA to become fellows as well. They were unhappy to learn that they would need to apply as individuals and be subjected to the same stringent review procedures as any other architects applying for membership.[44] When James Wahrenberger applied for AIA membership in 1890, N. J. Clayton, one of the original WAA members, wrote the AIA secretary, J. W. Root, that "[Wahrenberger] is one of the very few men, practicing the profession in this State, whom I can conscientiously recommend and endorse as an Architect in every sense . . . by previous training and honorable practice, to be entitled to membership in the Institute."[45]

When Gordon was informed that his membership application was denied, he admitted that the denial "cuts me to the quick." He continued to say, "I regret to feel that a few of my brother architects, all of whom treat me with every degree of courtesy to my face, should, prompted by jealousy alone, stoop to league themselves together to stab me in the back, under the cover of secrecy."[46] Despite Gordon's charge that the eight WAA members kept their colleagues out of the AIA, there is no evidence of the group's colluding to do so and no evidence of Dodson's opposition. But the unhappiness of those Texas architects not accepted into the AIA caused much dissension within the TSAA. Several years later, in 1895, the AIA gave Dodson a provisional charter authorizing him to start a Texas state chapter of the AIA. He attempted to do so but found that relationships among the Texas architects had become so strained over the membership issue that "it was impossible to get men together to organize under it." Reluctantly, he returned the charter to the AIA.[47]

Although Dodson had been re-elected president of the TSAA for the 1890 term, he resigned from the association before the 1890 meeting. The friction among the members over the AIA situation was undoubtedly one of the reasons for his resignation.[48] Moreover, the unethical and divisive behavior of his colleagues, particularly architects disparaging the work of others, deeply troubled him. As he said in his 1889 presidential address: "We cannot expect success if each is trying to work the ruin of others by deprecating all merit and by innuendos and evil speaking, seeking to pull others down that we may rear ourselves upon their ruin. Remember that if we are to accomplish anything, it is to be by a united effort and to attain to a united effort, self-respect and respect for other must unite us into a band of workers, each rejoicing in the success of his associates. If this principle in regard to our associates is not acted upon by each member, we are needlessly spending our time and our money in any effort to effect the objects of our association."[49]

For four years, Dodson devoted a great deal of his time and energy to the TSAA organization. He had great hopes for what architects could accomplish working together. He shared his highly romanticized vision with the architects at the TSAA meeting in 1889: "Sheltered within its walls the architects will keep abreast with the wants of this great state in all its improvements, until its sunny hills and umbrageous valleys rejoicing in the handiwork of man, will smile with their tasteful dwellings and gorgeous palaces, the picture of refined intelligence and a scene of beauty."[50] Given the rancorous situation, he may have concluded that his time could better be spent elsewhere. As an AIA fellow, Dodson continued working to help architects gain respect as professionals. He also continued focusing on his own architectural work, the most important of which was erecting safe, functional, and beautiful courthouses and other public buildings.

# Building the Cathedrals of Texas

Had he lived in an earlier historical period, Wesley Clark Dodson might have built cathedrals. In the Middle Ages, the cathedral stood as the focal point of major cities. The church provided the foundation for society, establishing the rules of conduct and setting expectations. It recorded the life transitions of birth, marriage, and death and provided the fabric that held society together. As in Europe, the towns in New England were laid out with the church and its towering spire centrally located on the town green. In Texas, by contrast, it was the courthouse, with its bell tower and clock, that assumed the prominent place on the town square.

Wesley arrived in Texas with his family during the post–Civil War era. They found Texas to be rife with lawlessness and disorder, and they searched for a place with what they considered a "good society,"[1] where they could raise their children properly. That required an area where homes were not regularly broken into at night; where drunkards, prostitutes, and gamblers were not visible on the streets; where children obeyed their parents, and their parents obeyed the law. Wesley later recalled that he "could not find a public building worthy of the name nor a dwelling with convenience or construction which would meet the requirements for which it was erected."[2] There was a great need for well-designed, well-built, and tastefully adorned churches, schools, jails, and courthouses, and Wesley was determined to help fill that need.

As Reconstruction ended and the economy began to stabilize, the population in Texas continued growing. The Texas Constitution of 1876 established county commissioners courts, consisting of four elected commissioners and one elected judge, to be responsible for administering county government. The state legislature laid out the counties and designated the center of the county for the county seat, reasoning it would give all citizens equal access to their government. Then, in 1881, the legislature passed a law allowing counties to issue bonds to finance the building of courthouses—a measure that opened the way for a surge in new courthouse construction.

When county commissioners decided to build a new courthouse, they would generally conduct a design competition, advertising in newspapers for architects to submit proposals. The competition's winner would be paid a fifty- or one-hundred-dollar premium.[3] For smaller projects, commissioners might seek proposals from contractors only;[4] occasionally, they would open competitions to both contractors and architects.[5] County commissioners tended to know little about architectural design. They knew they wanted a building that would become the focus of the county's political and social activities, and they usually wanted something bigger and grander than what neighboring counties had built, something that would make a statement about their own county's importance. Sometimes, to become better informed, commissioners traveled to inspect newly built courthouses in nearby counties to see what different architects were designing. Occasionally, commissioners would note a favored architectural style, but requests for bids varied widely in the amount of detail provided. Mostly, the commissioners were concerned with the building's cost and size.

As courthouses were built in the 1880s and 1890s, they soon became symbols of law and order. Courthouses held the records of land transfers, wills, and other legal agreements. The courts settled disputes among citizens and issued decisions enforced by the county sheriff. County officials appraised property and collected taxes. They called on able-bodied men to maintain the roads and all men to serve on jury duty. The commissioners court even provided aid for indigent citizens.[6]

The courthouse was also economically important to the county seat. The courthouse square was generally surrounded by a number of business establishments, many of which had dealings in the courthouse. The square became the meeting point for farmers who came into town a few times a month to buy and sell their goods as well as the place for festivals and celebrations that fostered patriotism and civic involvement. Courthouses were often the only place for local people to gather, either for political party conventions and public lectures or for dances and social gatherings. Sometimes, the courthouse was made available to newly established church congregations who had yet to build their sanctuaries. Other times, the courtroom was used for the free public school.[7] Often rooms in newly built courthouses that were not immediately needed for county officials were rented to local lawyers or businesses. W. C. Dodson's architectural office was in the McLennan County Courthouse for a number of years.[8]

In the 1880s, a number of Texas architects competed for courthouse work. Often fifteen or more architects would contend for a given project. One of the most noteworthy architects who vied with Dodson for commissions was Alfred Giles. Born in England, Giles had received his architectural training in a two-year apprenticeship at a London architectural firm. He moved to hot and dry San Antonio for his health in 1875 and designed a number of buildings in Mexico and South Texas. In the early 1880s, Giles became the leading San Antonio architect, winning a number of courthouse commissions. His buildings varied in style and evolved with the trends of the time. For example, he built the Gillespie County Courthouse (1882) in Italianate; the El Paso County Courthouse (1885), the Goliad County Courthouse (1893), and the Lockhart County Courthouse (1893) in Second Empire; the Webb County Courthouse (1909) in Beaux-Arts; and the Brooks County Courthouse (1914) in Classical Revival. Almost all of Giles's still-remaining buildings have been designated Recorded Texas Historic Landmarks and are on the National Register of Historic Places.[9]

Other notable architects in the competition for courthouse contracts were Eugene T. Heiner and the Ruffini brothers. Eugene Heiner was born in New York City to German immigrant parents. He trained with a Chicago architect as a young man and went to Germany for additional study. After working as a draftsman in Indiana for three years, he moved to Texas in 1876 and settled in Houston. During the 1880s, he built sixteen jails, several college buildings, and a number of courthouses. Three of his courthouses—those in Colorado, Old Brazoria, and Lavaca Counties—were later listed on the National Register of Historic Places.[10]

The Ruffini brothers, Oscar and F. E., were born in Cleveland to Italian immigrant parents. They gained their training as young apprentices to Ohio architects. When they came to Texas in the 1870s, F. E. Ruffini settled in Austin and eventually designed twelve courthouses, including those in Gregg and Concho Counties. His brother Oscar, with whom he sometimes worked, settled in San Angelo for health reasons and designed, among others, the Sutton County Courthouse (1891).

Other contemporary architects were Charles Wheelock, who built the Lamar County Courthouse; W. W. Larmour of Waco, who designed the Tom Green County Courthouse; and James Edward Flanders, who drew the plans for the Shackelford County Courthouse. Like Dodson, this group of architects primarily designed in the Second Empire style, a style that had developed in Europe during the reign of Napoleon III. Widely used in new Paris construction, such as with the Louvre's addition in the 1850s, the style became popular in the United States during the mid-nineteenth century for use in public buildings. Both the State, War, and Navy Building (1871–75) in Washington, DC, and Philadelphia City Hall (1871–1901) were built in this style.

In 1874, the main building at the Agricultural and Mechanical College of Texas (later Texas A&M) near Bryan, designed by Jacob Larmour, became the first Second Empire building erected in Texas.[11] Dodson may have seen and admired that building and its style, and he probably saw other Second Empire buildings in the architectural magazines of the era. The stately lines might have seemed appropriately dignified for public buildings, and its elegance might have appealed to his aesthetic sense. Dodson and the other Second Empire architects often incorporated Italianate, classical, or other styles into their designs to personalize them.[12]

Although Second Empire was the most popular style used in the 1870s and 1880s, other styles were incorporated in the 1880s. Jasper N. Preston and F. E. Ruffini designed the Bastrop County Courthouse in Renaissance revival, Wahrenberger and Beckman of San Antonio built the Maverick County Courthouse (1885) in Romanesque revival with Second Empire influences, and J. J. E. Gibson built the Shelby County Courthouse (1885) in a Gothic Revival style. J. N. Preston and Son of Austin built the Bell County Courthouse (1884) in the Renaissance revival style.[13]

In the late 1880s, J. Riely Gordon, thirty-five years younger than Dodson and representing the next generation of architects, became another noteworthy competitor for architectural commissions. Born in Virginia, Gordon moved to San Antonio in 1874 with his family when he was eleven years old. In 1881, he began a yearlong apprenticeship under W. K. Dobson, perhaps cut short when the architect left San Antonio. Gordon then worked as a draftsman for J. N. Preston and his son, Samuel A. J. Preston, for another two years. When the Prestons left Texas for California in 1884, Gordon opened his own office, partnering with Frederick B. Shelton. In an early attempt to solicit business, Gordon developed a set of generic plans that he sold to contractors. The contractors then used these plans to bid on projects advertised "for contractors only." Occasionally, Gordon would then get the contract to supervise the construction. His first public project, the Val Verde Jail (1885), was done that way.

In the 1890s, many of Gordon's courthouses were built in the Romanesque revival style, made popular by influential architect Henry Hobson Richardson and sometimes referred to as "Richardson Romanesque." Gordon probably learned this style in 1887 when he worked on the Romanesque revival San Antonio Post Office and Federal Building for the Office of the Supervising Architect of the Treasury in San Antonio. In later years, Gordon abandoned Romanesque revival to design in the Beaux-Arts and Renaissance revival styles. Eighteen Texas courthouses were built using Gordon's designs. The twelve that survive today are designated Recorded Texas Historic Landmarks and are on the National Register of Historic Places.[14]

In the 1870s and 1880s, most architects used a cross-axial design for courthouses; this was the floor plan that Dodson used for most of his 1880s courthouses. With entry doors on all four sides, leading to crossing corridors in the center, the design allowed for convenient placement of county offices and courtrooms and good cross ventilation. Regardless of the building's style, architects using the cross-axial plans typically placed the large district courtroom, extending the length of the building, on the second floor. If the towers were centered over the building, as they generally were when the courthouse was placed on the town square, then the towers were supported by wooden trusses affixed to the courtroom walls.

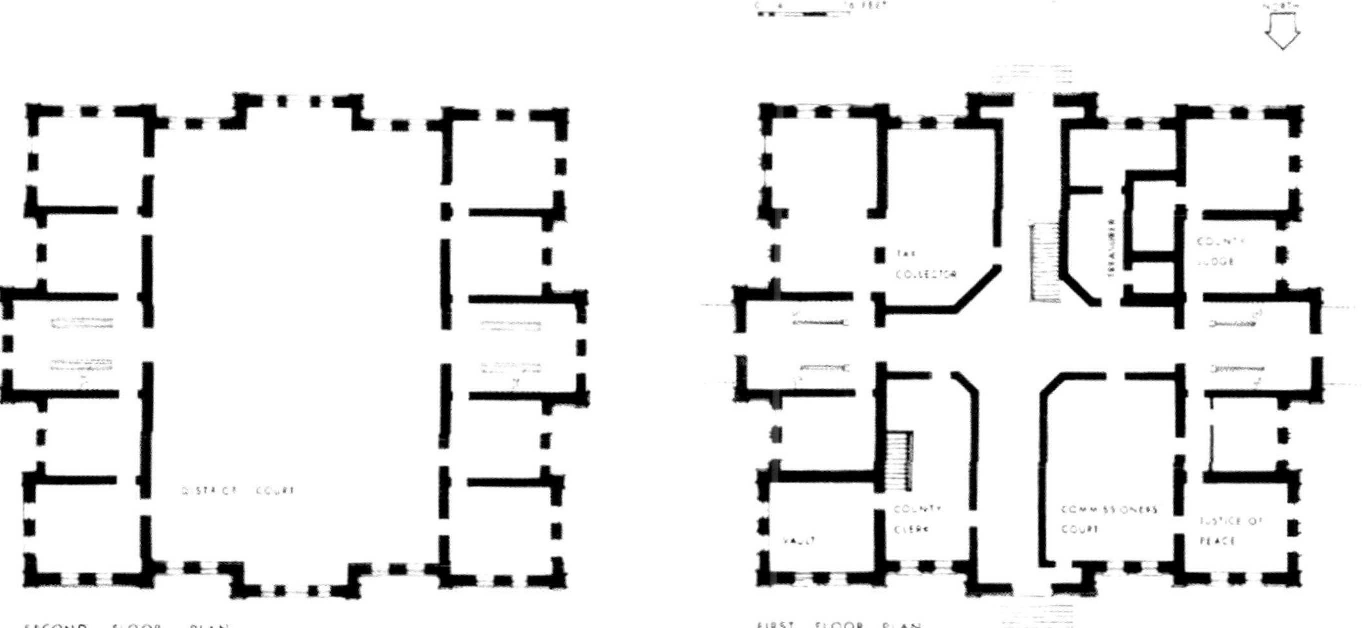


Floor plan for W. C. Dodson's Parker County Courthouse. Credit: Floor plans measured and drawn by Willard Robinson, *Texas Public Buildings in the Nineteenth Century* (Austin: University of Texas Press, 1974), 200.

The architectural plans for Dodson's early courthouses have all been lost, and no evidence exists to provide insight into the arrangement of the interior space. Photographs show that, with the exception of the Camp County Courthouse, all were cross-axial, with entrances of equal prominence on all four sides. Judging from his later courthouses that survive and his later writings, it seems likely that Dodson located the smaller county courtroom on the first floor, along with the offices of the county judge, county clerk, tax assessor and collector, county auditor, sheriff, and perhaps the land surveyor. These offices drew the most people into the courthouse on a daily basis to conduct business. The large district courtroom was likely centered on the second floor, with high ceilings to accommodate balcony seating accessible from the third floor. Paying attention to a smoothly functioning courthouse, Dodson probably would have placed the judge's office, district attorney's office, jury rooms, witness room, and district clerk's office in places with convenient access to the courtroom. This is exactly what he did in Parker County and in later courthouses for which floor plans exist.[15]

In 1888, when designing the Fannin County Courthouse, Dodson made an important improvement in courthouse design. His revised plan featured a seven-bay composition—not the three- or five-bay plans that he had been

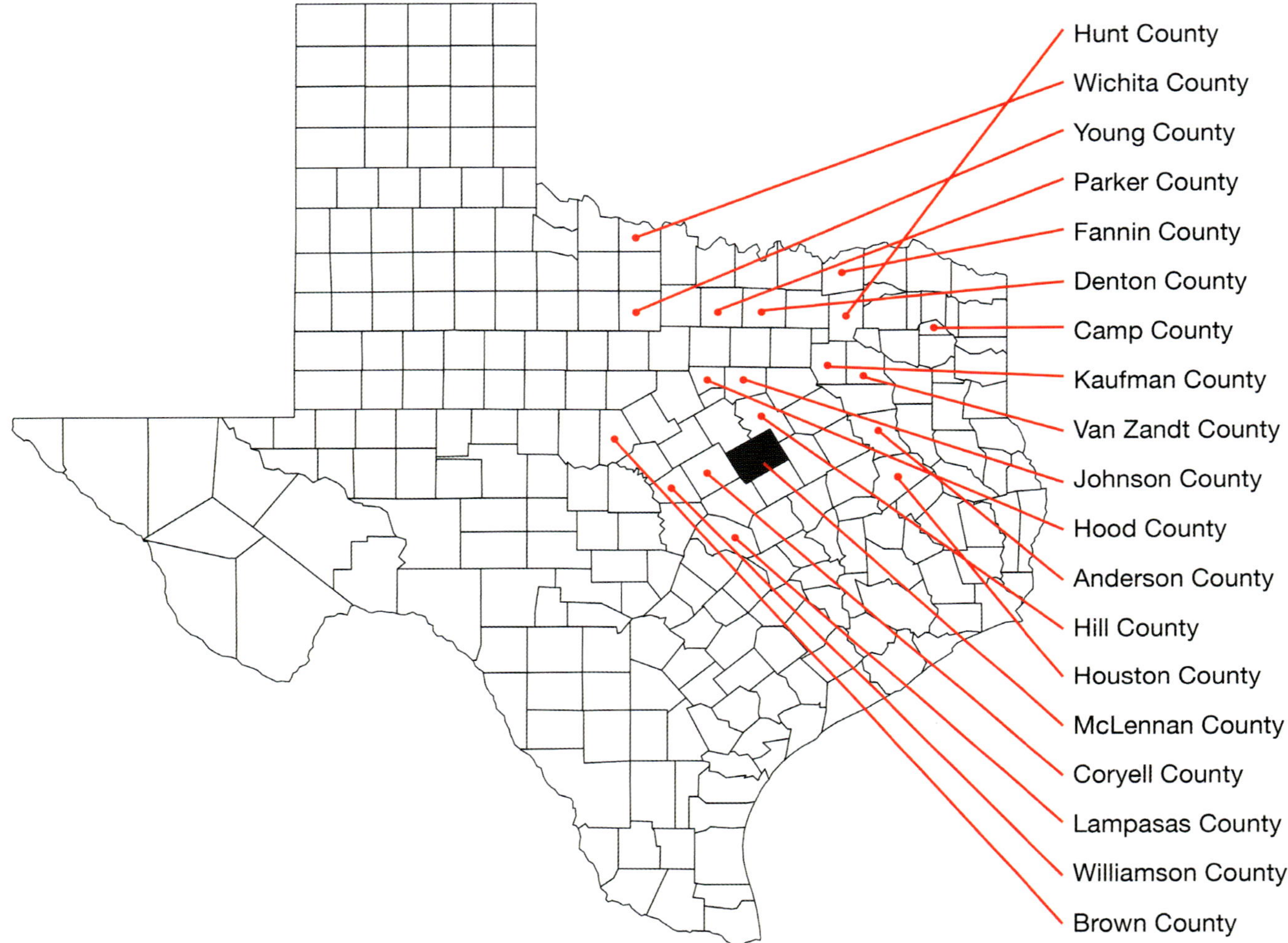


Location of W. C. Dodson's courthouses and jails. Credit: Dave Benbennick, (Wikimedia Commons). Marked by author to show courthouse and jail locations.

using. The additional space in the floor plan gave him the room needed to locate the second-floor courtroom to the side of the central corridors rather than in the center of the building. In turn, this enabled him to support the centrally located tower from the ground up, discarding the wooden trusses previously used. Dodson's new technique would prove to be indispensable in supporting the heavy masonry central towers in his later courthouses.

J. Riely Gordon's initial courthouse design had a floor plan that differed from the predominant cross-axial plan of the 1870s and 1880s. In his Aransas County Courthouse (1889), built in the Moorish style, and in his later Romanesque revival courthouses in Fayette, Erath, and Victoria Counties,

Gordon featured a square central atrium. This open-center plan may have been inspired by Henry Hobson Richardson's Allegheny County Courthouse Complex (1884) built in Pittsburgh. The open center produced good natural light and ventilation for all of the rooms placed around the courtyard. Gordon placed outside entry doors in the middle of all four sides with the corridors leading to the central court.

In 1894, Gordon shifted to a cruciform plan, which put the entry doors at the building's four corners (at the reentrant angles), with a central staircase where the atrium space had been in earlier designs. This floor plan was well suited for constructing a tower that rose from the building's center as it permitted the masonry footings to extend to the ground floor. Gordon used this floor plan in a design that was used to build the Brazoria, Hopkins, Gonzales, San Patricio, and Van Zandt County Courthouses, all built in 1894.[16]

Dodson spent thirty years designing and supervising the construction of public buildings. Beginning with the McLennan County Courthouse (1876) in Waco and for the remainder of his architectural career, Dodson faced a number of issues common to courthouse construction. Sometimes the county seat's location, and thus the courthouse's location, became a political issue, with debates delaying award or completion of contracts. Populist opposition to government spending sometimes sparked resistance to the construction of a new courthouse. Some counties struggled to afford the buildings they desired and had to scale back or completely abandon their building plans. Local political squabbles sometimes spilled over into courthouse deliberations. Finally, competition for courthouse commissions could be time-consuming and expensive—sometimes even underhanded and unethical. In the course of his career, W. C. Dodson encountered all of these issues.

# Dodson's Early Courthouses, 1876–1884

Dodson designed his first courthouse in 1876. That was followed by a five-year period with no courthouse contracts, during which time Dodson focused on designing local Waco buildings. Then, in 1881, when county commissioners were given the authority to issue bonds to finance courthouse construction, it set off what became known as the golden age of courthouse construction. Suddenly, a number of county commissioners sought architectural designs for new courthouses. Dodson soon had as much work as he could manage. Over the next three years, he had contracts for five courthouses and, when one of them burned, he built its replacement. He also supervised the construction of all these buildings. In this period, Dodson personalized his interpretation of the Second Empire style, varying his use of mansard roofs, developing a central tower design, and incorporating a variety of architectural detailing.

### McLENNAN COUNTY COURTHOUSE, WACO, 1876–1877

In March 1873, McLennan County received approval from the state legislature to levy a special property tax for three years to secure the funds needed for a new jail and the county's third courthouse.[1] Its first, built in the early 1850s at a cost of $400, was a thirty-by-thirty-foot log cabin. The second courthouse, built in 1856 at a cost of $11,500, was brick with a tin roof. By the early 1870s, that courthouse was falling apart and dangerous to the people working in it. Two people were killed exiting a second-floor door that led into thin air. A larger, safer courthouse was needed.[2] In 1874, the county commissioners court adopted a proposal for a jail and jailor's house offered by a local builder, R. Andrews. The new jail was quickly constructed, and the old jail and jail lot were sold.

The commissioners court then turned its attention to building a new courthouse. Initially, in a split vote, it selected plans offered by Andrews and his partner Doughly, paying them fifty dollars. The divided commissioners could not agree on the location of the courthouse, arguing over three possible sites, including one on the corner of Second and Franklin, a block off the public square, which had been offered to the court for free. By the time the commissioners finally agreed to build on this land, the location was no longer being offered for free, however, and the court paid $4,750 for the site. They then discarded Andrews and Doughly's plan and voted to build the courthouse according to the plans of W. C. Dodson.[3]

Why Dodson was ultimately selected as the courthouse architect is unknown; the court minutes contain no reference to a competition or any requests for plans. Dodson had just arrived in Waco the previous month with his plans to build the Fifth Street Methodist Church. Since some

McLennan County Courthouse, 1876. Credit: Courtesy of Leonard Lane.

on the court disapproved of Andrew's 1874 plan, the court may simply have asked Dodson if he could submit a better design. Dodson's first courthouse commission may have been the result of a divided McLennan County Court.[4]

Dodson designed Waco's third courthouse in the Second Empire style. He proposed a rectangular building with five bays on the longer sides and three on the shorter sides. The building was to be brick with limestone quoins.[5] He featured hooded arched windows and mansard roofs, both hallmarks of Second Empire buildings.[6] Hooded dormers jutted out from the corner mansards. Dodson finished the design by positioning a clock tower over the main entrance. Stacked convex and concave mansards created the tower, and iron cresting topped all of the roofs. This design, Dodson's first

The McLennan County Courthouse, Waco, Texas. Credit: Courtesy of the Texas Collection, Baylor University.

courthouse, was later considered "an interesting but simple composition of both convex and concave mansards."[7]

Happy with the design, the county commissioners advertised in the *Waco Daily Reporter* and the *Waco Daily Examiner* requesting contractor bids for a courthouse to be built "according to the specifications of W. C. Dodson." When local contractor Lee Slaughter, who had the low bid of $25,000, was unable to post the required bond, the contract was awarded to Trice and Harris, who had bid $29,865.[8] The commissioners paid Dodson $450 for his design—admittedly, more than they paid Andrews and Doughly in 1874 but considerably less than the 3.5 percent of the building's cost, which would soon become standard. Dodson also received $150 for supervising the construction, with an additional $45 for expenses.[9] Before construction was completed, the courthouse fund ran out of money, forcing the commissioners court to borrow from other accounts to finish the building. Trice and Harris's final payment of $9,865 was made in warrants paying 10 percent interest, with money to come from the special property tax being levied.[10]

At a town ceremony held on July 12, 1877, County Judge Maxey accepted the keys to the courthouse from the contractor. The *Waco Daily Examiner* praised the "beautiful brick structure" as an "elegant courthouse," noting that the "style of architecture exhibits the finest taste."[11]

In 1884, when the court started outgrowing its building, the commissioners hired Dodson to make improvements to the courthouse that would "keep the records of the court conveniently at hand." According to the *Waco Daily Examiner*, "Mr. Dodson is preparing the plans for a two-story vault back of District Clerk Beasley's present office, to be thoroughly fire-proof, with room for the accommodation of all the records and papers belonging to the office."[12]

## CAMP COUNTY COURTHOUSE, PITTSBURG, 1881

Some Upshur County residents complained that creek flooding too often prevented them from reaching the county seat at Gilmer and inhibited their ability to conduct important business. This group successfully petitioned to break off from Upshur County, establishing Camp County in 1874. A referendum was held to select the county seat, and residents chose Pittsburg over the other contending towns of Leesburg and Center Point. Functioning from offices in a rented wooden building, the new county commissioners began planning for a more permanent courthouse. William Pitts, a local resident, offered the donation of a building lot, which the commissioners gratefully accepted.[13]

In 1881, Dodson replied to Camp County's advertisement in the *Dallas Daily Herald* for new courthouse plans and specifications. Dodson submitted a design for a red-brick courthouse with white limestone accents for the hooded windows and corner trim. The roof was gabled; over it sat a simple bell tower topped with iron cresting. No clock looked out from the tower. One main entrance led into the rectangular space, which was approximately sixty by forty-five feet. The lower floor probably accommodated the six offices needed by the county officers as well as a fireproof vault, with a courtroom, jury room, and witness room housed upstairs.

The Camp County Courthouse. Credit: Courtesy of Keith Vincent.

The commissioners chose Dodson's design and authorized Judge John D. Polk to advertise for contractors to build according to Dodson's plans and specifications.[14] D. P. Smith, a local Pittsburg builder, won the contract with a low bid of $9,800.[15] He began construction immediately and made steady progress. As construction neared completion in December 1881, an observer wrote: "The new court house of Camp county will be one of the prettiest buildings in the state."[16]

### HUNT COUNTY COURTHOUSES, GREENVILLE, 1881–1883 AND 1884–1885

In the early 1880s, two railroads—the East Line & Red River Railroad and the Missouri–Kansas–Texas Railroad—began running through Hunt County, intersecting in Greenville, the county seat.[17] These lines provided local farmers with several ways to ship their crops to market and led to increased cotton production.[18] As the *Galveston Daily News* later reported, "The merchants were anticipating a business boom of unprecedented prosperity, for which ample preparations were being made." The people "were proud of their town and all Hunt County gloried in Greenville's prosperity."[19]

The Hunt County Commissioners were also preparing for the future. Their third courthouse, a brick building constructed in 1859, had been badly damaged during a storm in 1870. The commissioners court lacked the tax receipts to repair the building properly, and in 1874, the building was condemned. The commissioners bought the Methodist church building to temporarily use as a courthouse. In turn, they sold the damaged courthouse to the Methodist Church, which cleared it from the town square, intending to use the bricks to build a larger church for its congregation. After the bond financing legislation of 1881, the Hunt County Commissioners were eager to proceed with building a new courthouse. Led by County Judge J. S. Sherrill, they made plans to build a $40,000 brick structure on the town square.[20]

Dodson won the competition for Hunt County's fifth courthouse with a Second Empire design. He planned a brick building with stone quoining and five bays on each face, larger than the three-by-five-bay Waco courthouse. Over the corner pavilions, he placed unusually short mansard roofs with small gables projecting into them. These corner gables balanced the large gable roofs placed over the central entrance pavilions.[21] For the first time, Dodson placed the clock tower, constructed of two stacked segments—a cubed section and an Italianate top—in the center of the building over the second-floor district courtroom. All sides of the building were now virtually identical, with all appearing to be main entrances. This was important to Dodson since the Hunt County building was situated on a large town square, approachable from all four directions, unlike the courthouses in McLennan and Camp Counties, which were situated on street corners. Dodson skillfully added a great deal of additional architectural detailing to the windows, doors, and bracketed cornices that had not been included in the Waco courthouse, resulting in an elegant building. For his work, he was paid $1,226.

D. P. Smith of Pittsburg, the contractor for the Camp County Courthouse, won the contract to build the Hunt County Courthouse with the low bid of $35,600.[22] The foundation was soon laid and the cornerstone set. By November 1881, the brickwork was finished, and plans were being made to erect the roof. When the tower went up, the local citizens realized with excitement that the courthouse was going to be visible from eight to twelve miles in every direction.[23] The majestic courthouse was dedicated in June 1883.

The next year, a fire swept across Hunt County's town square. On Sunday, August 17, 1884, at three o'clock in the morning, an arsonist started a fire in wooden buildings that were occupied by a grocer and a furniture dealer. A strong wind blowing from the south spread the fire with alarming speed. Greenville's fire department had burned down just a few months earlier,[24] but officials telegraphed the fire department in Dennison, which put its truck on a train to Greenville. Meanwhile, local citizens formed a bucket brigade to fight the fire. Their efforts were not enough to stop the blaze, and the Dennison fire equipment arrived too late to save the town square.[25] Over two blocks of buildings were gone. "To the sorrow of everyone," the Greenville newspaper reported, "the flames also took hold of Hunt County's fine $40,000 courthouse and it was totally consumed in spite of the efforts of the fire company and the citizens." The business district of forty structures, "half of them excellent brick building," was destroyed by a "dastardly incendiary." It was a desolate day for Greenville, with losses totaling over $300,000.[26]

Fortunately for Hunt County, the commissioners had bought two fireproof steel vaults, and no county records were lost. The commissioners had also fully insured the courthouse. With $29,000 in insurance payments, they proceeded immediately with rebuilding.[27] Dodson was already in town supervising the construction of a new jail, so they contracted with him to oversee the building of the county's sixth courthouse, "almost an exact replica of the 5th."[28] In October 1884, the commissioners secured bids from contractors to dismantle the still-standing courthouse walls, "saving all materials which the architect felt could be reused, and to clear the site before beginning construction of the new building."[29] Dodson met with many of the nine contractors who were in Greenville examining the plans and preparing their bids for the new courthouse.[30] The commissioners awarded the contract to the low bidders, Ellis and Graham, for $31,675; they were just finishing the Hunt

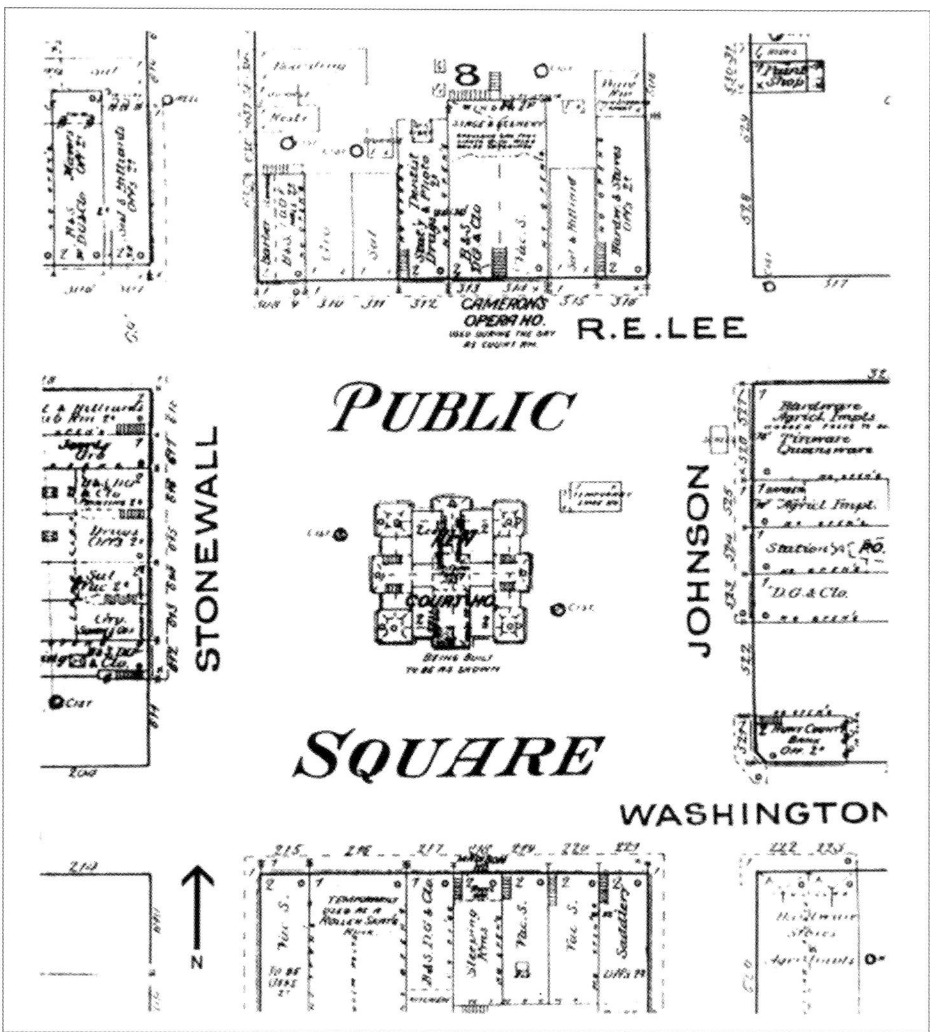


The fire of 1884 destroyed the Hunt County Courthouse and forty surrounding businesses. Credit: 1885 Sanborn Fire Insurance Map, Texas SP Hunt County Courthouse, National Register of Historic Places Registration Form.

County Jail. Construction soon began. As it proceeded, Dodson gave monthly progress reports, and the contractors were paid for work completed to that point.[31]

By October 1885, the courthouse was nearly complete. Built on the foundation of the earlier courthouse, and containing many of the original courthouse's bricks, the building was virtually indistinguishable from its predecessor. It was acclaimed as "a very imposing structure, being indeed, one of the finest public buildings in Texas."[32] At the same time as the courthouse was being rebuilt, twenty-five or more brick buildings were under construction on the town square, most of them replacing burned-out, old wooden build-

The Hunt County Courthouse.
Credit: Courtesy of Keith Vincent.

ings.[33] With the new opera house, the Odd Fellows Hall, the Masonic Temple, and a large brick hotel all nearing completion, Greenville's town square was almost fully recovered from the fire.[34]

### JOHNSON COUNTY COURTHOUSE, CLEBURNE, 1882–1883

In 1882, Dodson saw a "Notice to Architects" in the *Galveston Daily News* requesting proposals for a new courthouse for Johnson County. The county's population had more than tripled in the 1870s, reaching eighteen thousand inhabitants in 1880. That year, the Gulf, Colorado & Santa Fe Railroad had completed its line through Cleburne, making the city an important transportation center. With the advent of the railroad, the commissioners expected more growth in the county's leading industries of livestock and cotton. They knew the growing county needed to replace its inadequate 1869 courthouse. At their February 1882 term of court, the commissioners instructed County Judge W. J. Ewing to advertise for plans and specifications.[35]

Dodson submitted a proposal to Johnson County for what was a highly sought-after commission. At their April meeting, the commissioners spent four days carefully examining the sixteen plans submitted by architects.[36] According to the press release given to the *Galveston Daily News*, "The commissioners were gratified by the response to their request." They announced that they had "adopted the plan of W. C. Dodson, of Waco," on the condition that the courthouse could be built for $40,000. They agreed to pay Dodson 5 percent of the cost of the courthouse for his design and supervision of the construction. The press release noted Dodson's proposed stone-and-brick courthouse had "all the modern conveniences, and when completed will be one of the finest court houses in Texas."[37] Referencing the *Galveston Daily News* article, the *Waco Daily Examiner* concluded that "the Waco courthouse and several others in the state, are practical evidences of Mr. Dodson's capacity, and the community will be gratified to learn of a townsman's latest success over fifteen competitors."[38]

For Johnson County, Dodson designed a Second Empire building that resembled his earlier Hunt County Courthouse in overall plan, but that was unique in the treatment of the windows, roof, and tower. He divided each side of the massive square building into five bays and specified the use of red brick accented with limestone quoins and moldings. Above the entrance doors on two sides of the building, he placed pairs of tall rounded windows. The entrance doors on the opposite sides featured three tall windows with the center window topped by another round window and unifying architectural elements. The roof design combined mansard features over the corner pavilions and gable features over the entrance pavilions. Dodson added a number of small gables that projected into the corner mansards, into the dormer windows, and over the entry doors. For the first time, he added a third segment to his centrally located tower. On the lowest segment, he positioned two hooded windows on each face of the mansard; on the central straight segment, he situated a bell behind louvered windows; and on the third, a convex mansard, he placed hooded clocks on every face. On the top of the tower, he added a deck and wrought-iron cresting.[39]

On June 7, 1882, Dodson returned to Cleburne to present the commissioners with his final plans and specifications. His seventeen pages of specifications included detailed instructions about the entire building, from the foundation to the final painting. His instructions for building the tower supports, which were needed to position the tower over the district courtroom in the center of the building, were indicative of his precision and thoroughness. "All towers and trusses," he wrote, are "to be fastened and bolted to wall plates as shown on plans. These wall plates are to be fastened down to brick walls with one inch iron rods extended down 5′ 0″ in the walls, with wooden brick on lower ends and fastened at top with nuts and washers. . . .” He called for “angle washers and iron shoes for [the] feet of trusses to [the] roof. Iron truss rods,” he continued, would be “placed and secured as shown upon the section and detail drawings for the same, . . . with threads to rods thoroughly cut and nuts fitting exactly. Every part of the floors, roof and tower,“ he concluded, were “to be mortised, tenoned, spiked, nailed, bolted, braced and otherwise secured as to make not only a first-class workman like job, but one warranted free from start of trouble and so to remain.”[40]

After approving the final plans and specifications, the commissioners advertised in the *Galveston Daily News* for sealed bids from contractors.[41] They awarded the contract to Lee Slaughter, a Waco contractor whose bid of $38,485 was the lowest submitted. The commissioners agreed to pay Slaughter $5,000 upon signing the contract and then provide monthly payments based upon Dodson’s assessment of the amount of work completed, with the balance upon the commissioners’ acceptance of the building.[42]

According to his contract, Slaughter was responsible for supplying all materials, which were to be “of the best marketable qualities.” He was also responsible for hiring the workmen, subcontractors, and foremen. As the supervising architect, Dodson had considerable control over construction. He had the “full power and authority to reject any work or materials which, in his opinion, [were] not in accordance with the plans and specifications, and his decision on work and materials [was] to be final and conclusive.” Additionally, “if there [were] anything omitted in these Specifications, or that is not fully shown on the plans which would be necessary for the full completion of the building according to the full intent and meaning of these specifications and accompanying drawings, the same is to be done at the expense of the contractor without extra charge.”[43]

Once the commissioners arranged to finance the courthouse, construction began immediately. Dodson made the 150-mile round trip from Waco to Cleburne regularly, conferring with Slaughter, checking on the work accomplished, and reporting progress to the commissioners. For each trip, he was reimbursed $4.50 for his “traveling expenses.” By December 1883, the foundation had been laid as well as fifty thousand bricks. By February 1884, an additional seventy-five thousand bricks had been laid, and additional cut stonework was completed. By March, one hundred fifty thousand more bricks were laid, and eight fireproof vault doors were set. Each month, Dodson reported additional bricks laid and work completed, and as he made each report, both he and Slaughter received additional payments. By the summer of 1883, the work began to focus on the interior, with carpentry, painting, ironwork, and tinwork proceeding. Looking toward completion,

An admirer called the Johnson County Courthouse "the handsomest architectural design in the state" Credit: Courtesy of Keith Vincent.

the commissioners ordered tables, chairs, bookcases, and desks—all the furnishings that the new courthouse would need.[44]

During the courthouse's construction, the Johnson County Jail burned down, making it necessary for the sheriff to relocate prisoners to the Dallas County Jail. Because the need for a jail was urgent, the commissioners dispensed with newspaper advertisements. Dodson submitted a plan, as did James J. Ligon of Palestine, Texas, an agent for the Pauly Jail Building and Manufacturing Company. The commissioners accepted Ligon's plan and appointed a local architect, A. N. Dawson, to supervise construction. Dodson probably did not compete for the position as supervising architect. By

The Johnson County Courthouse in 1890. Credit: Courtesy of the Johnson County Historical Commission and the Portal to Texas History, University of North Texas Libraries.

The commissioners accepted the proposal of the Pittsburg contractor D. P. Smith to build the courthouse for $15,480. This figure seems exceptionally low, given that the bid on the Johnson County Courthouse had been $38,485 for a similar building. Perhaps some materials were not supplied by the contractor, or some other work was not done. Smith was to finish the building by December 1, 1883.[51]

When Smith presented the courthouse to the commissioners in January 1884, they refused to accept it, saying it was "not in accordance with the plans and specifications of the architect." Apparently, Smith had disagreed with Dodson about some work that was required, and instead of making the corrections Dodson insisted on, he refused to complete the building. The commissioners brought suit to recover damages from Smith. The construction issue is not known nor is the outcome of the suit. The following month, however, the commissioners hired a contractor to fix a leak in the courthouse roof, possibly the source of the disagreement.

In July 1884, the courthouse fund was closed, with the $500 remaining in the account being transferred to the general account. The building was apparently finished. The opening of the new courthouse, situated in the middle of the town square, helped revitalize Crockett's economy.[52]

### LAMPASAS COUNTY COURTHOUSE, LAMPASAS, 1883–1884

In 1871, unscrupulous land developers were attempting to encroach on the lands of individual farmers in the county. A fire deliberately set in Lampasas County's first courthouse destroyed all the county's land records. A courthouse was needed so that, at a minimum, accurate land records could be kept to protect the farmers' ownership rights. A financial panic in 1873, however, made it almost impossible to borrow money, so the commissioners limped along for almost a decade without a suitable courthouse.

In 1882, the Gulf, Colorado & Santa Fe Railroad extended its line to Lampasas, sparking a period of growth. In 1883, District Judge W. A. Blackburn and members of the Lampasas County Grand Jury petitioned the commissioners, calling for a more durable, imposing county building. In response, the commissioners ordered that a "suitable substantial courthouse be built and that immediate steps be taken to have said courthouse built."[53]

As a first step, the court authorized the four commissioners "to inspect such courthouses as they may deem proper, to consult (and if necessary) to employ an architect to procure plans and specifications for a new court house."[54] Two commissioners inspected the new courthouses in Austin, Dallas, Fort Worth, McKinney, and Decatur and became better informed about the process of building a courthouse. According to the *Wise County*

*Messenger*, the commissioners concluded that the Decatur courthouse, which was a Second Empire design, "was the best and came nearest filling the wants of Lampasas."[55]

Next, the commissioners consulted with Dodson about possible courthouse plans and costs. They soon hired Dodson as the architect and superintendent for their new courthouse, agreeing to pay him 2.5 percent of the construction costs for his plans and specifications and 1.5 percent for supervising the construction. This was less than the 5 percent that was becoming the standard fee for architects, which suggests that the commissioners were concerned about keeping costs down. Dodson may have agreed to the lower fee as it allowed him to avoid the uncertainty of going through an architectural competition.[56]

For Lampasas County, Dodson designed a rectangular Second Empire building, with five bays on two identical facades and three bays on the other sides. Smaller than his buildings in Johnson, Anderson, and Houston Counties, all of which were five bays by five bays, the Lampasas County Courthouse was also less expensive. The native limestone building had vermiculated ashlar walls, with the quoins, belt course, jambs, window lintels, and entrances all done in smooth-faced ashlar.[57] Gabled roofs were placed over the entrance pavilions. The mansard roofs placed over the corner pavilions had unusually short lower slopes and steep upper slopes, something the architectural historian Paul Goeldner called a "highly personalized" design.[58] Dodson's two-segment bell tower featured louvered windows and a convex mansard segment housing four clock faces. At the top of the tower, Dodson placed a deck with iron cresting. From the exterior, the building appeared to be two stories tall, with two levels of windows and a dividing stringcourse. On the interior, however, the building was actually three levels, with the upper level divided into two floors. The upper-level windows provided light to both the second and third floors. The wide band in the middle of the upper-level windows, as seen from the exterior, marked the floor of the third level.

On July 1, 1883, having approved the final drawings submitted by Dodson, the commissioners advertised for contractors.[59] They chose a local firm, the Scottish-born Kane Brothers, as general contractors and Tom Lovell and Company as the stone contractor. Lovell, who had emigrated from Scotland to Texas in 1881, resided in Brownwood. He later moved to Denton, where he headed Lovell and Sons Contractors and Builders. This was the first project on which Dodson and Lovell collaborated. Lovell would go on to serve as the contractor for eleven courthouses, including working with Dodson on the Hill, Denton, Coryell, and McLennan courthouses as well as the Williamson County Jail. Henry Kane would later form a partnership with John Cormack and build Dodson's Fannin County Courthouse.[60]

The Lampasas County Courthouse. Credit: Courtesy of the Lampasas County Museum.

The site chosen for the courthouse was a large square of land donated to the county by Lampasas's former mayor, Tilman Weaver. The commissioners accepted Dodson's recommendation that the courthouse be centered on the square from north to south and one hundred feet back from Live Oak Street, the property's western edge. Work began on July 23, 1883, with trees being cleared in preparation for excavating the courthouse basement. Waterlines were dug, anticipating the availability of public water, "an assured thing," according to an Austin Waterworks spokesperson. With the foundation laid, the commissioners held the cornerstone-laying celebration. The festive ceremony, led by the Lampasas Masonic Lodge and attended by many county residents, was testimony to the new courthouse's importance to its citizenry.[61]

Construction proceeded, with the county advertising for twenty stonecutters to work on the courthouse at four dollars a day. Convicts, who had previously laid tracks for the Santa Fe Railroad, did much of the construction work. By March 1884, the roof was completed, and the commissioners authorized the city of Lampasas to place a clock in the courthouse tower. The inside finishing work then began. On May 12, 1884, Dodson declared the courthouse complete.[62]

Although the stonemason's name is not on the cornerstone, Tom Lovell's work is recognized by this arch, which joins a pair of tall, round-headed windows into a single semicircular arch. This unit is above the first-floor entrance and extends to the roofline. Credit: Courtesy of Leonard Lane.

In his final report to the commissioners, Dodson indicated that the Kane brothers had found it necessary to install additional downspouts, and he thought it only just that they be reimbursed an additional fifty dollars. He praised them "as honest and upright men and as builders with but few equals." He also congratulated Tom Lovell and Company for being knowledgeable stonemasons who "faithfully performed their work." And finally, he thanked the commissioners for their "uniform courtesy" and their confidence in trusting him to design and oversee the construction of their new courthouse.[63]

As the keys to the courthouse were turned over to the commissioners and the courthouse dedication speeches completed, champagne was served to the assembled throng. "To the Temple of Justice," called out one toast, followed by Capt. F. D. Wilks, who responded that "everyone extends a word of praise for the architectural beauty, convenience and also superior manner in which it is built, and the consummation of a want long felt."[64] The county's celebration continued with a barbeque and a ball in the courthouse the following week.[65] "This event," noted the local newspaper, "is one which will be long remembered in the records of this city and county."[66]

The construction of the courthouse stimulated Lampasas's economy and led to a building boom. Lawyers and other professionals who had business dealings at the courthouse built offices. After Dodson's daughter Anna moved to Lampasas around 1905, Dodson became a frequent visitor. Upon his death years later, the local paper acknowledged that he was "well remembered by many of the older citizens of Lampasas."[67]

# 9 Dodson and Dudley Courthouses, 1884–1889

In 1884, Dodson formed a partnership with W. W. Dudley, a partnership that lasted five years and seven courthouses. Minutes from various county commissioners courts indicate that it was Dodson who both met with the commissioners during the architectural competitions and supervised the courthouses' construction. Apparently, Dudley concentrated his efforts on local Waco projects while Dodson focused on courthouse designs. After the partnership dissolved, Dudley never designed another courthouse but continued working as an architect in the house-building industry.

In this period, Dodson employed some new technologies and constructed his largest courthouse to date. He also experienced a number of delays: two from disagreements over the location of the county seat, one from the difficulty in floating bonds to pay for construction, and one from the murder of a building contractor by the contractor's partner.

## WICHITA COUNTY COURTHOUSE, WICHITA FALLS, 1884–1885

Wichita Falls considers its founding date to be September 27, 1882—the date the first Fort Worth and Denver City Railroad train arrived in town. Within a short period, the railroad land company sold a number of town lots, and homes and stores were built at a frenzied pace. Wichita Falls was fast becoming a transportation and distribution center with stockyards and feeding lots. An iron bridge was under construction that would allow cattle herds to be driven across the Wichita River. The herds would all be driven north from the railhead. In April 1884, the railroads delivered forty cars of cattle and horses in one week. Two additional railroads were awaiting a congressional grant of a right-of-way across Indian Territory. They planned to cross into Texas at Wichita Falls, which would further boost the town's economy. Before the end of the 1884 season, three hundred thousand head of cattle would be shipped to Wichita Falls.[1]

In the booming town, the Presbyterians had built a church and were loaning their facilities to other denominations until they could erect their own sanctuaries as well. The public schools already had one hundred seventy students enrolled. At the February 1884 election, voters passed a fifty-cent tax on every hundred dollars in property valuation to support the public schools, which the *Dallas Weekly Herald* called "a noble start for a town only 16 months old."[2]

The county commissioners began planning for a needed courthouse and jail. As the *Galveston Daily News* reported, they wanted both buildings modeled "after the latest pattern and arranged with every convenience."[3] Good quality stone was available nearby, and the commissioners were pleased to learn that "brick can be laid in the wall here at $11 a thousand."[4] This information apparently assured the commissioners that the county could both secure and afford the materials needed for solid construction. The Wichita County voters authorized the courthouse bonds, passing a bond tax of twenty-five cents on every hundred dollars in valuation.[5] In March 1884, under County Judge J. H. Barwise, the commissioners advertised for architects to submit designs for brick or stone courthouses not to exceed $40,000.[6] At least six architects submitted plans and specifications. Dodson's entry, the first plans entered into a competition under the Dodson and Dudley name, was "adjudged the best." The court awarded Dodson and Dudley the contract and agreed to pay the firm $1,172.50 in warrants (3.5 percent of the $33,500 contract price) plus an additional $300 in warrants for superintending the construction.[7]

Dodson designed a courthouse that, while smaller than his Hunt, Houston, and Johnson buildings, resembled those earlier Second Empire buildings. He used the same red brick with contrasting white stone quoins, stringcourses, and arches that he had used in the Johnson and Hunt County buildings. He made the roof a distinctive style of mansard with gables jutting into the mansard at the entrance pavilions. The Wichita County tower was composed of two segments, like the Hunt and Lampasas County towers; unlike those, it was built in the Italianate style, with an octagonal belfry and an octagonal cupola topping the building. Because of the building's smaller footprint, it had only one courtroom, which would prove to be a problem in a growing community.

The commissioners disagreed over the location of the new courthouse. R. E. Montgomery, the railroad's townsite company agent, offered to donate block 149, a fourteen-lot block, for the courthouse square. Judge Barwise and Commissioner T. J. Williams, however, preferred block 175 as a site for the courthouse.[8] Sales of lots around both proposed sites were brisk as buyers anticipated profiting from the resale of lots at a highly prized location. At the next meeting of the court, Commissioner Williams switched his vote and agreed to accept the railroad company's block 149 offer. This enraged the judge, perhaps because he suspected Williams had a financial interest in that outcome or perhaps because he had his own financial interest in block 175. In any event, the courthouse site at block 149 was adopted. Soon new brick buildings including a bank, retail stores, and a law office sprung up on the lots surrounding the courthouse square.[9]

In August, the commissioners advertised in the Galveston and Dallas newspapers for contractors to build the Dodson-designed courthouse.[10] The

The Wichita County Courthouse. Credit: Courtesy of the Wichita County Texas Archives.

commissioners chose the firm of G. C. Mays, M. Broderick, and W. Davidson, with the low bid of $33,500.[11] Foundation work began in September 1884, just as the county was preparing to celebrate its second anniversary.[12]

That fall, progress stalled on two fronts. The first problem concerned the contractor's bond. Whenever contractors won a construction bid, they were required to post a "good and sufficient bond" backing up their commitment to fulfilling the contract. The bond that Mays, Broderick, and Davidson first offered in November was rejected as insufficient. They were given until December, and then until January 1, and then until January 17 to provide a bond. Finally, the court informed the contractors that unless the commissioners received a satisfactory bond by February 9, 1885, it would cancel the contract. It was on this last date possible that the contractors filed a bond accepted by the commissioners.[13]

The second problem was difficulty floating construction bonds. Initially, the commissioners authorized $24,000 in courthouse bonds, only to be told by the state comptroller that the county had surpassed its debt limit.[14] The commissioners then rescinded the authorization, reissuing bonds five separate times in an effort to raise the funds needed. They reduced the denomination of the bonds from $500 to $300, increased the interest rate from 6 percent to 8 percent, and reduced the total amount from $24,000 to $15,000. Then, in January 1886, when a new assessment justified it, the commissioners authorized another $6,500 in 8 percent bonds.[15]

Work finally resumed in the spring of 1885. As payments to the contractors came due, the court signed over unsold courthouse bonds.[16] The court made the final payment by transferring the last available $5,500 in courthouse bonds. When Mays and Broderick sought payment of $2,943 for extra work and materials, the court agreed to pay them in bonds but only "when in the judgment of the court the assessments of the county will justify it."[17] The commissioners were so short of cash that they were unable to pay for the courthouse furniture outright. On an order of $2,475, they agreed to pay $500 in cash thirty days after delivery, with the balance paid over three years at 8 percent interest.[18]

In February 1886, the town celebrated as the courthouse officials moved from their temporary quarters in the Knights of Pythias Hall into the new courthouse. In aspiring to have more than they could readily afford, the county commissioners had somehow managed to build a magnificent public building. They boasted that, for the money spent, the new courthouse was "not excelled by any, anywhere for convenience, comfort, or architectural beauty."[19]

**YOUNG COUNTY COURTHOUSE, GRAHAM, 1884–1885**

In 1884, Young County was growing. The town of Graham, the county seat, had only seven hundred residents, but three new church buildings were underway.[20] Wanting to present an appearance in keeping with the county's economic prosperity, citizens petitioned to replace the county's twenty-by-forty-foot frame courthouse with a larger stone building.[21] In February, with the petition in hand, the commissioners gave County Judge R. F. Arnold authority to advertise in the *Galveston Daily News*. They were seeking architectural plans and specifications for a "thoroughly modern" courthouse, "sufficient to the needs" of the county but not to exceed $30,000.[22]

Dodson presented the Young County Commissioners with plans for a courthouse with the same footprint as the plans he had submitted to the Wichita County Commissioners just days earlier.[23] Instead of the brick used in Wichita, Young County's plans called for limestone walls. All four facades were similar, appropriate for a building that was to be set in the center of Commerce Park, approachable from all sides.[24] Dodson proposed a two-segment Italianate tower over the center of the building. Unlike the Wichita County Courthouse, this building featured gable roofs over the entrance pavilions.

Courthouse planning was briefly interrupted when the county seat's location became a political issue. There was a faction of residents who wanted the county seat moved to the exact center of the county, nine miles away, and they forced an election in late March 1884. The town of Graham survived as the county seat by forty-five votes.[25] With the location issue presumably resolved, the commissioners carefully evaluated the proposals submitted by a number of architects and selected Dodson's plan, judging it "the best and most suitable for the demands and necessities of Young County." They also chose the firm of Dodson and Dudley to supervise construction. For their work, the commissioners agreed to pay the firm 5 percent of the courthouse's contract price.[26]

Having advertised for contractors in the *Dallas Daily Herald* and the *Galveston Daily News*,[27] the commissioners intended to award the building contract at their April meeting. Once again, delays occurred when J. W. Proffitt and others filed suit contesting Graham as the courthouse location. The district court issued an injunction, restraining the commissioners from further action.[28] The suit was quickly dismissed, the injunction lifted, and at their May meeting, the commissioners awarded the contract to John Solon and W. B. Aubrey, Waxahachie contractors, with the low bid of $29,907.[29] To finance the building, the commissioners used some existing county funds and floated $28,000 in fifteen-year bonds paying 6 percent interest.[30]

The Young County Courthouse. Credit: Courtesy of Graham Archivist Project, Old Post Office Museum and Art Center, Graham, Texas.

Construction began immediately, with Irish stonemasons cutting stone in a quarry east of town. As work progressed, the supervising architects presented progress reports to the commissioners. The contractors were paid in five stages as the walls, the roof, and the interior were completed, with 20 percent of the money being held back at each stage until the courthouse was accepted by the commissioners.[31] With the first progress report, in September 1884, Solon and Aubrey submitted a bill for $558 for extra work done on the building's foundation, a claim the commissioners initially denied. Dodson supported his contractors, explaining that because of ground conditions, the depth of the foundations required by the specifications "did not give a satisfactory substrature for the building." He continued: "[To] render the stability of the building certain, we had the foundations made one foot deeper." This required both extra excavation and extra stonework. Dodson told the commissioners, "Your contractors should be paid for the same."[32] With the third report, made in December, Dodson noted that the contractors were doing a "faithful and good job of work, and that everything is coming up to the requirements of the plans and specifications."[33] On May 13, 1885, the commissioners accepted the completed courthouse.[34] N. J. Rosenquist, the Swedish chief stonemason, later said that the Young County Courthouse was one of the finest buildings he had ever built.[35]

### BROWN COUNTY COURTHOUSE, BROWNWOOD, 1884–1885

In the spring of 1884, Brown County's courthouse square was bustling with wagons and teams belonging to farmers and merchants, who made the square their major trading point. The wheat crop was good, cotton looked promising, and large quantities of wool were being marketed.[36] The community was discussing plans for a new courthouse to replace the 1876 building, which had burned in 1880.[37] The fire had apparently been set by men anxious to destroy all the land ownership records. At the time, ranchers, who wanted the land to remain open range, were confronting farmers, who were fencing in their land with barbed wire. Farmers needed their proof of ownership held in a secure courthouse vault. For the new courthouse, citizens envisioned spending $60,000 to $70,000, an enormous amount for a small county. According to the newspaper: "The people want a court house to which they can look with pride as Brownwood grows in prominence and favor."[38]

The Brown County Commissioners were anticipating a more moderate $35,000 to $45,000 expenditure.[39] They visited some newly built courthouses in nearby counties and examined those buildings' plans and specifications. In July 1884, after receiving architectural proposals, the commissioners chose Dodson's design.[40] Dodson had proposed a three-story limestone building with the same footprint as his Wichita and Young County Courthouses. As he had done with both those buildings, he designed an Italianate tower with an octagonal belfry for Brown County. He capped the corners of the building with short mansard roofs and covered the four entrances with tall mansards featuring dormers, as he had in Wichita. Distinctive to Brown County, though, all entrances featured Classical Revival porticos supported by pairs of columns on each side.

The commissioners sought bids from contractors, and in August, they accepted the low bid of $45,000 offered by Lee Slaughter, the Waco contractor and builder of Dodson's Johnson County Courthouse. To finance the building, the commissioners issued bonds sold at par to several private banks in Brownwood. Construction started immediately, and before long, the contractors had dug the basement and laid the foundation. On October 25, 1884, Brownwood hosted thousands for the celebratory Masonic cornerstone-

The Brown County Courthouse. Credit: Courtesy of Keith Vincent, Courthousehistory.com.

laying ceremony. In the summer of 1885, when the elegant new building was completed, the county officials moved into their offices.[41]

**ANDERSON COUNTY COURTHOUSE, PALESTINE, 1885–1886**

In December 1884, a grand jury report on Anderson County's 1856 courthouse found the building in dire need of repair. The report noted "the walls badly sprung and cracked in many places" with a "perfectly rotten" foundation and concluded "the building is unsafe and liable at any time to tumble down on the occupants." The grand jury condemned the building and recommended "the construction of a court-house which will be, at once, safe, beautiful, and a source of pride to the citizens of Anderson county."[42]

When the commissioners advertised for architectural plans in January 1885, Dodson submitted his proposal.[43] The next month, the commissioners met to examine the submissions, and Dodson and his competitors were in Palestine to explain their plans and specifications. The commissioners chose

The elegant Anderson County Courthouse. Credit: Courtesy of Palestine Public Library and the Portal to Texas History, University of North Texas Libraries.

Dodson's design for their new structure, asking him to return on March 29 with his final drawings.[44]

In late March, Dodson presented his final plans to the commissioners.[45] His design incorporated many features employed in his earlier works, including multiple pavilions, mansard roofs, and a central tower. But he also included a number of architectural details that gave the Anderson County Courthouse a more stately and refined appearance.[46] Designed in the Second Empire style, with each side having five bays, the exterior walls were brick with sandstone quoins. The heavy limestone accents offered a striking contrast to the dominant dark red brick. The corner pavilions featured mansard roofs while the central pavilions had gable roofs. The three-segment central tower was topped by a convex mansard and extended the total height of the building to seven stories. Moldings and other architectural details on the tower brought an elegance to the imposing structure. Dodson finished all sides of the building almost identically, which as he later explained, was appropriate in public buildings "with open spaces on all sides and all parts of the building exposed to view." He made a practice of treating each side "in such a manner as to give unity of design" to the building regardless of the point from which it was viewed.[47]

The commissioners approved the plans, advertised for contractors, and accepted the low bid of $40,000 offered by George Wright.[48] Construction began in May 1885 and proceeded uneventfully.[49] When the building was completed a year later, in May 1886, the courthouse was turned over to the commissioners, and officials began occupying their new offices.

### PARKER COUNTY COURTHOUSE, WEATHERFORD, 1884–1886

In 1877, the Parker County Commissioners found it necessary to replace their deteriorating 1858 courthouse. The commissioners court agreed to build a two-story, one-hundred-by-one-hundred-foot building. The first floor would have six county offices and fireproof vaults, and the second floor would have district and county courtrooms and additional rooms and vaults. Satisfied with their own design, the commissioners instructed Judge B. L. Richey to "procure the services of some efficient person to draft plans and specifications of said building."[50] They then hired contractors to do the construction and, when the building was completed, moved their offices into it.

In time, however, the courthouse officials found that the building they had designed did not function particularly well. It also lacked the stature or beauty of the courthouses being erected in the neighboring Hunt, Houston, and Johnson Counties, all of which made statements about the importance of those counties. In 1884, when the courthouse and all its records were destroyed in a fire, the commissioners decided to seek out the assistance of a skilled architect for a new design.[51]

In late March 1884, Dodson was in Weatherford, as were a number of other architects, to present plans and specifications to the commissioners.[52] After lengthy deliberations, the commissioners chose Dodson's design, satisfied that it "will make a house that is best suited to the interests of the county at large."[53] According to the *Waco Daily Examiner*, Judge A. J. Hunter was pleased with the final plans for the county's fourth courthouse. "It resembles to some extent the Johnson County courthouse, but is, I think, a finer building and more commodiously arranged. Each officer of the county will have a commodious office, and six fire-proof vaults will insure the safety of the records of Parker County in case of another fire." Judge Hunter proudly declared that the proposed courthouse would be "one of the finest in appearance and most convenient in arrangement of any in the state."[54]

The "commodious" courthouse that Dodson designed was a towering three-story building with a fourth story attic and a three-story central tower. His 102-by-88-foot building was divided into five bays on all facades. Constructed of local cream-colored limestone, the building's strong vertical lines were embellished with handsome sandstone carving. Dodson introduced a new roofline, placing large convex, curved mansard roofs over the end pavilions. Each mansard had four dormers featuring arched windows and decorative moldings. The courthouse's 114-foot tower would be clearly visible to people from miles away.[55]

With the final plans and specifications approved, Judge Hunter ordered the placement of a notice to contractors in the *Fort Worth Daily Gazette* and the *Galveston Daily News*.[56] The construction firm J. H. Milliken, builder of the Rusk County Courthouse, submitted the lowest bid of $55,335.[57] To finance the courthouse, the County sold $45,000 in 8 percent bonds, and supplemented that with $16,000 from insurance payments for the burned courthouse.[58]

Milliken began work immediately. When the foundation was finished in April 1885, county officials held a cornerstone-laying ceremony. It featured a grand parade led by the Weatherford Brass Band and included several hundred members of the Knights of Pythias, three hundred Masons, and a number of Odd Fellows. The day's celebration ended with a banquet prepared by the women of the Baptist church. All the townspeople were out to celebrate because, as the *Dallas Daily Herald* noted, reflecting on the competitiveness of the counties concerning their courthouses, "It is a fact . . . that this is to be the best court-house in Texas."[59]

A few months later, tragedy interrupted the construction. On July 15, 1885, at nine in the morning, James Milliken walked up to his partner James Lee, who was reading a newspaper, and shot and killed him. Apparently, the partners had an unresolved dispute concerning their financial accounts. Feelings in the town ran high as people took opposing sides. Milliken had been a Weatherford resident for twenty-five years and was well respected in the area. His brother was the president of the First National Bank, which had bought all the courthouse bonds. James Lee, the father of three small children and a member of the Masonic Temple and Knights of Honor, was a similarly well-regarded member of the community. Given the men's ties to the community, Milliken requested a change of venue for his trial; it was moved to Granbury in Hood County, where seating an impartial jury was

The Parker County Courthouse. Credit: Courtesy of Keith Vincent.

still difficult. The trial eventually resulted in a hung jury. After a witness was charged with perjury, and witness intimidation was alleged, a second trial produced another hung jury. Milliken was not charged again. He subsequently moved to El Paso.[60]

With the murder of one contractor and the arrest of his partner, construction on the Parker County Courthouse ground to a halt. Work eventually resumed, with Milliken workers seeing the building through to completion, six months behind schedule. The company forfeited twenty dollars per day for the delayed finish. Although Dodson was not paid extra for his additional time spent supervising, he was reimbursed an extra forty dollars for the eight to ten additional trips to Weatherford.

On June 29, 1886, Dodson met with the commissioners and reported that, with minor exceptions, the building was completed "in accordance with the plans and specifications." Dodson approved the final estimated payment of $9,783.70 due on the contract, paid in a warrant to the First National Bank. Dodson and Dudley received a final payment of $389.62 and half a cent for superintending the courthouse construction. Dodson praised five of the Milliken workers for their crucial roles in completing the building. Finally, he thanked the court for its "courtesy and assistance" during the construction process and for "the trust reposed in us." He then turned the keys over to the commissioners.[61]

### KAUFMAN COUNTY COURTHOUSE, KAUFMAN, 1886–1887

In 1879, the town of Kaufman became entangled with the town of Terrell in a fight to retain the Kaufman County seat. Terrell was founded at a stop on the Texas and Pacific Railway, which connected to markets in Dallas and Fort Worth; and the town had just surpassed Kaufman in population. Terrell argued that, with more people and more wealth, it should be the county seat. In a county referendum, however, Terrell was defeated. Several years later, in 1885, Terrell again raised the issue. By then, the Texas Trunk Railroad and the Texas Central Railway had formed a junction in Kaufman, sparking the town's growth. According to the *Austin American-Statesman*, two churches and an "elegant and substantial stone jail, to cost $25,000" were under construction in 1884.[62] Additional homes and businesses were either planned or being built.

Terrell citizens argued that the existing courthouse in Kaufman, erected in the 1870s, was too small, in poor condition, and a fire risk. Perhaps to illustrate the point, someone attempted to burn down the building.[63] The arsonist saturated the stairs to the second-floor courtroom with kerosene and set it ablaze. Fortunately, the fire was discovered and extinguished before much damage occurred. Terrell promised that if the county seat were moved, its citizens would put up $30,000 to build a new courthouse and jail. Despite the offer to resolve the courthouse situation, voters chose again to retain Kaufman as the county seat. The town held a parade and set off fireworks to celebrate its important victory in what had been a hotly contested campaign.[64]

The county still faced the problem of replacing its existing courthouse, though. The fifty-by-fifty-foot frame building had long been too small for all the county officials. To alleviate overcrowding, the clerk's office had been moved to a nearby brick building. That location became so unsafe, however, that even after the crumbling brick walls were braced, the county clerk was ordered to move himself and the county records to a safer location in the jail's front room.[65] Commissioner G. E. Chilcoat finally addressed the necessity of a new building, resolving "that we [the commissioners] proceed at once to erect a new stone courthouse of reasonable dimensions with the proper vaults and safes necessary to protect the public records of the county." Even

The 1887 Kaufman County Courthouse prior to removal of its tower in 1910. Credit: Edward Cave Collection.

given the dire situation, two commissioners voted against proceeding. Judge J. E. Dillard broke the tie by voting in favor of building.[66]

In late 1885, the county commissioners solicited designs for a new courthouse. The submissions included plans from two noted Dallas architects: W. H. Wilson, who had designed the Red River County Courthouse in a mix of Second Empire and Renaissance revival styles; and James Flanders, who had designed the Shackelford County Courthouse in the Second Empire style. In the end, the commissioners chose Dodson's plans for a three-story Second Empire building that closely resembled the Parker County Courthouse. They also named Dodson as superintendent of construction.[67]

To finance the building, the commissioners authorized Judge Dillard to float $60,000 in bonds. He was also authorized to advertise for sealed bids to erect the courthouse according to Dodson's specifications.[68] In March 1886, the commissioners opened sixteen bids and awarded the building contract to Aubrey, Solon, and Laude with "the lowest and best bid" of $69,569.[69] Before long, the cornerstone was laid, accompanied by a parade down Mulberry Street and a ceremony conducted by the Masons on the town square.

Construction went smoothly, with the contractors completing the building months ahead of schedule. On July 9, 1887, county officials accepted the building from the architect and began occupying their offices.[70]

Building the courthouse seemed to bring renewed energy to the town and with it an end to the efforts to move the county seat. Over the next few years, a number of brick buildings were built around the courthouse square, and the town of Kaufman flourished.[71]

### FANNIN COUNTY COURTHOUSE, BONHAM, 1888–1889

In March 1887, Dodson responded to a notice to architects placed by the Fannin County Commissioners in the *Fort Worth Daily Gazette*. Fannin County's decaying brick courthouse had recently been deemed beyond repair and condemned.[72] With both a growing population and a booming economy, the county commissioners agreed they had the means to build a suitably imposing courthouse. On March 9, 1887, they ordered "that advertisements be placed in the *Fort Worth Gazette*, the *Dallas News*, and one of the St. Louis papers for submission of plans by architects for a new courthouse in Bonham to be built on the town square." After reviewing all submissions, the commissioners chose the plans of Dodson and Dudley as "the most suitable of any submitted" and appointed them as architects and superintendents of the new courthouse. For contractors, the commissioners chose the Lampasas firm of Henry Kane and John Cormack, which had submitted the low bid of $77,000. To finance the courthouse, the commissioners ordered the issuance of $75,000 in fifteen-year bonds.[73]

As he designed more courthouses, and as counties were able to afford more expensive buildings, Dodson innovated on his Second Empire designs. For Fannin County, Dodson included many Classical Revival and Italianate features. He enlarged the footprint from his earlier three or five bays to seven bays and used a more complex organization of the space within. Instead of centering the large district courtroom on the second floor, as was typically done, he placed the courtroom to one side of the main corridor. Moving the courtroom to the side allowed Dodson to provide ground support for the central tower. In his earlier buildings, he had used wooden trusses to support a wooden tower, a technique he later referred to as "the old fashioned way."[74] This design was only possible with a light tower—a heavier tower required ground-based supporting structures. Dodson's new design was key to erecting heavy masonry towers in two of his later courthouses.

Dodson made all the facades for the Fannin County Courthouse essentially equal, but he introduced variations in window designs and architectural detailing to add interest. He produced strong vertical lines by placing rectangular windows on the first and second floors and using arched windows topped by a keystone on the third floor. He included soaring two-story raised Classical porticos over all the entrances. Paired two-story columns supported the roofline arch. Below them, heavy buttresses on each side of the entrances supported the columns. Across the porticos at the base of the columns, he placed wrought-iron railings. Abandoning the mansard completely, Dodson employed only gable roofs. Freed from the weight restrictions of wooden trusses, he positioned an Italianate three-story tower with a bell and a clock over the center of the three-story building. Stone columns stood at each corner, and an octagon-shaped cupola covered with fish scales topped the tower. The *Fort Worth Daily Gazette* judged Fannin County's courthouse as "second in magnificence to only . . . the state capitol."[75]

In constructing the building, Dodson employed a new technology that had been developed by the US Army Corps of Engineers but that had never before been used in Texas. Because the ground was unstable, he built the Fannin County Courthouse upon a foundation of 922 bois d'arc trees. (*Bois d'arc* is a French term meaning "bow wood." The tree was common around Fannin County and had been used by the Native Americans to make their hunting bows.) The trees, the majority of which were twelve inches in diameter at the butts and fourteen feet long, were driven into the ground. Concrete footings were then placed over this foundation. Architectural historian Willard Robinson noted: "While W. C. Dodson is recognized for the distinguished character he imparted into his designs, he must also be accorded a place in Texas history for his contributions to technology."[76]

Dodson's eighteen-year-old son Lee Jefferson accompanied him while he supervised the building process. Dodson may have wanted to spend time with his son, to have his company during the evenings away from home.[77] He may also have wanted his son to see what a career in building would be like. But given Dodson's attitude about making oneself useful, it is almost certain that Lee contributed to the project somehow, perhaps as an assistant, available to help with any matters beyond his father's physical capabilities. Lee later reported on the stonemasons, who had been brought over from Scotland. They had hand dressed fifteen million pounds of stone at a local quarry before the stone was brought to the construction site. During the evenings, Lee related, after the long workday was complete, the Scots would sit on the porch of Bonham's Barney House, where they were rooming, light their pipes, and listen as their bagpiper piped "On the Banks an' Braes o' Bonnie Doon" and other Scottish tunes. The "brawny Scots" also engaged "in a wee bit of conversation aboot Edinborrrrgh and them ere other towns where the thistle grows."[78] The *Bonham Daily Favorite* reported at the time that the

(Top) Laying the cornerstone of Fannin County Courthouse, May 16, 1888. Credit: Courtesy of Fannin County Historical Commission.

(Bottom) The 3,300-pound marble cornerstone, noting Dodson and Dudley Architects. Credit: Photo by author.

The Fannin County Courthouse, ca. 1900. Credit: Courtesy of Fannin County Historical Commission.

stonemasons "greatly amused the citizens with their brogues, manners, and bagpipes."[79]

The day the cornerstone of the Fannin County Courthouse was laid was a day of celebration in Bonham. The *Fort Worth Daily Gazette* reported that the day "had been one of the most auspicious for Bonham and Fannin county ever experienced in the history of the city and county." An estimated five thousand people were in town to witness the ceremonies. Over four hundred Masons, from lodges all over the county, marched in a parade, accompanied by the Bonham band and a large mixed-voice chorus. At the ceremony, a pure-white marble cornerstone weighing thirty-three thousand pounds was put in place. The day concluded with a gala banquet and evening festivities.[80]

On June 6, 1889, the courthouse was dedicated at another impressive ceremony, attended by about twelve thousand people and covered by the *Austin American-Statesman*. "A grand procession, headed by the Bonham cornet band, included members of the Masonic lodges, all dressed in formal attire, Knights Templar, Knights of Labor, Farmers' Alliances, Paris Light Guards, and city officials riding in carriages. With music and speeches, the county proudly celebrated the completion of its courthouse that, according to the *Austin American-Statesman*, was "the most magnificent courthouse in the whole state of Texas."[81]

# Dodson's Later Courthouses, 1890–1898

The 1890s was a tumultuous time in Dodson's courthouse work. It began with the building of his most elegant Second Empire design and ended with his designing a courthouse in the newly popular Beaux-Arts style. But the Depression made it a difficult decade for both Dodson and county commissioners.

### HILL COUNTY COURTHOUSE, HILLSBORO, 1890–1891

In the late 1880s, Hill County's economy was booming with over two hundred thousand acres planted in cotton. The new railroads crisscrossing the county made it easier to get the cotton and other crops to market.[1] The resulting prosperity led a confident citizenry to petition its commissioners to replace their two-story brick courthouse built in 1874 with something more befitting their county. Although they also received remonstrances against rebuilding, the commissioners concluded that a majority of their citizens wanted a new courthouse. Accordingly, they invited architects to submit proposals.[2]

Dodson drew up plans and was in Hillsboro on September 11, 1889, to submit them to the commissioners. That day, the commissioners considered all the plans and specifications submitted, heard the architects' explanatory remarks, and asked questions. In these situations, Dodson felt he had an advantage over his competitors because his plans were always clearly drawn and he could use his effective speaking skills to help the commissioners visualize how his courthouse would function. At the end of the day, the commissioners chose Dodson as the architect.[3] When Dodson returned a month later with his final plans, the commissioners approved them, agreeing to pay him 5 percent of the courthouse cost for his design and for his supervision of the construction process.[4]

At the time, the county seat's location was not a settled issue. The commissioners decided against moving forward with courthouse construction until the November election confirmed whether the county seat would be in Hillsboro or Woodbury. When the results affirmed Hillsboro as the county seat, the commissioners contracted with Lovell, Miller, and Hood to construct the building for $83,000.[5] They then purchased a two-story brick building for $2,750 to serve as a temporary courthouse while the new one was being built and sold the old courthouse to C. J. George, who tore down the building and cleared the courthouse square of debris.[6] To fund the new building, they floated bonds on the open market in 1890 and then additional bonds that were bought by the Texas comptroller in 1891.[7]

The Hill County Courthouse. Credit: Courtesy of Keith Vincent.

For Hill County, Dodson designed his most ornate Second Empire building, incorporating Classical Revival and Italianate influences. Each side of the ninety-two-foot square limestone building consisted of five bays. At the four entrances, Dodson placed immense porticos with two-story Corinthian columns set on one-story stone bases, giving the building strong vertical lines. He added a great deal of decorative stonework, including large keystones, carved limestone panels, a belt course decorated with cotton flowers and leaves, and limestone trim around the windows, doors, and cornices. The segmented central tower that reached seven stories, visible for miles, was virtually identical to Parker County's. In the interior hallways, staircases, and courtrooms, Dodson placed elegant stained-glass panels depicting cotton leaves and flowers and historical scenes significant to the county. In March 1891, well after construction was underway, the commissioners authorized Dodson to draw the plans and specifications for a clock and bell to be placed

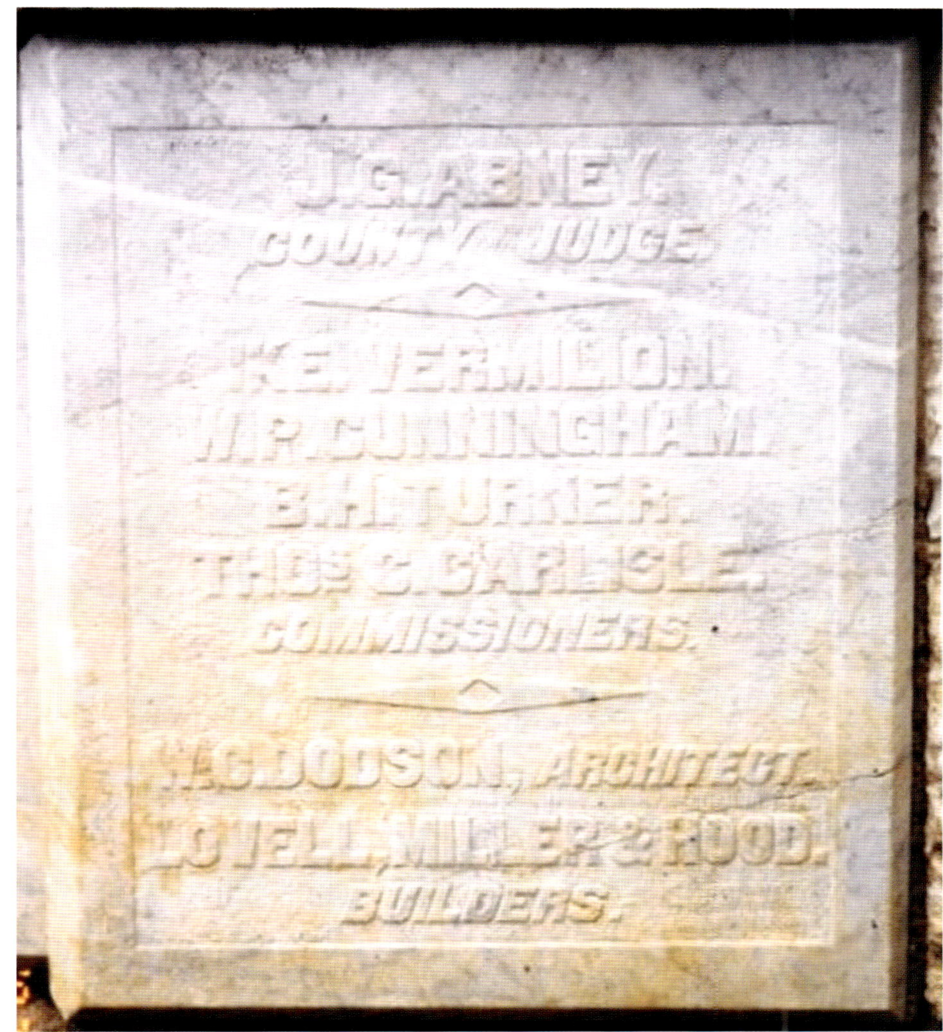


The Hill County Courthouse cornerstone, noting W. C. Dodson, Architect. Credit: Photo by author.

in the new tower. Although two commissioners lobbied to have Hillsboro's citizens pay for the clock and bell, since they were the principal beneficiaries, the commissioners agreed, in a divided vote, that the county would pay for the tower's additions.[8]

When construction began, Dodson made periodic reports to the commissioners on the materials purchased and work completed, authorizing payments to the contractors. As always, he certified that the work met "the requirements of the plans and specifications and the conditions of the contract."[9] By April 1891, it was clear that the project was running over budget and that the contractors needed money to purchase materials and pay their workers.[10] At their April meeting, the commissioners agreed that "a necessity exists" for allowing the contractors to draw $3,800 out of the money held in reserve, which was 10 percent of their payments. Lovell, Miller, and Hood agreed to pay 6 percent interest on the $3,800 until the courthouse was accepted.[11] In September 1891, after Dodson gave his final report, the commissioners accepted the completed building and made final payments to Dodson and the contractors.[12] Tom Lovell suffered a loss of $4,700 over the contract price. Likely because they were satisfied with the finished courthouse, the county's commissioners and citizens donated the money needed to cover Lovell's losses.[13]

### HOOD COUNTY COURTHOUSE, GRANBURY, 1890–1891

In 1890, Hood County officials were forced to demolish their fourth courthouse—a fifteen-year-old stone building that had been built using the previous building's foundation and still-standing burned walls. Like many of the other poorly constructed courthouses in the state, Hood County's was rapidly deteriorating. The commissioners had already added iron crossties in an attempt to support the cracked walls, but the building became too dangerous to be occupied. The commissioners resolved that it was "their imperative duty" to build a new courthouse that would safely preserve the county's public records and papers.[14]

In preparation, the county officials visited a number of new courthouses, probably including Dodson's in adjoining Hill County, to acquaint themselves with current trends in courthouse design. After securing proposals, they spent three days conferring with a number of architects and scrutinizing their plans and specifications. On September 25, 1890, the commissioners decided Dodson's plans for a Second Empire courthouse was "the most suitable."[15]

Dodson worked within budget constraints as the commissioners, who had originally hoped to issue $50,000 in bonds, found the state limited them to $34,500. The constraints made it impossible for Dodson to include the cut stonework and complex architectural details that he had featured in his Hill County courthouse. Nonetheless, he designed a structurally sound, three-story building that included recent technological advances such as iron staircases, arches, and beams.[16]

For Hood County, Dodson used an overall plan very similar to that which he had used in Parker County; each identical side consisted of five bays. This was Dodson's last courthouse to feature mansard roofs, which he placed over the corner pavilions, very much like he had in Lampasas. He used gable

A late-nineteenth-century postcard of the Hood County Courthouse. Credit: Courtesy of Keith Vincent.

roofs similar to Lampasas's over the central projecting entrance pavilions. His three-story central clock tower was identical to those in Parker and Hill Counties. He used contrasting quoins and pilasters as decorative touches to the outside corners of the projecting pavilions and to frame the arched entrances. Inside, Dodson located the district courtroom prominently and arranged the jury rooms, magistrates, constables, and county attorney's offices nearby to facilitate the courtroom's smooth functioning. The tax collector, sheriff, and county clerk were conveniently located for daily business on the first floor.

Contractors Moody and Ellis received the contract and began construction in late 1890. Work proceeded uneventfully, and by the end of May 1891, the tower was being finished and the roof was going on. Over the summer, the interior was finished, and the commissioners ordered furniture in preparation for occupying the building.[17]

The Hood County cornerstone with W. C. Dodson noted as architect. Credit: Courtesy of Leonard Lane.

As the courthouse was being built, Granbury's business community anticipated an improving economy and built twenty-two new two-story buildings around the courthouse square.[18] On the night of August 3, 1891, a fire broke out in one of the new brick buildings that housed the newspaper. The fire destroyed nine businesses, including the First National Bank. Fortunately, the just-completed courthouse survived unscathed.[19]

### SWISHER COUNTY COURTHOUSE, TULIA, 1891: THE DESIGN NOT BUILT

In 1891, newly organized Swisher County was just starting to grow. Although only two houses were within sight of Tulia, fifteen to twenty more were being built.[20] The commissioners had already built a two-story wooden courthouse for $2,000,[21] and they were planning to build a $2,000 schoolhouse.[22] But

Swisher County's 1890 wooden courthouse. Credit: Courtesy of Swisher County Archives and Museum.

County Judge C. T. Word, apparently, had even grander aspirations for the county. He wanted a respectable courthouse equal to those in the more established counties around Swisher. In the summer of 1891, the commissioners contracted with Dodson to develop plans and specifications for a stone or brick building of sixty by ninety feet. In September, the commissioners advertised for contractors to build the courthouse according to Dodson's plans, and on October 5, they chose a contractor with a bid of $35,000, agreeing that "construction is to commence at an early date."[23]

But construction never went forward. When the commissioners investigated financing, they found that Swisher County's tax base was too limited to support floating $35,000 in courthouse bonds—the same problem Wichita Falls had encountered seven years earlier. The commissioners were forced to cancel their plans. Swisher County operated from its wooden courthouse for eighteen more years until it was able to afford a three-story brick courthouse, which was designed by another architect and cost $55,694.[24] Among those present for the groundbreaking ceremonies in 1909 were W. G. Conner, J. M. Stapp, J. L. Stallings, and F. A. Scott—the first Swisher County Commissioners who, with Judge Word, had aspired unsuccessfully to build such a courthouse in 1891.[25]

### VAN ZANDT COURTHOUSE, CANTON, 1894: THE CONTRACT LOST

In 1893, the United States suffered an economic collapse that left Texas' economy depressed for the remainder of the decade. Numerous farmers fell into debt and lost their farms. Many banks folded. Contracts for new architectural work became scarce. Although county officials were reluctant to incur additional debt, the Van Zandt County Commissioners knew they needed to replace their deteriorating jail. Dodson won the 1893 competition and secured the contract. Then, in August 1894, the commissioners agreed that they also needed to replace their aging courthouse, which was nearing forty years old. Satisfied with Dodson's work on the jail, the commissioners awarded him the contract to draw up the plans and specifications and to superintend the construction of the new courthouse.[26]

Before Dodson could submit any drawings, however, Otto Kroeger, a San Antonio builder, approached the commissioners with a design drawn by J. Riely Gordon, which Kroeger proposed to build. As part of the contract Kroeger negotiated with the commissioners, he agreed to compensate Dodson $1,000. Why the commissioners broke their contract with Dodson and accepted Kroeger's deal is not known. Dodson's contract may have gotten caught up in several political fights going on at that time. The town of Canton had just fought with Wills Point over the location of the county seat. The Wills Point supporters opposed a new courthouse in Canton as it would strengthen Canton's position. The Populists, who had gained a stronghold in Van Zandt County by appealing to its struggling farmers, opposed the construction of any courthouse, hesitant to go into debt during the depression. In the next election, the Populists took control of the commissioners court. Once in power, they made Kroeger's situation difficult. They secured an injunction to halt work on the courthouse, an injunction that was eventually lifted. They halted the sale of the $50,000 courthouse bonds and partially paid Kroeger with $35,000 in Asher County school bonds already held by Van Zandt County. The day after canceling the $50,000 bond issue, they floated $26,000 in county bonds and turned over $14,000 of those bonds to Kroeger, thus paying off their obligation completely. The county then had $12,000 to enable it to function. It was Kroeger's problem to find the cash to pay for his materials and workers.[27]

While the Populists may have opposed Dodson's contract, it was clearly Kroeger's actions that cost Dodson the commission. Asking the commissioners to void a signed contract was unethical even if it was not unusual at the time. The design Kroeger presented was a replica of the Gordon design for the Brazoria County Courthouse, which Kroeger had just finished constructing. What he paid Gordon for the design is unknown. Also unknown is whether Kroeger gave kickbacks or other inducements to the commissioners to break their contract with Dodson. In any event, Dodson lost a scarce work opportunity. The sting of this loss was particularly felt since Dodson had just lost a competition for the Hopkins County Courthouse in Sulphur Springs to Gordon. Despite the Populist obstruction, Kroeger built the Van Zandt Courthouse, with H. A. Evans superintending, and completed the construction in 1896.[28]

Otto Kroeger developed a reputation for pressuring county commissioners to renege on signed contracts made with architects in order to work directly with him. He always presented designs he had secured from Gordon. When Gonzales County lost its courthouse to fire in December 1893 and needed to secure plans for a replacement, the commissioners chose the design of local architect T. S. Hodges from those submitted by eleven architects, including one from Dodson. The commissioners subsequently withdrew the commission from Hodges and asked for submissions directly from contractors and builders. Kroeger won the contract, again using a design by Gordon. Losing bidders accused Kroeger of giving $2,500 in kickbacks to the commissioners. These allegations were investigated but no charges ever resulted.[29]

The TSAA criticized the practice of anonymously supplying plans to contractors as unprofessional as it devalued the work of the architect. Contractors could reuse plans without compensating the architect for additional buildings. Moreover, commissioners who dealt only with contractors did not appreciate the importance of the architect's design and technical skills nor their knowledge of safe building practices. The TSAA also denounced architects offering their services to clients who had already contracted with one of their colleagues. Gordon was not the only architect who violated the TSAA's ethical standards. Alfred Giles also sold designs to contractors Martin, Byrnes, and Johnston, who used Giles's unattributed plans to win the contract for the Caldwell County Courthouse in 1893. Both Gordon and Giles later claimed credit for their courthouse designs.[30]

### DENTON COUNTY COURTHOUSE, DENTON, 1895–1897

On February 16, 1895, the Denton County Commissioners met to discuss the county's need for a new courthouse building. They assembled in Denton's third courthouse, built in 1877. By 1890, the poorly constructed brick building had already shown signs of needing extensive repairs. The plaster ceilings were crumbling, and the cracks in the walls were widening. In 1894, the courthouse was condemned as unsafe. An official presented a petition to the commissioners court, signed by every county official working in the building, expressing fears that the building could collapse on them at any moment. Either make the building safe, they pleaded, or provide an alternate space.[31]

The commissioners were hesitant to authorize a new courthouse that would put the county in debt in the midst of a depression. During a long debate on the possibility of repairing the existing courthouse, a prominent lawyer argued that the courthouse was fine, saying "he only hoped that he lived as long as the house stood."[32] His speech was interrupted by a sudden roar of falling material. The commissioners and spectators frantically evacuated what appeared to be a crumbling building. Someone, possibly courthouse office workers concerned about the building's condition, had sent a barrel filled with pieces of coal, tin roof, nails, and empty cans careening down a winding staircase to simulate a collapse. They made their point. Moved by the prank played on them, the commissioners finally agreed to issue $100,000 in bonds for a new courthouse.[33]

Fifteen architects submitted plans, including Dodson, but the commissioners could not agree on any of them. Finally, they chose the Romanesque revival building in J. Riely Gordon's plan. The commissioners asked Gordon to draw new plans, though, to satisfy some of the commissioners' concerns, especially those of dissenting commissioner C. W. Bates. Two weeks later,

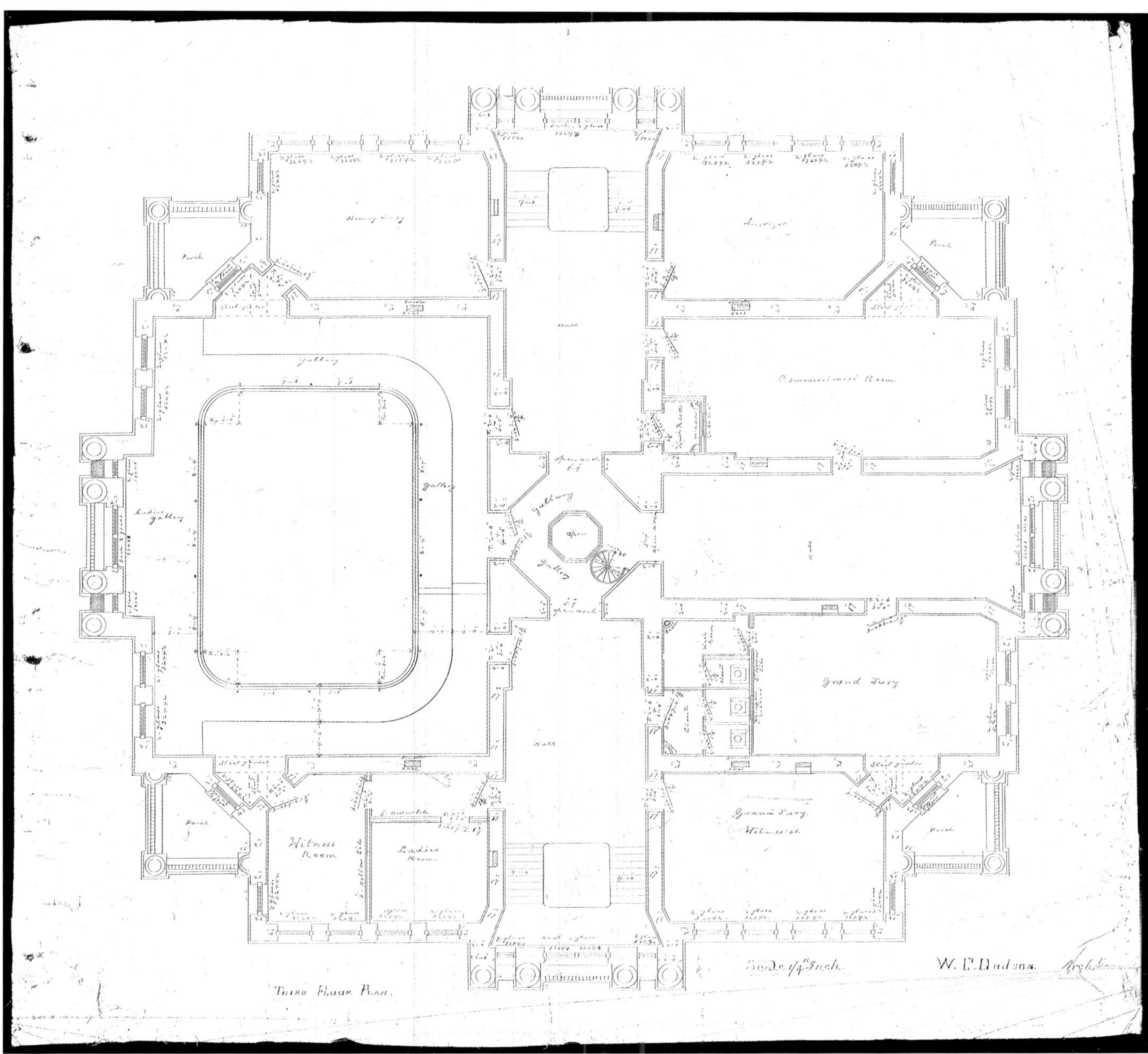


Dodson's original blueprints for the third floor of the Denton County Courthouse. Plans for the other floors have been lost. Credit: Courtesy of the Denton County Office of History and Culture.

Gordon returned with the revised plans. He proposed a three-story courthouse with a tower, a rotunda in the center, and entrances at the four corners. The courthouse featured several large offices, a district courtroom on the second floor, and a large third-floor gallery for spectators.[34]

For three days, the commissioners studied Gordon's plans and considered further changes, but before they could take a final vote, J. M. Miller, the other commissioner who had voted against Gordon's plans, declared that he had been offered a bribe to approve the plans. He did not identify anyone or provide any evidence except to say that Gordon was not involved. With this charge hanging, the commissioners voted to discharge Gordon without pay. They awarded the commission to Dodson, who was probably the architect originally preferred by Bates and Miller. The commissioners requested that Dodson prepare studies, drawings, and specifications for a Romanesque revival courthouse and supervise construction. For his work, Dodson was paid $7,500, or 5 percent of the building's cost.[35]

Dodson was undoubtedly pleased to have the commission. He had not worked on a courthouse since he had finished supervising the Hood County Courthouse construction in 1891. His Swisher County design of the same year had not gone forward, halted by lack of financial resources. His Van Zandt commission had been stolen by Otto Kroeger. His bid in 1894 to design the Gonzales County Courthouse, one of eleven submitted, had lost to the local architect T. S. Hodges. His submission in the Hopkins County Courthouse contest had lost to J. Riely Gordon's. Dodson may have found some work in Waco during the economic depression, but the Denton County Courthouse was a much-needed contract.

Instead of the Romanesque revival style requested by the Denton County Commissioners, Dodson probably would have preferred designing in what he saw as the cleaner, more elegant lines of the Classical Revival, Italianate, or Second Empire styles. He may have agreed with his fellow architect James Wahrenberger, who said in an address to the TSAA membership that it was "absurd that public buildings like courthouses . . . should be of such antiquated architectural style as to remind us of the dark days of the inquisition."[36] Given only a month to develop the final plans, Dodson probably revised his initial design, scrapping most of the Second Empire, Classical, and Italianate features that had been incorporated and replacing them with Romanesque features. These included heavy rounded arches, recessed entrances, and a 140-foot-high central octagonal tower surrounded by four cylindrical towers, all with ogival roofs. At each corner of the massive three-story, 105-by-105-foot building, he placed a series of balconies topped with ogival-roofed towers.[37]

The interior of the Denton County Courthouse featured oiled paneling and wainscoting, decorative ceramic-tile floors, and cast-iron stairs. Credit: Photo by author.

Dodson produced a strong polychrome effect by using tan sandstone for the exterior walls, light brown stringcourses and lintels, eighty polished pink granite columns, and red sandstone capitals. He used a variety of rustication to produce strong shadow lines in the stone. His decorative exterior features included bull's-eye window accents and a variety of carved-stone details, one in a basket-weave motif. His interior features included wainscoting in the corridors and stairways and wood paneling, oiled to bring out the wood's natural beauty, in the courtrooms. Cast-iron staircases placed near the main east and west doors led to the second floor.[38]

To construct the high central masonry tower, Dodson utilized the plan he had devised for his Fannin County project. He moved the location of the large second-floor district courtroom to one side of the central corridor, enabling him to place supporting walls for the tower in the center of the building. As was his usual practice, Dodson placed the tax assessor and collector's office, county clerk's office, and county courtroom—rooms most accessed by the public—on the first floor. The district courtroom, judge's chambers, and

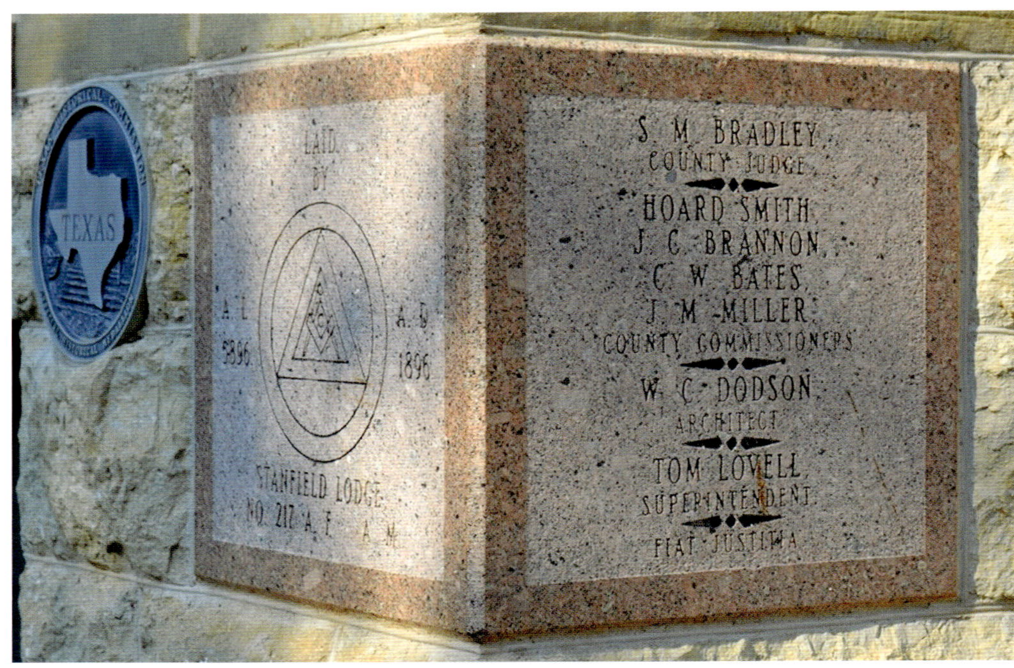


The cornerstone notes W. C. Dodson as the architect. Credit: Photo by author.

district attorney's office were on the second floor. The third floor housed the gallery over the courtroom, a meeting room for the commissioners court, rooms for the grand jury and its witnesses, and additional offices.

When the commissioners approved Dodson's courthouse plans in August 1895, they appointed him superintendent to oversee construction. A few months later, in November 1895, Dodson apparently recommended to the commissioners that Tom Lovell take over as superintendent. Although Dodson was noted for his careful supervision of construction, he may have felt that Lovell, a resident of Denton, would be able to provide better daily, ongoing supervision. Dodson may also have wanted Lovell, whose work he respected, to gain experience supervising construction. The commissioners agreed to pay Lovell $150 per month as superintendent. Dodson still made several 130-mile train trips from Waco to confer with Lovell about construction progress and to resolve any problems that arose. The commissioners paid Dodson for his travel expenses and the 5-percent commission originally agreed upon.[39]

Construction, which was expected to take eighteen months, did not go smoothly. In November 1896, the thirty stonecutters went on strike, demanding that their ten-hour day be shortened to nine with no change in wages. They finally settled on a nine-hour day and begrudgingly accepted a 10-

A late-nineteenth-century postcard of the Denton County Courthouse. Credit: Courtesy of Keith Vincent.

percent pay cut to $3.60 per day. The commissioners had trouble getting workers and advertised repeatedly for fifteen to twenty additional stonemasons.

By that time, it became clear that the building was going to cost considerably more than the $100,000 originally planned. The commissioners had already spent more than that amount and had let additional work contracts that would bring the total cost to $147,000. The courthouse budget became a campaign issue in the November 1896 election. Newly elected cost-conscious commissioners tried to cut corners by purchasing cheaper sandstone. Lovell resigned rather than use inferior stone, and Benjamin Brand finished supervising the courthouse construction. The building was completed in May 1897.[40]

Adding to the commissioners' woes, J. Riely Gordon filed suit against the county, demanding to be paid for his design work. The commissioners hired a law firm to represent them. Denton County's lawyers successfully argued that Gordon had never been hired officially and thus was not entitled to payment. Gordon appealed the decision but once again lost. Although the county won, the litigation cost it additional resources.[41]

Despite cost overruns and other difficulties, the Denton County Commissioners were satisfied with Dodson's work. They passed the following resolution: "Whereas, Maj. W. C. Dodson having been in the employ of Denton County during the past eighteen months as architect of the new Court House . . . and having discharged all the duties incumbent upon him as such architect, in a manner entirely satisfactory to the Commissioners Court of Denton County: *Therefore resolved* by the Commissioners Court . . . that we commend Maj. Dodson to any Commissioners Court desiring the service of an architect as an upright, honorable, Christian gentleman and a competent and skillful architect." Despite their disagreements with Lovell, the commissioners gave him a glowing reference for his work: "We cheerfully commend Mr. Lovell to any one in need of a first class contractor and builder and an honorable gentleman and we regard him second to none as a superintendent."[42]

### CORYELL COUNTY COURTHOUSE, GATESVILLE, 1897–1898

In 1897, the Coryell County Commissioners were ready to authorize a new courthouse and jail. They had been operating out of a cramped four-room building, built on the courthouse square in 1872, that was in poor structural condition and no longer adequate to meet the needs of a county with more than twenty thousand residents. In February 1897, the commissioners unanimously voted to build a new courthouse and jail suitable for the twentieth century.[43]

Led by Judge T. C. Taylor, the commissioners embarked on what Taylor called "an inspecting tour" to gain information about advertising, letting contracts, financing, setting taxation rates, and "all other pertinent information of value regarding the erection, construction, and building of [a] Court House and Jail for Coryell County." After seeing a number of courthouses, including Gordon's just-completed Ellis County Courthouse and F. C. Gunn's Tarrant County Courthouse, the commissioners advertised for architectural designs for the new building.[44]

The tour enabled the commissioners to craft their advertisement with a great deal of specificity. They indicated the new courthouse and jail were "to be constructed under the latest modern style." They called for Coryell County stone, for a fireproof vault, and for both an eight-hundred-pound bell and a Seth Thomas no. 15 clock for the tower. They expected both buildings to be wired for electricity and to have modern plumbing and heating systems. They also sought plans and specifications for the courthouse furniture.[45]

The Coryell County Courthouse. Credit: Courtesy of Keith Vincent.

On May 13, 1897, the commissioners reviewed the designs received from a number of architects, including one submitted by Dodson. Although the commissioners had declared Gordon's Richardson Romanesque courthouse "the prettiest house and equipment they had seen yet," they accepted Dodson's newly popular Beaux-Arts submission and asked him to draw the final plans and specifications. The commissioners also appointed him supervising architect of the courthouse.[46]

Dodson designed the Coryell County Courthouse in the Beaux-Arts style, which had earlier been used for the 1888 Boston Public Library and widely introduced in the United States at the World's Columbian Exposition of 1893. Taught at the École des Beaux-Arts in Paris, this style combined the classic forms of ancient Greek and Roman architecture with elements from the Italian Renaissance and French and Italian baroque periods.[47] Beaux-Arts would soon become the dominant architectural style of the late nineteenth and early twentieth centuries. Dodson placed the three-story building on a raised base of rusticated stonework. Using both red sandstone and white limestone, he created a rich polychromy. The white limestone exterior walls contrasted with the red sandstone columns, lintels, and stringcourses. The white limestone pediment over the main entry featured a red sandstone decoration with a Texas star. The raised first story, pediment, and statuary all were typical Beaux-Arts features.[48]

To accommodate the domed central tower, Dodson moved the courtroom to the side, as he had done in Fannin and Denton Counties, thus allowing him to position masonry walls to support the weight of a dome. On the exterior, the dome emerged from its own octagonal rusticated masonry base. The octagonal drum featured columns separating tall arched windows that in turn lighted a blue-and-gold stained-glass dome in the rotunda. The copper-clad dome featured four Seth Thomas clockfaces sitting atop pairs of columns and surmounted by rounded pediments. On top of the dome, an open belfry housed an eight-hundred-pound bell. Coryell became the first Texas courthouse to have a dome as its crowning feature. In the twentieth century, buildings with a dome and rotunda would become increasingly common as these features became symbols for democratic government itself. "Echoing state and national capitols," two architectural historians noted, the dome and rotunda "unmistakably reflected power and pride and expressed the dignity of authority the public admired." A third historian praised Dodson for his "virtuosity" in his Coryell County design.[49]

Dodson also innovated on another aspect of his typical courthouse plan. Usually, he treated all of the facades equally, giving no single one prominence. For the Coryell County Courthouse, however, he emphasized the south entrance, placing three large arched doorways on the ground floor. On the floor above, he set six Corinthian columns and a prominent portico leading into a large vestibule and rotunda. The less prominent north facade had a portico with four columns; the east and west facades had no porticos. All four corners of the building featured a projecting pavilion topped by a small dome painted to match the red sandstone trim.

The four entrances, placed in the center of the exterior faces, led to corridors that met at the central rotunda. In one quadrant, Dodson placed an oval-shaped county courtroom, as requested by the commissioners. In the others, he put the offices of the county clerk, tax assessor and collector, and sheriff. The cast-iron staircase, placed near the main door, led to the upstairs. On one side was the large district courtroom, also an oval, with a balcony. Offices for the judge, district clerk, and grand jury were near the courtroom. On the third floor, with its eight arched balconies, Dodson situated the jury room and additional offices. Dodson designed what admirers believed to be "one of the most interesting and charming nineteenth-century courthouses in the Southwest."[50]

To move forward with the building process, the commissioners advertised for bids from contractors and floated courthouse and jail bonds worth $85,000, paying 5 percent interest.[51] The commissioners awarded the building contract to Tom Lovell for $61,486. After some changes and additions, one of which was to make the north entrance more prominent, the final bid became $67,624. The commissioners vacated the existing courthouse to allow for its demolition and relocated to the J. B. Fauntleroy Rock Business House until the new courthouse was finished.[52]

On August 14, 1897, Dodson made his first progress report to the commissioners, and Lovell was paid for the work completed to that point.[53] Soon the foundation was laid, and the walls of the basement, which had ten-foot ceilings, were finished. The cornerstone, weighing 825 pounds, was laid on October 2, 1897, with the Gatesville Masonic Lodge conducting the ancient ceremony.[54] Thousands of visitors flooded Gatesville that day, including a number of Masons from the county's other lodges; they watched as the time capsule was deposited and the polished gray granite cornerstone was laid.[55]

Construction, including the addition of modern technical innovations, went smoothly. Electric wiring was strung, fixtures and globes were installed, sewer lines were connected to the jail's sewer line, and the fireproof vault was installed. Newly purchased furniture was placed, ready for opening. The grounds were cleaned, and sidewalks and fencing installed. The commissioners hired a janitor tasked with keeping the courthouse and its grounds in clean operating order. They contracted with the Gatesville Electric Light Company to light the entire courthouse "from base to dome" for thirty dollars per quarter.[56] On July 18, 1898, in his final report, Dodson told the commissioners:

> I have the pleasure to announce to you that your Contractor Mr. Tom Lovell has completed his contract for the building of the [courthouse], in spirit and intent of the plans, specifications and the requirements of the contract . . . and has been faithful and watchful in carrying out and fulfilling the obligations resting upon him as Contractor, and in such manner as to add another laurel to his reputation as a master builder. I wish also to notice the skill and faithfulness of his subordinates Miller, Douglass, Frank James and others in their several departments of construction and of finishing.
>
> I trust it is not out of place in this connection to say also that in my practice and experience I have hardly found a Court who jointly and individually has shown such care in the selection of plans and specifications, and in guarding the interest of the County in all contracts and in their execution, and in the diligence it has constantly shown

> to give your county the best and neatest and the most convenient and substantial Court House to be found in the State for the amount of money expended, and it is your privilege to be assured that you have succeeded in your effort to do so, and have built a monument to your memories which will out last the natural lives of yourselves and children.

Dodson concluded that he approved the building with minor exceptions.[57] Because it was impossible to check the roof's soundness until a substantial rain fell, Dodson recommended that $200 be withheld from the final payment due to Lovell until that occurred. The building, completed and furnished at a cost of $74,195, was ready to open. In July 1898, the commissioners and other county workers moved their offices into the new courthouse.[58]

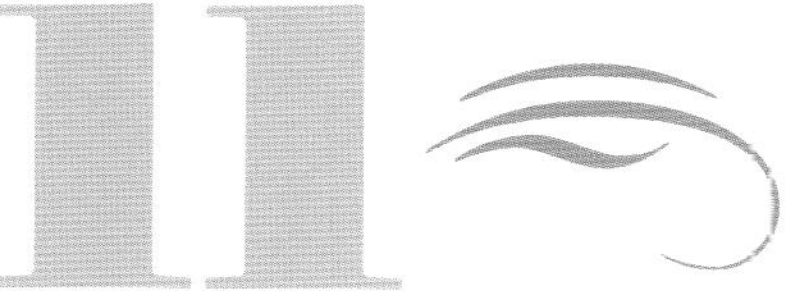

# Consulting and Supervising Architect, 1900–1902

## McLennan County Courthouse, Waco

By 1900, the courthouse that Dodson had designed at South Fourth and Franklin in 1876 was no longer large enough to handle the county's growing business. To house the 19th District Court and its records, the county had rented the basement and then eight rooms in the nearby Provident Building. When that did not solve the overcrowding situation, the commissioners began looking for a site for a new courthouse.[1] The 1893 depression was over, and prosperity had returned to the county. The cotton economy was thriving, and citizens were not hesitant to authorize public spending. Fifteen hundred McLennan County taxpayers signed a petition asking the "county commissioners court to authorize the building of a new courthouse and jail and to issue forty-year bonds up to $250,000 to pay for them." The proposal submitted to the electors in a special April 1900 election passed easily. The commissioners then sought plans and specifications from architects for a courthouse to be located on a new site.[2]

Dodson had served as the expert architect for the McLennan County Commissioners Court since 1890. In that capacity, he had reviewed and approved all preliminary architectural plans presented to the court.[3] In June 1900, recognizing that the selection of an architect and a design for the new courthouse required "technical knowledge possessed only by an experienced architect," the commissioners gave the project to Dodson for his consideration. They charged him with reviewing the ten proposals received and making the final selection.[4]

Dodson's appointment would have pleased the members of the TSAA. For years, the architectural association had opposed competitions overseen by county commissioners who lacked the qualifications to clearly frame the request for proposals and fairly judge the individual entries. In 1899, at the TSAA's meeting in Waco, Dodson, as president of the association, appointed a committee to draw up "a code of rules to govern members of the association in taking part in architect competition." As the minutes indicate, members would refuse to enter competitions unless the request for plans and the judging of entries were both done by "competent professional men."[5]

In September 1900, consulting architect Dodson reported to the McLennan County Commissioners that he had reviewed the ten plans submitted to the commissioners. He dismissed six on first review as "unsuitable in almost every respect for the building you desire." Another two he soon discarded as inferior to the final two plans. These last two, no. 8 and no. 9, he examined closely, both to see if changes were needed and to verify the estimated costs submitted.

Drawing on his years of experience designing courthouses, Dodson assessed the functionality of the buildings. It was important to him that the

The McLennan County Courthouse and Jail, 1902. The jail was later replaced by a courthouse annex. Credit: Courtesy of the Lee Lockwood Library and Museum, Waco, Texas.

location of the courtrooms give them "the prominence due them" and that they be situated so people arriving and departing one courtroom would not disrupt the quiet needed in another courtroom. The record rooms, fireproof vaults, library, and judges' private rooms needed to be "all in connection and all well grouped." Dodson checked to see that a private staircase led from the jury room to the courtroom and the judge's chambers were immediately connected to the county courtroom. The elevators and stairwells had to be convenient, and the traffic flow reasonable. He looked for unassigned rooms, which would be available to accommodate future courthouse growth. And he considered the lighting and ventilation to determine if they were adequate.[6]

Although plan no. 8 had "many excellent points worth consideration," it had others that Dodson judged to be "undesirable and hard to overcome." He was critical of no. 8's exterior design, which was a "novelty rather than a classic," and found "the treatment of the different fronts . . . unsightly and objectionable." One front had "painfully bare walls" one-hundred-feet long with no recesses, balconies, porches, columns, pediments, or ornamentation of any kind. For Dodson, who always maintained that the facades of public buildings should be treated similarly and convey a unity of design, plan no. 8 was "strikingly defective." The building did not have good proportions. The tower and dome were too small for the building, and the tower was constructed "the old fashioned way" with trusses that rested on walls, a method that Dodson had long ago abandoned. The architect of plan no. 8 had also put square- and circle-headed windows on the same line, "giving a bad effect."[7]

In contrast, Dodson liked the architectural style of plan no. 9, a Beaux-Arts building. The building's concept, with its wings, dome, and dominant entrance, was similar to that of the Texas Capitol. The "treatment of all its parts (internally and externally)," Dodson reported, "is delicate and scholarly" and showed a "unity of design in every part." Dodson did, however, propose some changes to the building. He felt that although the building's tower and dome were "of fine proportions . . . the plinth and drum are each too low" and needed reworking. He recommended modifying some room arrangements and assignments to improve their functioning. He suggested building a tunnel to connect the jail to the courthouse and advised eliminating the fountain planned for the rotunda. Finally, he suggested that some of the statuary could be eliminated without compromising the building's proper adornment. His report to the commissioners concluded with the recommendation that they adopt plan no. 9, which happened to be J. Riely Gordon's. "The whole makeup of the building," Dodson concluded, "is easy and dignified and if built with changes suggested will give you a public building with convenience, elegance and repose."[8]

Courthouse construction begins. Credit: Photo courtesy of the Lee Lockwood Library and Museum, Waco, Texas.

Speculation existed that Dodson and Gordon did not have a particularly cordial relationship. Dodson disapproved of Gordon's selling undesignated plans to the contractor Otto Kroeger—a practice the TSAA had criticized as unprofessional. Dodson believed Kroeger used unethical methods, such as bribery and kickbacks, to take signed contracts away from others. That included Kroeger stealing Dodson's commission to build the Van Zandt Courthouse at a time when work was scarce.

On the other side, Gordon may have resented the loss of his Denton County Courthouse commission to Dodson. He was also bitter that he had not been admitted to the prestigious AIA. Although no evidence has been found that Dodson was involved in Gordon's exclusion from the exclusive institute, Gordon apparently believed that Dodson and the other WAS members were responsible. In any event, in his contract with the commissioners, Gordon agreed to make himself personally available to work with Dodson for the project's duration. Evidently, the two men put aside any differences they may

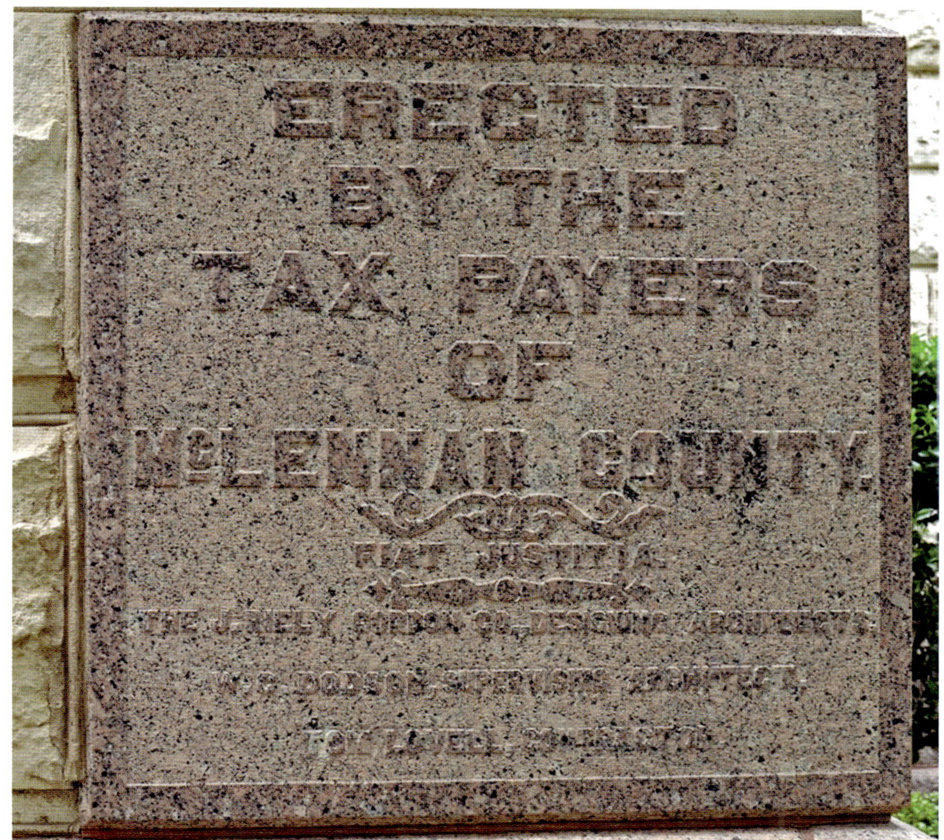


The cornerstone of the McLennan County Courthouse bears the inscription "built by the taxpayers of McLennan County." It also states: "Fiat Justitia (Let Justice be Done). The J. Riely Gordon Co., Designing Architects; W. C. Dodson, Supervising Architect; Tom Lovell, contractor." Credit: Courtesy of Leonard Lane.

have had, and they worked together to make the blueprint changes Dodson recommended. The resulting dome—the crowning feature of the building—was a testament to the cooperative work of the two architects.[9]

The day the cornerstone was laid, Waco hosted over twenty thousand people who had come on special excursion trains from all over the state. The day featured balloon ascensions, competitive military drills, a banquet for one hundred guests, a number of speeches, and a street parade with brass bands. In addition to the Grand Masons of Waco, the parade marchers included ten other visiting Masonic lodges, all escorted by the Waco Knights Templar. The Masons laid the cornerstone according to the Masonic rituals. County Judge G. B. Gerald, who presided over the proceedings, noted that he had also presided at the cornerstone laying of the Dodson-designed courthouse in 1876. As the *Houston Post* noted, "The entire occasion was a notable one in Waco's history."[10]

As supervising architect, Dodson was tasked with recommending the

The McLennan County Courthouse, "one of the finest Neo-Classical buildings in the state," as noted in its National Register of Historic Places narrative. Credit: Courtesy of Dave Fulp.

combination of materials for the facing, trimming, and interior finish. He chose the marble and granite for the flooring and columns, the walnut and oak paneling for the courtrooms and offices, as well as the staircase finishes, window trims, ceiling moldings, and much of the detailing that gave the courthouse its elegant appearance.[11] He also examined and inspected all the work that was done and was given the authority by the commissioners to "reject or condemn" any material or work not in accord with the plans and specifications."[12] Dodson worked well with the skilled and exacting Tom Lovell, who was awarded the $194,831 contract[13], and the construction went smoothly. An elevator, electric lights, and telephone wiring were all included in the building.[14] In March 1902, the keys to the completed new "temple of justice" were handed over to the commissioners. For their work, Dodson was paid $3,422, and Gordon $6,319.[15]

The courthouse was built on a cruciform plan with corridors leading in four directions from the central rotunda. The courtrooms were located at the ends of the corridors on the upper levels. The dome—the building's crowning feature—appeared to be a replica of St. Peter's Basilica in Rome. On top of the dome was a statue of Themis, the Greek personification of justice. Below her were two smaller statues, one a torchbearer, the other Justitia, the Roman equivalent of Themis. Surrounding the dome were a number of eagles.

Supervising the construction of McLennan County's courthouse marked the end of Dodson's career as an architect of Texas courthouses. By building courthouses, Dodson sought to bring order and civilization to Texas. In towns that had frame buildings, board sidewalks, and dirt streets crowded with horses and wagons, Dodson built "Cathedrals of Justice" from stone and brick, with tall bell towers and tasteful, ornate architectural details that gave the imposing structures refinement and character. He sought to build civic pride, instill respect for law and order, and create scenes of beauty and culture, all necessary components of a good society. Years later, a writer for *Harper's Magazine* characterized one of Dodson's courthouses as "a gem of its kind" that "rises above the town like a cathedral in a town in France."[16]

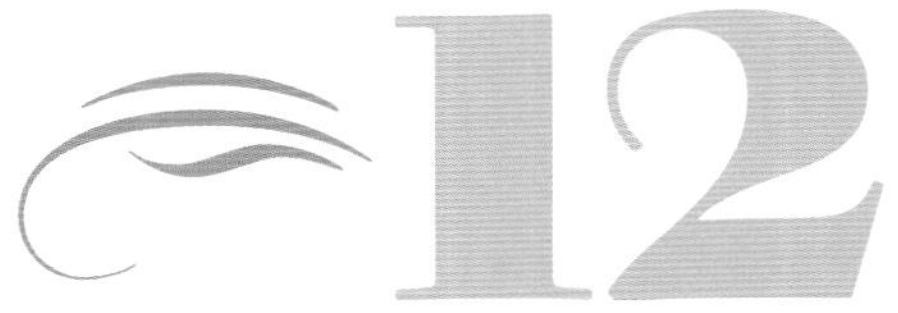

# Jails and Other Public Buildings

In the early days of Texas, jails were rather primitive. Law enforcement officials in some counties restrained prisoners as best they could, sometimes simply chaining a prisoner to a tree or to the town windmill—or, as in the case of Williamson County, confining prisoners in an upside-down Conestoga wagon.[1] Other counties, such as Coryell, jailed prisoners in a double-log building. It wasn't until 1879 that the Texas State Legislature required all county commissioners to "provide a court house and jail . . . and keep the same in good repair."[2] Then in 1884, the legislature allowed for the sale of county bonds to finance jails. A surge in the construction of jails followed.

Most jails built in the 1880s, particularly the smaller ones, were square buildings with jailor's quarters on the first floor and prisoners' cells on the upper floors. These buildings actually looked more like cubes, since they were usually as tall as they were wide and deep. If they had a tower, as in Mason County, it often housed a scaffold with a noose and a trap door for the rapid administration of justice. Larger jails were often built in a T shape, with the front of the jail, the crossbar, reserved for the jailor and his family, while the rear section, the stem of the T, housed the jail cells. Both F. E. Ruffini and W. C. Dodson designed jails on this floor plan. Other jails, such as the Eugene Heiner–designed Gonzales County Jail, were built on a cruciform plan, which accommodated more prisoners.

The 1880s saw many technological improvements in construction. Both concrete and iron beams were incorporated into building designs, as well as gas and then electric lights and improved water and sewer systems. Two companies provided most of the ironwork for the jail cells: the Pauly Jail Building and Manufacturing Company of St. Louis and Diebold Safe and Lock Company of Cincinnati. Both companies provided cells that could either be placed in buildings or mounted on the back of wagons to create moveable jails. Both also contracted to build and outfit jails designed by an architect. And, in a number of counties, both companies contracted to complete the entire project: the design, construction, and outfitting of the building with cells.[3]

The designers of jails sometimes used medieval castle components, such as crenelated parapets, to convey an image of strength and security. Alfred Giles, Oscar Ruffini, and Dodson all built jails with these features. In the 1890s, Romanesque revival features gained in popularity. Diebold Safe and Lock built a Romanesque revival jail for Fort Bend County with a design attributed to J. Riely Gordon.[4] Sometimes when the jail was situated on the corner of the town square, as in Wichita Falls,[5] it would be built to complement the courthouse architecture and include corresponding French, Italianate, Classical, or Romanesque elements. Other jails were built a block or two away from the courthouse, nearby but removed from the town square.

When county commissioners could afford to hire an architect to design their jail, they did so. They often asked for buildings with style and decorative features, and they usually wanted buildings that would make a statement about their sturdiness and security. A number of architects competed for these jail commissions, including Alfred Giles, the brothers F. E. and Oscar Ruffini, and Eugene T. Heiner. Heiner was the most prolific of the group, designing sixteen jails in the 1880s, three times the number designed by each of the others.[6]

### HUNT COUNTY JAIL, GREENVILLE, 1884

In March 1884, at three o'clock in the morning, a fire of unknown origin broke out in the Malone and Matthews livery stable on the northeast corner of Greenville's public square. Fed by the piles of hay and dry feed, the fire spread rapidly, destroying ten frame buildings including the nearby fire engine house, the post office, the Western Union Telegraph office, the Pacific Express, a saloon and grocery, and the Washington Hotel. Also destroyed, according to the *Dallas Weekly Herald*'s account, was "the famous, or rather infamous, Red-Light bagnio, which disgraced our town for such a long time." The fire quickly spread to the public square itself and threatened the newly built courthouse. By keeping a steady stream of water on the building, the fire fighters kept it from catching fire. They were not, however, able to save the city hall or the county jail. The eight to ten prisoners locked in the jail were rescued and taken to the jail in McKinney.[7]

The commissioners had already been planning to replace their two-story jail built in 1870. They had secured a design from Dodson for a stone or brick building as part of his proposal for the county courthouse. Judge J. S. Sherrill had just returned from Austin, where he had tried, unsuccessfully, to negotiate the sale of $15,000 in Hunt County jail bonds to the state school fund. At that time, the state school fund had no money available to draw against; therefore, the county would have to offer the bonds on the open market.[8] Because the county urgently needed a jail, the commissioners immediately called for construction bids and appointed Dodson as the project's supervising architect.[9] Greenville's Ellis and Graham won the construction contract,[10] and P. J. Pauly was awarded the contract for the jail's cells and ironwork.[11] Built at a cost of $13,500, the finished jail was turned over to the county commissioners on October 15, 1884.[12]

### WILLIAMSON COUNTY JAIL, GEORGETOWN, 1888

In 1888, the Williamson County Commissioners knew their Georgetown jail was neither secure nor large enough to hold all the prisoners the county needed to detain. To alleviate overcrowding, they had already moved nonviolent prisoners to the county farm, putting them to work on road repair crews. But a vocal group of Populist farmers continued insisting there was nothing wrong with the existing jail that repairs could not fix.[13] They opposed a new jail, primarily because they feared a tax increase at a time when crop yields were poor and farm incomes down. Despite facing sizable opposition, including a movement to divide the county, the commissioners agreed to seek architectural designs to replace the existing overcrowded jail. To lighten the burden on the taxpayers and mollify the opposition, the commissioners agreed to fund the jail with a $22,500 bond issue for fifteen years at 6 percent.[14]

The firm of Dodson and Dudley submitted the winning plans, which, according to the *Waco Daily Examiner*, won over "strong competition from all over the state."[15] The building was designed in a style evocative of the French Bastille, with eighteen-inch-thick rusticated stone walls and contrasting corner quoins. The roofline's crenellated stonework gave the jail the appearance of a secure military fortress. Designed with a T-shaped floor plan, the two-story building contained ten secure cells, each of which would hold four prisoners. In front of the jail room was a room with two of the old jail cells and the guard room that connected to the jailor's residence. An iron stairway led from the guard room up to two more rooms—one with two new cells for "females and insane persons," and another with two of the old cells for "misdemeanor cases." Thus configured, the cells allowed for the segregation of different types of prisoners as was deemed appropriate at the time. At the front of the building was a jailor's residence with three large, well-furnished rooms on each floor.[16]

The commissioners advertised for contractors in February 1888,[17] but before contracts could even be awarded, a jailbreak occurred at the existing facility. Six prisoners escaped by crawling through a hole cut in the ceiling. A second jailbreak occurred while construction was under way, clearly demonstrating the need for a more secure facility. To prevent yet another break, the county moved its prisoners to the Austin jail.

The Brownwood firm of Lovell and Miller won the construction contract with a bid of $20,966, and the Diebolt Safe and Lock Company was chosen to supply the jail cells.[18] Both firms completed their work by December 1888. After the new jail cells were tested and approved, the county's prisoners were brought back from Austin. The jailor moved into his spacious new residence, considered "one of the best houses in town."[19]

The Williamson County Jail. Credit: Evans Studio, Texas Historical Commission, and the Portal to Texas History, University of North Texas Libraries.

**HILL COUNTY JAIL, HILLSBORO, 1893**

In November 1892, shortly after Dodson's work on the Hill County Courthouse was finished, a fire broke out in Hillsboro. Sparks from a passing railroad engine ignited cotton bales stored next to the Missouri–Kansas–Texas Railroad line. Twenty-eight hundred bales of cotton, valued at $100,000, caught fire. The blaze quickly spread to the nearby Hill County Jail, badly damaging it. The commissioners realized that attempting repairs would be futile and decided to construct a new building.[20] Lacking insurance on the jail, they filed suit against the railroad company to recover $25,000, the jail's estimated value.[21]

Because of the pressing need, the commissioners dispensed with a competition and asked Dodson, their courthouse architect, to draw up plans and specifications for a new jail. When he presented the drawings on January 31,

The 1893 Hill County Jail. Credit: Renelibrary (Wikimedia Commons, CC BY-SA 3.0).

1893, the commissioners asked that he revise his plans to include four additional felon cells. After approving his final plans, they hired him as supervising architect and agreed to pay him 5 percent of the contracted costs.[22] Tom Lovell and William Hood, now operating without W. R. Miller, submitted the low bid of $26,200 for the county's third jail.[23]

For Hill County, Dodson designed a massive, two-story building with a T-shaped floor plan. The front portion of the building, the crossbar of the T, served as the sheriff's and jailor's quarters, with large rooms featuring eleven-foot ceilings. The rear portion, the stem of the T, was designed to hold prisoners. Taking advantage of the technology becoming available at the time, Dodson placed a concrete floor in the basement under the jail cells. He also designed the first and second floors and the roof out of concrete. Semicircular corrugated-steel barrel vaults served as the first-floor ceiling and as support for the concrete floor above. The high-strength steel cells were placed toward the center of the rooms, with corridors on the outside along the windows. This allowed for the placement of tall, narrow windows, which afforded both light and ventilation in the cell area without compromising security. To reinforce the building's fortification-like appearance, Dodson placed notched battlements on the roof edge and corbiesteps up the sides of the gables. He used metal sheeting to cover the gutters and steep gable roof. For decorative features, he included a stringcourse above the windows on both floors and added limestone lintels above the windows.[24]

In March 1893, construction began with the excavation of the foundation and the pouring of the basement floor. Dodson made periodic reports to the commissioners as work progressed, with the contractors being paid for the materials purchased and the work finished.[25] On October 2, 1893, Dodson made his fifth and final report, turning the finished jail over to the county.[26] His construction design, built by Lovell and Hood, resulted in a structurally sound and secure jail. Prisoners could neither dig tunnels through the concrete floors nor cut holes in the concrete ceilings.[27]

### VAN ZANDT COUNTY JAIL, CANTON, 1894

At the start of the depression in 1893, the Van Zandt County Commissioners reluctantly agreed that they needed a more secure jail facility. They requested designs from a number of architects and chose the one submitted by Dodson.[28] Similar to his other jail designs, Dodson's plans called for a T-shaped brick building with the sheriff's quarters in the front and his office and the jail cells in the back. The Pauly Jail Building and Manufacturing Company won the contract to build the structure "in compliance with detailed specifications written by J. W. Dodson [son of the architect] and architect W. C. Dodson" and to supply the jail cells at a cost of $18,775. The building was completed on August 14, 1894, and turned over to the county.[29]

### CORYELL COUNTY JAIL, GATESVILLE, 1897

While supervising the construction of the Coryell County Courthouse, Dodson was asked by the county commissioners to supervise, "without extra charge," the construction of the new Coryell County Jail, located a block from the courthouse square.[30] Although the supervision was additional work, for which he would usually have been paid 1.5 percent of the contract price,

Sheriff Cicero Rusk with his family on the steps of the Van Zandt County Jail. Credit: Courtesy of the Elvis Allen Collection, Van Zandt Historical Commission.

The 1898 Coryell County Jail. Credit: Coryell County Museum and Historical Center.

Dodson agreed, probably because he was already in Gatesville overseeing the courthouse construction and could complete the job without additional trips from Waco.

The plans and specifications for the jail were drawn by the Pauly Jail Building Company, which designed a square building with quarters for the jailor on the first floor and jail cells for thirty prisoners on the second. The commissioners stipulated that the second-floor ceiling be seventeen feet tall, which would allow for them to later divide the space into two floors with additional cells. The building's tower included a hanging platform.[31] Pauly was also chosen to construct the building and outfit it with steel cages or jail cells.[32] Construction began immediately after the contract was signed on July 5, 1897. Construction continued at a good pace, and on December 16, 1897,

Dodson issued his last progress report, authorizing Pauly's final payment.[33] The jail was turned over to the county, and prisoners transferred to the secure facility.

### MCLENNAN COUNTY JAIL, WACO, 1903

After the McLennan County Courthouse was completed in 1902, the commissioners turned their attention to building a needed jail. They awarded the contract to develop the plans and specifications to Dodson. He designed a building that featured a tower topped by a crenellated roofline, similar to the one used in his fortresslike Williamson County Jail. Because the nearby courthouse did not feature a clock, Dodson removed the clock from his still-standing 1877 courthouse tower and positioned it toward the top of the jail tower. For his design, Dodson was paid 3.5 percent of the contracted price, or $874.77. On July 4, 1903, the commissioners accepted the bid from P. A. Harris of $24,991 to build the jail according to Dodson's plans and specifications.[34]

Dodson was also tasked with supervising the construction. As work progressed, he made monthly reports, estimating the work completed and the materials delivered. The commissioners then paid Harris the money due him, minus 10 percent, which was held back until the jail was completed, ready for occupancy.[35] In December 1903, Dodson reported that the "jail had been completed in a workmanlike and satisfactory manner in accordance with the contract specifications." Harris was given a final payment of $5,474.96, the balance due minus $50 withheld until the roof could be tested by rain. Dodson was paid $378.20, 1.5 percent of the building's cost. With the jail completed, the county commissioners ordered the transfer of prisoners to the new facility.[36]

### ODD FELLOWS WIDOWS' AND ORPHANS' HOME, CORSICANA, 1886

The Independent Order of Odd Fellows was a philanthropic fraternal society with roots in England dating back to the early 1700s. The Odd Fellows operated through local chapters or lodges and undertook important service projects. Orphanages were their most important projects. In 1885, the Grand Lodge of Texas Odd Fellows resolved to build a home for the widows and orphans of deceased Texas members. They hoped, as the exploratory committee reported, it would be "the crowning glory of our organized and practical system of benevolence and charity."[37] A committee of six, including Waco member and real estate agent John T. Walton and Grand Master and Waco attorney Marcus D. Herring, located a two-hundred-acre site in Corsicana

The McLennan County Jail, 1903. Credit: Lee Lockwood Library and Museum, Waco, Texas.

Texas Odd Fellows Widows' and Orphans' Home. Courtesy of Ron Maxfield.

that seemed most appropriate for the home, selecting it over Waco, Terrell, and several other towns that had sought the orphanage.[38] When the purchase was completed, they opened the home, temporarily using an existing building on the property.[39]

As soon as Walton and Herring returned to Waco, they sent Dodson on the narrow-gauge railroad to Corsicana to view the grounds and to draw plans and specifications for the permanent building. They envisioned a two-story brick building with two wings, which they intended to build one at a time as space was needed.[40] Dodson designed a Second Empire building that would accommodate up to one hundred residents. It featured mansard roofs, tall and rounded windows, a stone stringcourse, and other stone accents. At one corner, a series of bay windows was topped off with a tall, concave mansard roof containing three hooded dormers. The Waco builder John H. McNeil, who had built three Dodson-Dudley–designed Waco school buildings, was given the construction contract.[41]

The cornerstone was laid on April 25, 1886, the anniversary of the Odd Fellows order, before a large turnout of Odd Fellows from lodges all over the state. They were joined by members of the Knights of Labor, the Knights of Pythias, and the Brotherhood of Locomotive Fireman, plus numerous fire companies, bands, and local Sunday school classes. After a day of speeches reflecting on the need to help the poor and suffering and praising the Odd Fellows' practice of doing good works, the crowd enjoyed a basket dinner.[42]

The first wing of the building was soon finished at a cost of $15,000. The building provided a home for a number of widows and orphans until 1905—that year, a fire tore through the entire building, burning it to the ground. Several children were injured jumping from the second-floor windows to escape the flames.[43]

### FIRST PRESBYTERIAN CHURCH, PALESTINE, 1887–1888

While Dodson was in Palestine supervising construction of the Anderson County Courthouse, he probably went to services at the First Presbyterian Church. He knew the minister and one of the elders from attending the Presbyterian synods. In 1887, likely impressed with Dodson's work on the town's courthouse, the leading church elders asked him to design a new building for their growing congregation. He accepted the commission for the firm Dodson and Dudley.[44]

Dodson designed a building that evoked ecclesiastical authority by combining several elements of medieval church architecture. In the sanctuary, his decorative buttresses and numerous tall, arched stained-glass windows were reminiscent of Gothic Revival. The four front windows with the contrasting stone arches suggested the Romanesque revival style. The single corner tower with the pair of tall, rounded windows evoked Italianate bell towers. The building was wired for electricity, and was the first church in Palestine to have lights. Hooked up to city water, the church had all the modern conveniences of the day. The church's contractor, Joseph Frederick Wolff, was unable to build the delicate 130-foot steeple Dodson had designed, and thus the church was dedicated in July 1888 without it. The next year, C. S. Maffitt, a new church member who had come from North Carolina, offered to design a shorter steeple. Although the deacons were skeptical, they gave him a contract. Builder G. T. Scott erected the seventy-foot steeple. A bell, brought from the former church, was installed in the belfry.[45]

The Palestine First Presbyterian Church, front view, 1900. Credit: Palestine Public Library and the Portal to Texas History, University of North Texas Libraries.

The Palestine First Presbyterian Church, side view. Credit: Courtesy of Carol Kennedy, Texas Historical Commission, and the Portal to Texas History, University of North Texas Libraries.

Palestine Central High School. Credit: Palestine Public Library and the Portal to Texas History, University of North Texas Libraries.

**CENTRAL HIGH SCHOOL, PALESTINE, 1888**

In May 1881, the citizens of Palestine voted to establish a free public school system. They took over the operation of the Palestine Female Academy, which had been educating both boys and girls. Within a few years, the growing enrollment made a larger building necessary. In 1887, the city council and the school commission decided to raze the academy and erect a two-story brick high school for $25,000. The academy was located on Avenue A, next to where the Dodson-designed Presbyterian church was about to be built.

Old Main with wings, as planned, 1903. Credit: Courtesy of the TWU Libraries Woman's Collection, Texas Woman's University.

Perhaps because he was a respected architect already in Palestine, Dodson was given the commission to design the high school. George Wright, who had just finished work on the Anderson County Courthouse, won the job as contractor. The Palestine Masonic Lodge conducted the cornerstone-laying ceremony at the Avenue A site. Construction proceeded rapidly, and the building was ready for the opening semester in 1888.[46]

### THE INDUSTRIAL INSTITUTE AND COLLEGE OF TEXAS, DENTON, 1902–1903

In 1901, the Texas State Legislature passed an initiative providing for a school for women intended to offer practical training, "fitting and preparing such girls for the practical industries of the age."[47] The commission charged with finding a suitable site selected Denton from fourteen possible cities. Denton was already highly regarded as the location of two colleges, the public North Texas State Normal College and the private John B. Denton College, which would change names and locations several times before becoming Abilene Christian. Denton also was deemed to have "an elevating moral and social atmosphere," a healthy environment, and a location easily accessible for a great number of students. The donation of sixty-seven acres for the new school campus and a grant of $16,050 from the people of Denton probably influenced the commission as well.[48]

Girls Industrial Institute and College of Texas. Credit: Courtesy of the Denton Public Library and the Portal to Texas History, University of North Texas Libraries.

On May 2, 1902, the Board of Regents, the state's university system governing body, met and called for architects to submit designs for "Main," the first building of the Industrial Institute and College of Texas. The board wanted a building that "would be adequate to the wants of the institution but which would not be finished in its entirety at the present time."[49] The board met again on July 1 and 2, and, after examining the plans and specifications of nine architects, chose Dodson's submission. His winning design included a core building with space for classrooms, laboratories, a library, auditorium, and administrative offices. It also included wings on both the east and west sides of the central portion that could be built as funds were available and additional classroom space was required for growing enrollments.[50]

At that time, Dodson had formed a partnership with a young Waco carpenter and draftsman, Milton W. Scott. Why Dodson took on a partner at this late stage in his career is unclear. He undoubtedly saw much of himself reflected in the young man. Like Dodson, Scott had lost his father when he was a young boy and had felt a responsibility to support his mother and sisters. Scott had worked as an apprentice carpenter since age eleven. Also like Dodson, Scott was studious and widely read, but he had not been able to secure a formal college education. He was serious about his work and interested in building schools and churches. Dodson must have liked Scott personally and seen in him a promising architect who could advance the profession, designing quality, long-lasting buildings. Dodson had remarked earlier to his colleagues that his generation of architects would soon "have to cease our labor, with our task unfinished, and leave to those who come after us the completion of that which we began."[51] Presumably, he took Scott on not as an employee but as a partner to mentor him and further his architectural career.

The seventy-three-year-old Dodson also might have wanted the assistance of an excellent draftsman in carrying out one of his last public projects. Whether Scott had any influence on the design is not known. Dodson had already built public-school buildings and was comfortable laying out classrooms and administrative offices. Scott's major responsibility was probably drafting most of the plans. The young architect was later known for being an excellent draftsman, meticulous and exacting in his work.[52]

The exterior of "Main" bears a strong resemblance to Dodson's Coryell County Courthouse. Like the courthouse, the base of this four-story brick building was built of rusticated native limestone.[53] The main entrance, like Coryell's, was recessed and accessed through five Romanesque arches. Many of the building's neoclassical features had also been used in the Coryell courthouse, including a center dome and six two-story marble columns placed above the entrance and topped with a triangular pediment. Dodson's four-story Classical Revival building with Romanesque influences was an imposing structure with sufficient elegance to benefit a "temple of knowledge."

The board awarded the construction contract to Dennis Mahoney of Waxahachie, Texas, for $45,462. On January 10, 1903, the cornerstone was laid in a festive ceremony featuring the stonecutters from the Masonic Lodge. The school motto, "We learn to do by doing," was inscribed on one side of the cornerstone. The *Dallas News* later reported that after "the stone was lowered in place, the public grand honors given, the square, level and plumb applied to the stone, the . . . implements of masonry [were] turned

Old Main cornerstone. Credit: Photo by author.

over to the architect."[54] The first classes were held in the fall of 1903 in the newly renamed Girls' Industrial College of Texas. By the fall of 1916, more than fourteen hundred young women had enrolled in the school.[55]

By the end of his career, in addition to his courthouses, Dodson had designed five schools, five jails, three churches, and a widows' and orphans' home. He had also supervised the construction of another jail and two other churches. According to the *Waco Morning News*, Dodson had designed "many other important buildings in Waco,"[56] but no records of those structures have been found. Dodson's public buildings are the legacy of an architect who sought to build the institutions needed for a good society.

# The Fate of W. C. Dodson's Buildings

### THE 1876 McLENNAN COUNTY COURTHOUSE

In 1900, when the commissioners decided the county needed more space for offices and courtrooms, Dodson's courthouse building from 1876 was still structurally sound and functionable. Thus, upon completion of the new courthouse, the commissioners put the old building, along with the jail, up for sale. The Crow Brothers bought the courthouse for $10,000. They moved their business, the Waco Steam Laundry, there and operated as a laundry and a bathhouse for dusty travelers until 1926. The building was razed in the early 1930s.[1]

### JOHNSON COUNTY COURTHOUSE

At 12:30 a.m. on April 16, 1912, a fire broke out in a jury room on the second floor of the Johnson County Courthouse and quickly spread. Albert Bledsoe, the assistant city fire marshal, was on the second floor directing the firemen battling the blaze when an outer wall collapsed, burying him under a pile of brick and stone. Another firefighter hit by the falling bricks was dragged from the building but later died. The fire completely destroyed the structure and all the county records. The commissioners moved quickly, and in September 1912, they secured voter approval to issue bonds for a new courthouse.[2]

### ANDERSON COUNTY COURTHOUSE

In 1913, Palestine resident Percy Wynne was indicted for burglarizing a pool hall. Intent on destroying the documents supporting his indictment, Wynne set fire to the courthouse early in the morning on January 6, 1913. By the time anyone discovered the blaze, it was too late to save the building. The indictments and other papers dealing with criminal cases were lost, but the county records survived, having been stored in a fireproof vault. Wynne was later convicted and sentenced to the state prison for fourteen years (four years for the pool hall burglary and an additional ten years for setting fire to the courthouse); his three small children were taken to the state orphan home. Although the courthouse was insured for $35,000, it was not rebuilt with Dodson's design but was replaced by a building in the Renaissance revival style, designed by C. H. Page.[3]

### WICHITA COUNTY COURTHOUSE

When Wichita County built its courthouse in 1884, it lacked the tax base to fund a larger courthouse. The building's small footprint accommodated only one courtroom. By 1915, however, one courtroom wasn't sufficient to handle all the county's business. The commissioners temporarily solved this problem by dividing the second-floor courtroom, enabling it to serve both

The Waco Steam Laundry in the old McLennan County Courthouse. Credit: Private Collection of T. B. Willis and the Portal to Texas History, University of North Texas Libraries.

(Top) Johnson County Courthouse shell after the April 15, 1912 fire. Credit: Courtesy of the Layland Museum, Cleburne, Texas.

(Bottom) The cornerstone of the 1884–86 Anderson County Courthouse sits at the North Church Street entrance of the current courthouse. Credit: Courtesy of Leonard Lane.

The 1884 Wichita County Courthouse. Credit: Courtesy of the Wichita County Texas Archives.

the 30th and 78th District Courts. But more space was still needed for adequate jury rooms and officials' offices with fireproof vaults for the preservation of records. By 1916, the county had a tax base large enough to support $225,000 in bonds. That year, after securing voter approval of a bond issue, the commissioners authorized the construction of a courthouse designed by Fort Worth architects Fields & Clarkson, Sanguinet & Pate. When the new building opened, the local civic league and the extension department of Texas A&M University made plans to use the old courthouse.[4]

**BROWN COUNTY COURTHOUSE**

By 1917, Brown County's thirty-two-year-old courthouse was deteriorating and in need of repairs. The commissioners undertook renovations, expecting to spend $65,000. Before the work was completed, however, the commissioners had spent $100,000, with the vault and a few stones as the only parts of the original courthouse still remaining. A local critic claimed that the "repair" was "contrived" to permit the financing of the building with warrants instead of with voter-approved bonds and that a new building was the commissioners' goal the entire time. The cornerstone for the brick building was laid on November 4, 1917. The ceremony, conducted by the Masonic Grand Order of Texas, was attended by several masons who had assisted in the laying of the courthouse cornerstone in 1884.[5]

### CENTRAL HIGH SCHOOL, PALESTINE

In 1916, a new school was built for the high school students of Palestine. The Dodson-designed Central High School building was rededicated as Davy Crockett Junior High School and served students another nine years. In 1925, it was torn down to make space for a new Davy Crockett building.[6]

### CAMP COUNTY COURTHOUSE

By 1928, Dodson's Camp County Courthouse had served the community for forty-seven years. The two-story, sixty-by-forty-foot courthouse was too small to continue managing the county's daily business. Under County Judge Joe R. Hooton, the commissioners court agreed to build a new courthouse on a lot north of the old courthouse, built in 1881. They gave the design contract to architects Smith and Praeger and chose Wentzel and Wood as the contractors. Construction on the new courthouse began June 1, 1928, and was completed a year and a half later at a cost of $77,000. The 1881 courthouse was torn down in 1930 to provide a site for a new fire station.[7]

### HUNT COUNTY COURTHOUSE AND JAIL

Built in 1885, the courthouse served Hunt County citizens for nearly half a century. Then in 1928, it was declared unsafe and demolished to make way for a new courthouse and jail building at a cost of $400,000. Many of the bricks from the old courthouse, which were made from clay from the banks of the Sabine River near Greenville, were saved and reused in the new building.

In the jail's final week of service, thirty-seven prisoners were confined in the lower-level cells. Because of overcrowding, two more prisoners were held in the second-floor hospital ward pending their arraignment on violation of Prohibition's liquor laws. Those two prisoners dislodged bricks from the outer wall using bed slats and slid to the ground on blankets they had tied together. When the new jail on the fifth and sixth floors of the just-completed courthouse opened the following week,[8] the remaining prisoners were transferred. The old jail was then demolished.[9]

The east doorway arch of Young County's 1884 courthouse. Credit: Courtesy of Susan Smith, Young County Historical Society.

**YOUNG COUNTY COURTHOUSE**

In 1932, Young County built a new courthouse adjacent to its existing one. The lot on which Dodson's building from 1884 stood was deeded to the federal government as the site for a new federal building. The commissioners sought bids to tear down the old courthouse and clear the lot for the new building. When all the bids to demolish the courthouse were deemed too high, the commissioners told their citizens that they could take away any parts of the building they wanted to reuse as long as they hauled away an equal amount of debris. One citizen took the stair railings and used the wood to make new gavels for the county judges. Many took stone from the outer walls. Before long, the site was cleared, and the courthouse materials were being used for new buildings around the city of Graham. All that was left standing was the stone arch that had surrounded the courthouse's east door.[10]

A few years later, when new streets were cut through Commerce Park, the arch was left on what became a small island in the center of the downtown square. A dispute ensued between those who wanted to remove the arch to improve traffic flow and those who felt the arch must be preserved as a reminder of Young County's early days. The preservationists won out. The arch continues to stand, as one Young County resident said, representing "early day law and order."[11]

### HOUSTON COUNTY COURTHOUSE

In 1907, needing more courthouse space, Houston County erected a two-story brick structure on the southeast corner of the courthouse square. It housed the county clerk's office, vaults for the storage of county records, and a jury room. In 1934, when oil was discovered in Houston County, officials oversaw the construction of a frame annex, completed within two days, to handle the crush of people wanting to access land records. The additional space provided by these two buildings allowed Dodson's 1883 courthouse to serve the people of Houston County until 1938.

At that time, in the midst of the Great Depression, the Public Works Administration (PWA) initiated a program to encourage the construction of public buildings by making funds available to states, counties, and municipalities. While this program provided employment for workers, it unfortunately led to the destruction of many of Texas's late-nineteenth-century courthouses. Houston County applied for $90,000 in PWA funds. Once granted, the county sold its elegant Second Empire courthouse to D. J. Duncans for one dollar; he agreed to tear down the building and clear the courthouse square, making way for the construction of an undistinguished modern structure.[12]

### KAUFMAN COUNTY COURTHOUSE

In the decade after the Kaufman County Courthouse was built in 1887, lightning struck the courthouse tower several times. The tower was so damaged that, in 1910, the top two sections were removed, and a dome was added to cover the remaining base section. In 1922, when the original foundation was found to be unstable, a reinforced-concrete foundation was put in place. In 1941, the county commissioners secured a $125,000 grant from the Works Progress Administration (WPA) that would partially fund a new courthouse

The Kaufman County Courthouse, ca. 1930s. Credit: Image courtesy of Texas Department of Transportation.

and jail. They had hoped to replace the building soon after, but because the United States was drawn into World War II, the project never went forward.[13]

By the 1950s, the building, now over sixty years old, appeared "sound from the outside" but showed signs of deterioration inside, with visible cracks and crumbling mortar. In 1954, the commissioners voted to build a new building for $600,000 and demolished the existing courthouse to create a site for it. The groundbreaking ceremonies, held March 13, 1955, were attended by a large crowd, including three men who had attended the same ceremonies for the earlier courthouse. One of them, Marion Fox, had been the printer at the *Kaufman Sun* newspaper and, according to the *Austin American*, had "set the type describing the ceremonies at the first courthouse 69 years ago." The cornerstone from 1887 was placed on the grounds of the new courthouse.

The Fifth Street Methodist Church after the 1953 tornado. Credit: Lee Lockwood Library and Museum and Museum, Waco, Texas.

Unfortunately, another seventy years later, by 2025, the sandstone had deteriorated so badly that the inscription was barely legible.[14]

### FIFTH STREET METHODIST CHURCH, WACO

In 1953, a tornado severely damaged the sanctuary and steeple of the Fifth Street Methodist Church. The church was repaired and continued to be used for another ten years. It had housed the congregation for eighty-seven years when it was razed in 1963 to erect a new building.[15]

In March 1963, Dodson's granddaughter Lallie Dodson Gibson was invited to attend the last service to be held in the church. She reported to her

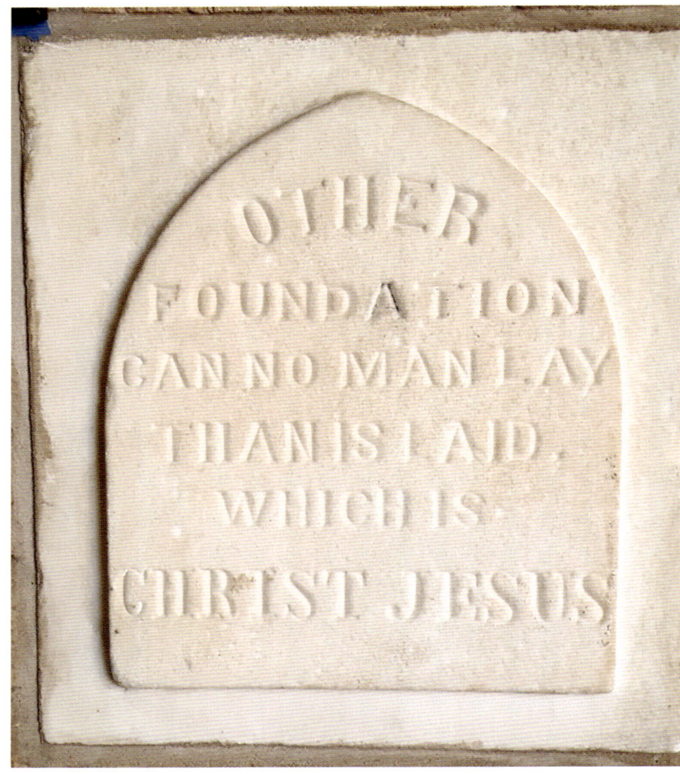


Fifth Street Methodist Church cornerstone, now in the narthex of the 1963 building. Credit: Courtesy of T. Bradford Willis.

cousin Charles Henry Dodson: "They had removed the old cornerstone, polished it all up, and put it on a pedestal and it will be placed in the foyer of the new church. Grandpa's name really shone . . . They were very cordial in their honoring me as his granddaughter and high in their praise of a man who could build like that."[16]

### VAN ZANDT COUNTY JAIL

The Van Zandt County Jail housed prisoners securely from 1894 until the 1930s. In 1935, the county commissioners secured a WPA grant of $86,000 to assist in building a new courthouse with a jail on its top floor. When the building, which cost $190,000, was completed in 1937, the prisoners were transferred to the new facility. The old jail stood empty. During World War II, the county gave the jail building to the US Army "for the duration," so that it could strip the old jail cells from the building. Using cranes, blocks and tackles, oxy-acetylene torches, and other scrap-cutting tools, the army salvaged tons of steel for its scrap metal drive. The Office of Price Administration, the wartime ration board, conducted operations in the old jailor's

The jail is part of the Williamson County Courthouse Historic District. Credit: Photo by Another Believer (Wikimedia Commons, CC BY-SA 4.0).

residence until 1947. After that, the Veterans Service Office and the Van Zandt County Farm Bureau used the old building. In 1969, despite the efforts of the Van Zandt Historical Society to save it, the jail was torn down.[17]

**WILLIAMSON COUNTY JAIL**

In 1934, the Southern Prison Company of San Antonio remodeled the interior of the Williamson County Jail. It provided new cells, added a hospital ward, and increased the prison's capacity from thirty-five to sixty-seven prisoners. With the $40,000 renovation, the building continued to be used as a jail until 1989 when it was replaced by a larger building. The jail, referred to as a "striking two story limestone fortress," was designated a Recorded Texas Historic Landmark in 1965. In 1977, it was included in the Williamson County Courthouse Historic District that was listed in the National Register of Historic Places.[18]

**HILL COUNTY JAIL**

In 1981, the Hill County Jail became a Recorded Texas Historic Landmark and was listed in the National Register of Historic Places, lauded as "an excellent example of nineteenth century Texas public architecture." The jail continued to house prisoners until 1983 when a larger facility was completed. After it was vacated, the Hill County Historical Commission obtained the structurally sound ninety-year-old building to serve as the Hill County Cell Block Museum. In 2022, major structural problems were discovered in the building's foundation, requiring extensive repairs. Recognizing that historic buildings, such as the jail, were part of the county's cultural heritage, the commissioners asked the historic preservation firm Architexas to develop a master plan for needed renovations. In 2024, having secured the needed funds, the commissioners had the foundation reinforced and leveled.[19]

**THE INDUSTRIAL INSTITUTE AND COLLEGE OF TEXAS, OLD MAIN**

The Industrial Institute and College changed names several times over the years, becoming the Girls Industrial College in 1903, the College of Industrial Arts in 1905, the Texas State College for Women in 1934, and Texas Woman's University in 1957. In 1916, in order to accommodate a growing enrollment, the college added wings to the east and west sides of Old Main. This, according to Dean Mary Evelyn Huey, brought Dodson's "full original plans to completion."[20] In 1974, Old Main, "the original, and for many years, the only building" on the campus, was recognized, as Dean Huey noted, for being "central to the life of the University." For this, as well as for its historical and architectural value, Old Main was designated a Recorded Texas Historic Landmark.[21]

**PALESTINE FIRST PRESBYTERIAN CHURCH**

Over the years, as membership continued to grow, two additions were added to the Palestine First Presbyterian Church. In 1998, the church was declared a Recorded Texas Historic Landmark. The same year, it was listed in the National Register of Historic Places for being a "premier example of late 19th century Gothic Revival ecclesiastical architecture." In 2024, over 140 years after its dedication, it was the oldest church still serving a congregation in Palestine.[22]

**CORYELL COUNTY JAIL AND COURTHOUSE**

Coryell County's jail, whose construction Dodson supervised in 1897, housed prisoners until 1930 when it began to show signs of deterioration. On August

Old Main. Credit: Photo by author

First Presbyterian Church, Palestine. Credit: Photo by Renelibrary (Wikimedia Commons, CC-BY-SA-4.0). Cropped by author.

The Coryell County Jail cornerstone now sits on the north side of the courthouse. Credit: Courtesy of Sherry Lawrence, Coryell County Genealogical Society.

30, 1930, the commissioners contracted for a new jail.[23] In 1934, the old jail was pronounced "structurally insecure" and was demolished. During a later courthouse renovation, a complete set of the original jail blueprints was found. One blueprint showed gallows at the top of a stairwell, with suitably strong ceiling supports, and a man hanging from a rope from the ceiling. The blueprints were framed and hung on the first floor of the courthouse.

The Dodson-designed Coryell County Courthouse remained structurally sound. During the Great Depression, the county judge arranged to have an unwanted carload of cement delivered to Coryell County, enabling WPA workers to finally finish the courthouse basement's dirt floors.[24]

In 1977, the Coryell County Courthouse was recognized as a Recorded Texas Historic Landmark and listed in the National Register of Historic Places.[25] In 1986, the Coryell County Historical Commission inspected the courthouse and recommended a series of updates and repairs. The commissioners sought volunteers to do the renovations and asked for twenty-five-dollar contributions from local residents.[26] Before long, the commissioners

The Coryell County Courthouse was added to the National Register of Historic Places on August 18, 1977. Credit: Wayne Wendel.

realized that the renovations would be a much bigger project than anticipated. The columns in the bell tower had deteriorated and required major work. An elevator had to be installed, or the county would lose federal revenue-sharing money. Accessible entrance ramps and restrooms were needed, as were fire stairs and fire-detection systems. The commissioners hired a preservation and restoration consultant to develop a comprehensive restoration plan and seek available grants for what might be a million-dollar project. "The courthouse is built well and will last another 100 years," said the Historical Commission

Chair, D. W. McDonald. "We can fix the bell, redo the district courtroom back to its original state and when the work is finished it will be something we can be proud of for years."[27]

In November 1986, the Coryell County Commissioners authorized the complete restoration of the courthouse. To finance the work, they secured a million dollars in loans from local banks. During the renovation, workers replaced the thirteen-foot zinc statues of Liberty and Justice that stood on the roofline with fiberglass replicas. They mounted a replica of the missing eagle statue on the top of the bell tower. By removing a false ceiling in the district courtroom, the workers were able to uncover and restore the courtroom balcony with its hand-tooled leather railings. They also restored the newly exposed third-floor arches, cornice work, and an exquisite round stained-glass dome. In September 1988, on the ninetieth anniversary of the building, Coryell County held a rededication ceremony.[28] In July 2023, on the building's 125th anniversary, it held another celebration.[29]

### HILL COUNTY COURTHOUSE

On January 1, 1993, the Hill County Courthouse went up in flames. The New Year's Day fire began in the tower and soon burned out of control. After its supporting timbers burned, the entire tower and its bell collapsed into the center of the building, igniting all three floors of the courthouse. By the time the fire companies finally extinguished the blaze, the interior was completely gutted. Only the exterior masonry walls of the one-hundred-year-old structure remained.

The citizens of Hill County were proud of their courthouse, which had been recognized as a Recorded Texas Historic Landmark and listed in the National Register of Historic Places in 1971.[30] They opposed any plan to construct a new modern building, choosing instead to rebuild their historic courthouse. They contracted with Architexas to develop the reconstruction plans and specifications. Architexas sorted through the fire's remains and used historic photographs to reconstruct the courthouse as closely as possible to the original. It took several years and $8 million to restore the building. Local fund-raising, insurance payments, and two concerts by Hill County–native Willie Nelson helped pay for the building. When the county sought and secured grants from the Texas Department of Transportation to help with the restoration, it sparked a movement to save other endangered courthouses. On April 24, 1999, the courthouse was rededicated at a daylong festival that included a speech by then Governor George W. Bush and an evening fund-raising concert featuring Willie Nelson.[31]

Gov. George W. Bush speaking at the rededication ceremony. Credit: Photo by author.

The Hill County Courthouse on fire. Credit: Courtesy of Architexas.

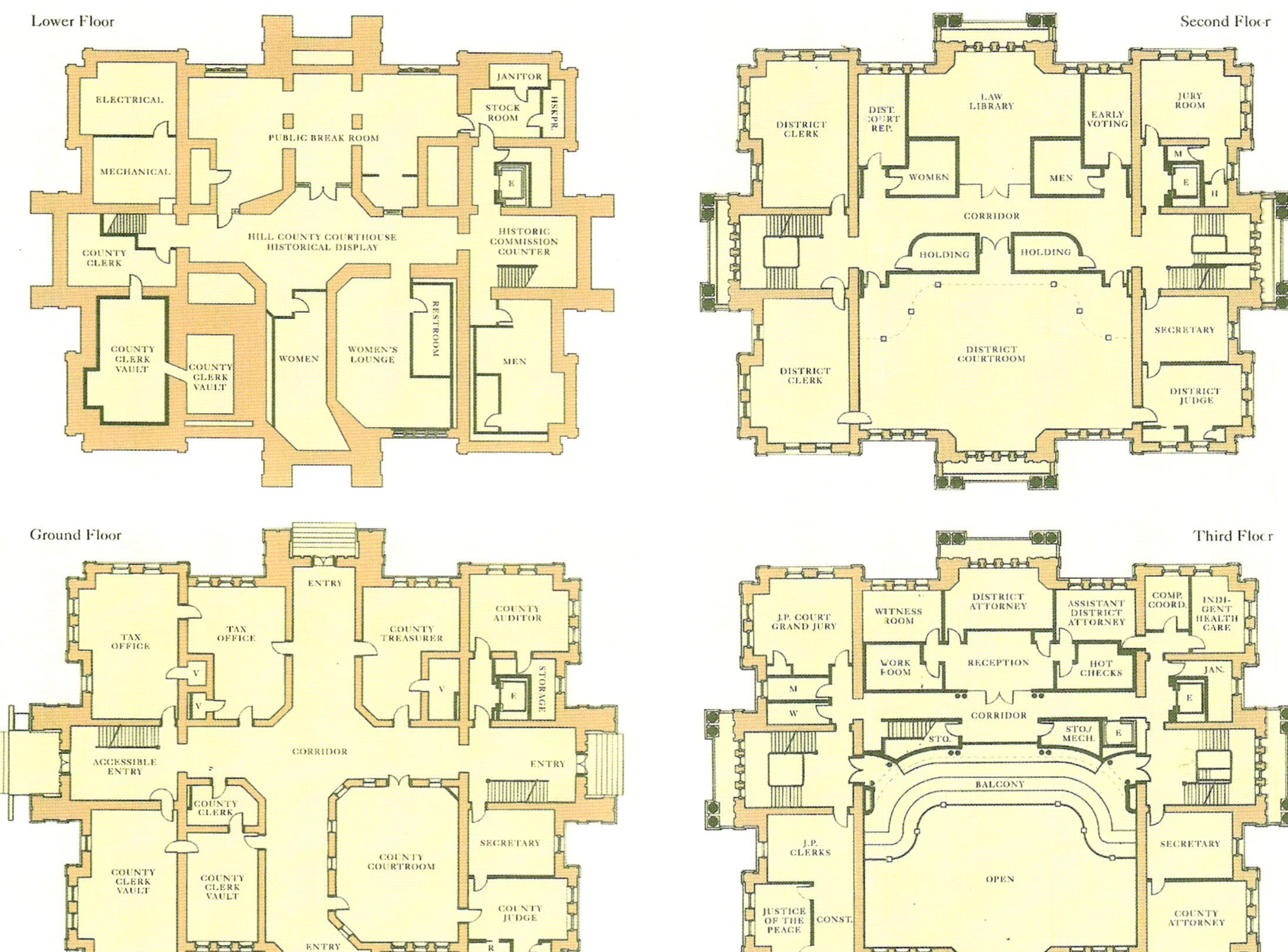


After the fire, the district courtroom was restored to its original two-story appearance with a large spectator gallery. Credit: Hill County Historical Commission, Hillsboro, Texas.

The Hill County Courthouse became a Recorded Texas Historic Landmark in 1964 and was listed on the National Register of Historic Places in 1971. Credit: Photo courtesy of Jordan McAlister.

The Lampasas County Courthouse, admired for its geometrical details carved in stone, became a Recorded Texas Historic Landmark in 1965. It was placed on the National Register of Historic Places in 1971. Credit: Courtesy of Wayne Wendel.

**LAMPASAS COUNTY COURTHOUSE**

In June 1999, with the support of Governor George W. Bush, the Texas legislature established the Texas Historic Courthouse Preservation Program to help counties preserve their historic buildings. In 2000, the Texas Historical Commission began making planning grants available to help counties develop the architectural plans and specifications for needed repairs, as well as offering emergency grants to address immediate problems and construction grants to correct long-term problems. By 2024, the preservation program had provided grants for the full restoration of seventy-eight courthouses and grants for planning or emergency repairs to many others.[32]

(Opposite) In 1970, the Denton County Courthouse was named a Recorded Texas Historic Landmark. In 1977, the courthouse was listed on the National Register of Historic Places. In 1982, the city of Denton designated it a historic landmark. Credit: Courtesy of Jordan McAlister.

In 1965, the importance of the Lampasas County Courthouse was recognized when it became a Recorded Texas Historic Landmark, and in 1971, it was listed in the National Register of Historic Places.[33] In 2000, Lampasas County officials received a $2.3 million partial matching grant from the Texas Historical Commission. The grant enabled the county to correct poorly engineered repairs that were made to the building over the years following various floods, fires, and lightning strikes. The county was also able to undo alterations made to the interior, replace or restore damaged windows, update old and faulty mechanical systems, and make modifications needed to comply with the Americans with Disabilities Act.[34] As the renovations began, the community held concerts, bake sales, and other events to raise the required matching funds. On March 2, 2004, more than three hundred people attended a festive rededication ceremony celebrating their courthouse's restoration. One local volunteer was asked about her work on the project. Reflecting her pride in the courthouse, she replied, "Other than raising my family, that was the most important exercise of my entire life."[35]

### DENTON COUNTY COURTHOUSE

The Denton County Courthouse was recognized as a Recorded Texas Historic Landmark in 1970 and listed in the National Register of Historic Places in 1977.[36] In the 1980s, Denton County began major restoration work, done in three phases over a number of years and helped by a grant from the Texas Historical Commission. Architexas, the architectural firm overseeing the restoration, removed a floor that had been constructed over the courtroom, restoring the courtroom to its original appearance with a surrounding balcony. They located replacement stone at the quarry where the original stone had been cut. They procured stone to rebuild entry steps, enabling the courthouse to reopen its south entrance, which had been closed since 1965. Workers removed inferior replacement windows and installed wood windows that replicated the original design. Architexas called the Denton County Courthouse "one of the most significant and impressive examples of public architecture in Texas,"[37] and the chair of the Denton County Historical Commission called it "the most treasured building in the county."[38] The building was rededicated in 2004.

### PARKER COUNTY COURTHOUSE

The Parker County Courthouse was recognized as a Recorded Texas Historic Landmark in 1965 and listed in the National Register of Historic Places in 1971.[39] In the 1990s, the Texas Historical Commission gave the county several grants to restore the building's exterior. County officials used the funds

The central bell tower is one of the distinguishing features of the courthouse. Credit: Photo by author.

In 1971, the National Register of Historic Places narrative noted: "The Parker County Courthouse is an eye-catcher." Credit: Courtesy of Wayne Wendel.

to replace the roof and windows and to repair the clock and clock tower. In 2002, with another $4.2 million grant from the historical commission, the county restored the interior to its original design. They returned the district courtroom, made smaller during earlier refurbishments, to its original size—one of the largest in the state. They returned the wooden balconies that had flanked the courtroom and restored the decorative wall and ceiling paintings. The brass squirrels that had held up the gaslights were kept to support the electric fixtures. Even the original floor pattern in the carpet was recreated.

The Parker County Courthouse's restored clock tower. Credit: Private Collection of Jim Bell and the Portal to Texas History, University of North Texas Libraries.

The building was made accessible, and the plumbing, mechanical, and electrical systems were updated. In 2005, the county celebrated its historic building with a rededication ceremony.[40]

### HOOD COUNTY COURTHOUSE

In 1968, a tornado damaged the Hood County Courthouse tower, leaving it tilting and in imminent danger of falling. The county commissioners planned to raze the tower and install a flat roof, but other more preservation-minded leaders argued to keep the clock tower and the building's original architecture. The Granbury Woman's Wednesday Club petitioned the commissioners to save the tower, saying that it considered "the historical significance and architectural beauty of the Hood County Court House in its present form of architecture to be an asset to the State of Texas and to Hood County in particular." Dismantling the tower would destroy "an important link with the past" that could "never be replaced." The club asked the commissioners court to "completely restore the clock, cupola and . . . existing tower" and to "maintain the architectural integrity and historical significance of said Hood County court house."[41] The commissioners accepted the arguments of the preservationists and contracted to have the damaged structure repaired, with the windows, clock, and ornamental work all restored to their original condition. To modernize the building, they added air-conditioning, heating, and an elevator. They also lowered the district courtroom ceiling, an "improvement" that would later be undone. The courthouse was designated a Recorded Texas Historic Landmark in 1970.[42]

The courthouse restoration provided the economic stimulus needed to revitalize all of Granbury's town square. Tourism became vitally important to the local economy as visitors came to see the historic courthouse, visit the museum located in the old jail, browse in the restored shops and restaurants, and see the old Victorian homes. The square continued to be the main site for county gatherings and patriotic celebrations. In 1974, the Hood County Courthouse and the surrounding town square became the Hood County Courthouse Historic District. It was the first town square in Texas to be listed in the National Register of Historic Places.[43]

In 1998, the commissioners undertook what was expected to be a $900,000 renovation of the courthouse. Work was to include repairs to the tower, roof, and windows, as well as plumbing and electrical repairs and improved accessibility. Workers soon found, however, that the original tin roof remained, covered by three additional layers, and that the tower was badly deteriorated. Both the roof and tower required more extensive repairs than had been anticipated, almost doubling renovation costs to $1.7 million.[44]

The Hood County Courthouse. Credit: Courtesy of Jordan M. McAlister.

In 2001, Hood County secured a planning grant of $345,000 from the Texas Historical Commission and, in 2008, a construction grant of $5 million. With Architexas as the preservation consultant and HDR as the project architect, the commissioners undertook the total restoration of the courthouse's interior, including that of the original two-story courtroom.[45]

When the building, widely considered the county's "crown jewel,"[46] was rededicated in 2012, over ten thousand people attended the ceremonies.[47] A local official noted the importance of the historic Second Empire building to the people of Granbury: "The Hood County Courthouse is the heart and soul of our community. Built of native limestone in the middle of a town square influenced by our native Upland South culture, the Courthouse gives Granbury its special sense of place and unique charm. Our courthouse reflects the past, significantly contributes to the present, and now heralds a shining future for Hood County."[48]

### FANNIN COUNTY COURTHOUSE

On New Year's Eve 1929, a fire started in the courthouse's Italianate cupola and soon engulfed the tower. As the *Bonham Daily Favorite* reported: "The tower is gone and the bell is in the basement, and the clock, a total wreck, lies by its side."[49] The fire also destroyed the building's elaborate gable roof. While in the midst of the Great Depression, the county commissioners could afford to do little more than secure the building by installing an undistinguished flat roof.

In 1964, the county commissioners approved a major modernization of the courthouse. They hired contractors to remove the remaining roof pediments, install new aluminum doors and windows, and cover the exterior stone with a smooth surface of Lueders limestone, transforming the courthouse into an art deco building.[50] One critic of this modernization noted: "All the original hand-dressed stone and architectural details were covered to produce a squat boxy building with no distinguishing architectural features."[51]

In 2008, local librarian Barbara McCutcheon began campaigning for the restoration of the courthouse to its original grandeur. County officials applied for a state historical renovation grant. Then, in November 2016, Fannin County voters passed a courthouse restoration bond proposal. This $12.5 million bond was partially matched by a $5 million grant from the Texas Historic Courthouse Preservation Program. Fannin County expected the bond and grant would provide sufficient funds to restore the courthouse to its original design from 1888.[52] But, largely because of damage done to the building's stone during the renovation in 1964, an additional $10 million, obtained through certificates of obligation, was required to complete the project.

The courthouse fire, 1929. Credit: Courtesy of Fannin County Historical Commission.

The courthouse after its remodeling in 1964. Credit: Courtesy of Leonard Lane.

Beginning the removal of the stone cladding that covered the original sandstone. Credit: Courtesy of Leonard Lane.

The restoration was completed in the spring of 2022. The finished project cost almost $30 million dollars. In a county of roughly thirty thousand people, this represented a remarkable commitment to preserving local history. At the courthouse's rededication ceremony, several restoration committee members reflected on the years spent completing the work. The *North Texas e-News* noted that for Architexas preservation architect Anne Stimmel, "this wasn't just another project. . . . She was leaving a piece of herself in this beauty." County Auditor Alicia Whipple added, "This beautiful lady will always have a piece of our hearts."[53]

The aluminum windows and doors and smooth stone overlay were removed. Credit: Courtesy of Leonard Lane.

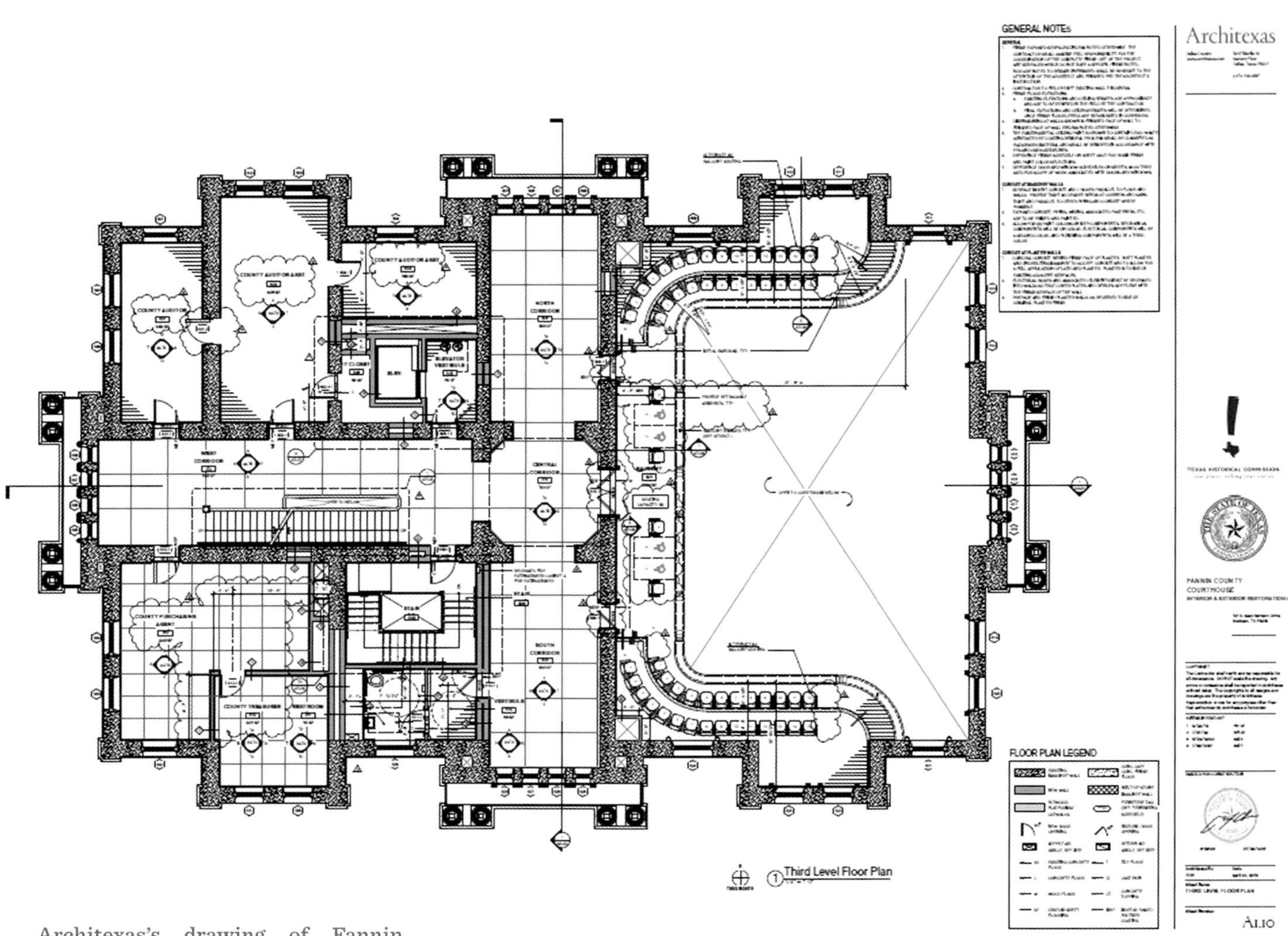


Architexas's drawing of Fannin County's courtroom design. Credit: Courtesy of Architexas.

The "grand lady" on the day of the rededication, March 10, 2022. Credit: Photo by the author.

(Opposite) The restored McLennan County Courthouse dome. Credit: The Lyda Hill Texas Collection of Photographs in Carol M. Highsmith's America Project, Library of Congress (Wikimedia Commons).

### MCLENNAN COUNTY JAIL AND COURTHOUSE, 1902

Dodson's McLennan County Jail was demolished in 1953 when the site was needed for a new federal building. The J. Riely Gordon–designed courthouse was designated a Recorded Texas Landmark in 1970 and listed in the National Register of Historic Places in 1978.[54] In 1999, the commissioners court requested that Architexas develop a site assessment and restoration master plan for the courthouse. The goal of renovation was both to accommodate the county's current and future needs for a courthouse and, to the extent possible, return the historic building "to its original design and appearance."[55] In 2012, some structural problems were discovered under the courthouse dome and roof. A $2.6 million restoration project corrected those problems and restored the dome and statuary to their original grandeur. In 2019, the commissioners secured an updated master plan so that additional restoration steps could be taken. Their goal was to ensure that the courthouse could continue serving the people for the indefinite future.[56]

The Texas Historic Courthouse Preservation Program has made grants of millions of dollars to restore a number of courthouses, including all surviving W. C. Dodson buildings that had not already been restored.[57] Because these buildings were judged worthy of preservation, and because efforts were made to protect them, seven Dodson-designed courthouses, and an eighth whose construction he supervised, are still in service over a hundred years after his death. These imposing buildings, standing in prominent central locations, were focal points of nineteenth-century community life in Texas and serve as reminders of the ideals and values of the people who built them. The courthouses continue to serve as centers of their twenty-first-century communities and have been key in the economic revitalization of many historic downtown squares. These cathedrals of Texas stand as W. C. Dodson's legacy today.

# 14 The Legacy of a Good Name

Photo of Wesley taken by his son-in-law William Dougherty, ca. 1910. Credit: The Denton County Office of History and Culture.

In the years after he moved to Waco, Wesley remained in close contact with his daughter Mollie Bet Board in Bryan. The society pages of the *Bryan Eagle* indicate that he made trips to visit Mollie Bet and her family several times a year. Frequently, he brought one or more of his younger children with him. Sometimes he left Anna, Mattie, and Bessie to visit with the Boards for an additional week. Other times Wesley took one of Mollie Bet's children back for a visit with his Waco family. Most of Wesley's Waco family was in Bryan in June 1901 for the wedding of Mollie Bet's daughter Mabel, and in June 1911 for the wedding of Molly Bet's daughter Ada.[1]

Wesley maintained a close relationship with his grandchildren, going to San Antonio in 1911, for example, with some of his children to visit Mabel and her husband and to see his daughter Mattie, who by then had married and had a baby son. In a letter to Mollie Bet, Wesley told her he had visited the Alamo, which he called the place "of most interest" to him in San Antonio's public areas. "I was acquainted with all of the events of its history which gave a zest to examining it in all its details—the place where the Mexicans made the breach in the South wall and gained entrance, and the place where Crocket died, and the spot where Bowie lay sick and helpless on a cot when he was assassinated—Ah, the Alamo, the 'Cottonwood.' The Cottonwood grove from which it took its name has disappeared to make room for buildings with no historic interest. How much of nature's loveliness, and of sacred spots has our so called civilization destroyed."[2]

Wesley and Mollie Bet's letters reveal the loving closeness between them. He consoled her over the loss of an infant grandchild, expressed his anxiety at times when Mollie Bet was ill, and indicated his pleasure that his younger children, Anna and Willie (James William), had come to see her. In one letter, he acknowledged receiving a photograph of Mollie Bet: "I am always glad to hear from you, and would like to see you, but can't tell when it will be. I am so glad you sent me your picture. It looks so much like you I had to kiss it. It is the best one of you I have seen."[3]

Wesley shared some light moments with Mollie Bet. When she thanked him for a picture of himself that he had sent, he replied: "It gave me much comfort to know that my picture was beautiful and just like me. It has been a mystery to me why women have taken on so about me, and now I understand it—it is because I am so good looking, and they admire the beautiful."[4]

He reminisced with Mollie Bet about her early years in Livingston, Alabama, a town they left when she was only five. Wesley had returned to Livingston in 1891 and found virtually nothing left of what they remembered fondly. The school buildings where Sarah had taught had all burned in the 1890s, as had Mollie Bet's "old childhood Academy." Their old Presbyterian

The Alamo featured on a 1906 postcard. Credit: Private Collection of T. B. Willis and the Portal to Texas History, University of North Texas Libraries.

church no longer stood. The people they had known were no longer there. "If you were there," he wrote, "it would be a very melancholy pleasure—old landmarks gone, and those you knew and who knew you, or me or your ma—with two or three exceptions—all gone. If you should ever go there, read 'Goldsmiths Deserted Village'[5] and see if a like feeling doesn't overcome you. There is nothing tangible of your ma's precious work done in the education of the girls left to be seen, as they too are dead; and but little left to call me to remembrance only a few of my buildings left, and my name, as a Confederate soldier, engraved in the solid marble Confederate Monument which stands in the Courthouse Square. . . . Your Grandma and your Aunt Juliett, with your two little brothers—Robert and Ernest, with two children of your Aunt Eliza's—lie in the old grave yard without a friend there to think of them or put flowers on their graves."[6]

Dodson headstones in Myrtlewood Cemetery, Livingston, Alabama. Credit: Provided by author.

Memorial to Confederate veterans bearing Wesley Clark Dodson's name, dedicated in 1908 near the Sumter County Courthouse in Livingston, Alabama. Credit: Courtesy of Dr. Valerie Burnes, Sumter County Historical Society.

**CIVIL WAR REMEMBRANCES**

In 1887, Wesley was a founding member of the Pat Cleburne Camp of United Confederate Veterans, and, for several years, was the group's commander or lieutenant commander. The camp was open to any Confederate veteran, and membership at one time numbered over three hundred men. In 1887, the majority of Waco men over the age of forty-five had fought in the Civil War. About fifteen hundred McLennan County men had volunteered to serve with the Texas forces. Other veterans, like Wesley, had served in other Southern states but had migrated to Texas after the war. The Cleburne Camp provided a way for the veterans to recall their contributions to the war effort, commemorate their heroes, and provide social support and financial assistance to those veterans in need. Since most of the men in the camp had served in the Civil War's western theater, they named the group after Col. Patrick Cleburne, a divisional commander in the Army of Tennessee. Cleburne had fought at the battles of Chickamauga, Missionary Ridge, and Ringgold Gap and had been killed at the Battle of Franklin.[7]

The group met on the first Thursday of every month. As camp historian, Wesley regularly made presentations on the events and people in the war. In 1900, for example, he made three presentations: one on events leading up to the battles around Chattanooga, another on the Battle of Lookout Mountain, and a third on the Battle of Missionary Ridge.[8] In 1909, the *Camp Cleburne Ledger* reported that Wesley had "made a very interesting address, detailing certain important events occurring during the war in 1862–3 and showing their great bearing upon the final disastrous issue." At another meeting it was reported that "the historian, W. C. Dodson, was present and promised to give the camp at its next meeting a continuation of his historical talks on the war in the southwest from 1861 to 1865."[9]

In the middle of one talk, Wesley digressed from his analysis of the bloody fighting to describe the field of battle.

> On a clear day, the view from Missionary Ridge was enchanting, with the Chattanooga valley spread out before you, in all the loveliness which a pleasing nature wears. Hills and plains interspersed with groves of trees, and dotted with farms and dwellings and shrubbery and flowers, reminding us of homes and loved ones far away, where once was peace and joy, and the family unbroken. Running in this valley . . . were numerous rivulets babbling in their beauty, and dancing in their joy, and sparkling in the sunlight like the dust of diamonds, as they ran their course to the Tennessee, where their individuality was forever lost. . . . Mountains, near and far, rise in unbroken lines, rank above rank, and

> head lifted above head, reaching for supremacy, and the valleys with running streams and winding waters—dark and shaded by the hills, with over-hanging cliffs and unbroken forests, fills the mind with awe, and a feeling of reverence at the comingling of the beautiful and sublime so intricately woven by Him, in whose hands are the destinies of Nations, that the soul of man is bowed in humility before the overwhelming scene.[10]

Even at the scene of death, Wesley found natural beauty and God.

In the middle of another talk at Camp Cleburne, Wesley digressed from his explanation of wartime events to ask: "And you, the sons and daughters of the men and women who suffered in body and mind in those perilous times, who met every danger with undimmed eye and cheek unpaled by fear, whose heroic blood gives you life today, do you use any means to inform yourselves of all they suffered for you? Do you know anything of the history of the Southern Confederacy?—a history of only four years, but a history that challenges the admiration and respect of all other nations, because in the short period of its life it fought more battles, won more victories, endured more hardships, exhibited more fortitude and died a nobler death than Any Nation that earth ever knew—died in a halo of victory, shrouded in the winding sheet of honor, unstained by any guilt and was never conquered, but struck for its home and its rights until it was annihilated."[11]

Wesley's talk echoed the "Lost Cause" mythology that developed in the South following the war and that surged in popularity during the Jim Crow era of the 1890s. At that time, organizations such as the Sons of the Confederacy, United Confederate Veterans, and Daughters of the Confederacy were formed. The movement was not led by the former planter class of slaveholders or by the Confederate leadership, as might have been expected, but by middle-class people and by the rank and file members of the Confederate army.[12] They erected statues, wrote articles and books, held ceremonies honoring the Civil War soldiers, and promoted the tenets of the Lost Cause as the Southern interpretation of the war. This romanticized version of history downplayed slavery as the underlying cause of the war and sometimes even defended slavery as a benevolent, paternalistic institution. It portrayed the war as the South's attempt to resist Northern aggression and to defend its legitimate states' rights. Ignored in the Lost Cause legend was the reality that the South seceded because it feared the institution of slavery was endangered. Also omitted were the divisions between the large planters and the middle-class merchants, professionals, and small farmers, many of whom had neither supported slavery nor favored secession.[13]

In 1895, Wesley attended the Fifth Annual United Confederate Veterans Reunion. The event, which was held in Houston that year, was advertised as "a grand gathering of the remnant of the brave legions who so valiantly strove for victory upon the battle fields of the south." Over twenty thousand veterans from over six hundred local camps converged on Houston for the celebration. Those who had served in the Alabama forces met at Camp Dick Dowling's headquarters, where Wesley found a number of his old army comrades. He enjoyed reminiscing with Gen. Stephen D. Lee, Wesley's commanding officer at Chickasaw Bayou. The reunion featured balloon ascensions, competitive drills, marches, seventeen-gun salutes, and fireworks—but most important were convention speeches designed to keep alive the memory of the Confederate soldiers and enshrine the South's interpretation of the Civil War as the "War of Northern Aggression" or "a conflict between the states."[14] "The moral question of slavery [was] not the cause of [the contest]," the historical committee reported.[15] As Gen. J. B. Gordon called the convention to order, he remarked, "Under the conquered flag we are come together again to honor the cause for which it waved. . . . They [the Confederate forces] fought for the great principle of local self-government and the privilege of managing their own affairs, and for the protection of their homes and residences." The United Confederate Veterans would work to ensure that school history books would be what they deemed a "true history."[16]

In accepting and advancing the Lost Cause theory, Wesley was undoubtedly trying to preserve the memory of his compatriots and himself as heroic and to see all of the injuries, deaths, and lingering pain and suffering as something given on behalf of a worthy cause. Although he suffered the rest of his life from his war wounds, he was probably comforted by the belief that he had fought to preserve the South's honor. Since the myth was widely embraced in both the North and the South, Wesley might also have felt vindicated for his participation in the war. Instead of portraying his actions as an attempt to destroy the union his grandfather had fought to create and his father had fought to preserve, the Lost Cause myth presented his actions as noble, hopefully to be seen by his children and grandchildren as honorable.[17]

Wesley became a scholar of Civil War battles. He scoured volumes of war records to find battle reports from many Confederate and Union officers. In 1897, when he went to a United Confederate Veterans reunion held in Nashville, Tennessee, he visited Franklin, near his boyhood home in Williamson County, the site of one of the worst Confederate military disasters. The cemetery there held the remains of fifteen hundred Confederate soldiers. "I examined very closely the old battleground and positions at Franklin, and was rather surprised to find that there are discrepancies in some maps of the battleground. I also went over the Confederate cemetery and noted every grave, with its inscriptions and the number from each state. That cemetery will be a perpetual monument to the patriotism, to the manhood and womanhood, of Franklin and of glorious old Tennessee."[18]

In 1908, when he learned of the death of Gen. Stephen D. Lee, Wesley wrote a tribute to him for the *Waco Times-Herald*. He praised the general for his leadership at Chickasaw Bayou, where Wesley and about six other Cleburne Camp members had served, and at the Siege of Vicksburg. Lee was a man of "unyielding and stubborn courage," Wesley wrote, "and this trait showed itself in all his military career. He is gone to join his old comrades who have gone before. May the memory of his virtues live in the minds and hearts of his comrades and his countrymen."[19]

Wesley also wrote articles dealing with the Civil War for the monthly magazine *Confederate Veteran*. In one such article dealing with the battles at Chickamauga, Lookout Mountain, and Missionary Ridge, he concluded, "There was a dense mental vapor in the minds of officials in charge of both armies in the maneuvers and battles on Lookout Mountain which caused discord and bitterness that never healed. Our commander [Bragg] had two of his lieutenant generals dismissed from his army [D. H. Hill and Leonidas Polk], both of whom asked for a court of inquiry, which the government refused. The Federal authorities had several courts of inquiry concerning their generals who were charged with the cause of defeat."[20]

Wesley never glorified war. He wrote about the failure of leadership in the Civil War campaigns in which he participated, particularly that of General Bragg's, and he praised the courage of soldiers who fought honorably, such as color-bearer Sergeant Gilder and Adjutant Ellerbe, who valiantly retrieved the colors left on the field at Resaca. As he said in the midst of the Civil War, there was never "a man happy at home, who was in favor of war!" It was "the Devil" who was behind war![21]

When the Spanish-American War broke out in 1898, Wesley criticized the "fool Congress" for getting the country into a war he could not support: The "yellow press" had whipped up war fever over an explosion on the USS Maine in Havana Harbor. "All who want to go can do so—if they know no better—but all that I can do will be to wish them well and weep at their funeral. I have graduated at that business and don't wish to take a post graduate course. *Experience* is a good teacher, but he doesn't keep a free school, and I was at his school between three and four years and paid a very high tuition."[22]

By 1909, Civil War veterans, "the wearers of the gray" as they referred to themselves, were aging and many of the men needed assistance. At each Camp Cleburne meeting, after the mortuary roll was called, the question was

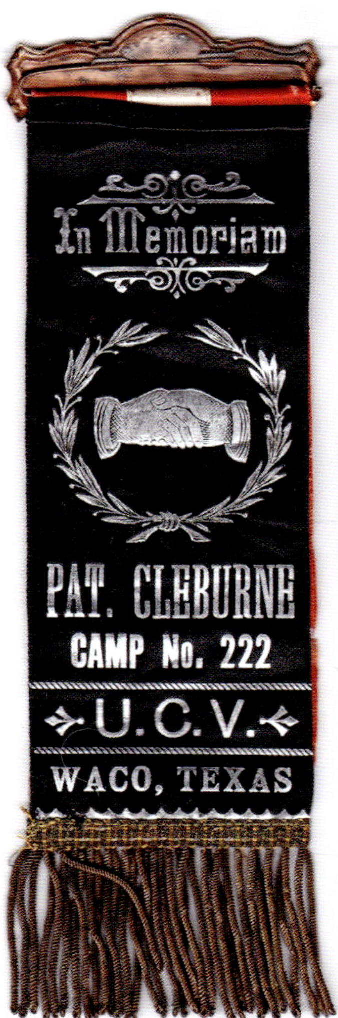


Wesley's Camp Cleburne Confederate badge of honor. Credit: Provided by author.

asked, "Is any comrade sick or in distress or out of employment?" As the *Waco Daily-Examiner* reported, help was offered to anyone mentioned.[23] In 1911, Wesley filed an application for a pension made available by 1909 Texas legislation to soldiers "who are in indigent circumstances." He qualified because "he had served in the military service of the Confederate States during the war between the States of the United States" and did not have an income more than $150 a year nor property worth more than $1,000.[24]

By 1913, membership at the Cleburne Camp had dropped to about twenty-five men. In October, when the camp held its annual memorial service for all members who had died within the year, they remembered thirteen veterans

—the most lost in one year. At the monthly meetings in both October and November 1913, the camp reported Wesley among the sick. As Wesley had told Mollie Bet in 1912, he was getting weaker, suffering from rheumatism that his doctor believed resulted from the war wounds to his hip and leg.[25]

### FAITH AND FAMILY

Wesley's strong religious faith came through in many of his letters. Because of a miscommunication, he missed his granddaughter Mabel's confirmation, which disappointed him greatly. "I wish so much I could be there tomorrow when Mabel joins the church but it is too late to do so now. God bless her, and keep her in this life, and preserve her soul and body unto eternal life in Christ Jesus."[26] When Mollie Bet was ill, Wesley wrote: "I am so much distressed, dear daughter, that you are not well yet, but trust and pray you will be soon. How it would rejoice my heart! . . . God bless you and spare you, dear daughter, if it be His Holy Will. . . . If no providential hinderance, I will go down next Saturday to see you, and take Anna."[27] For his granddaughter Lucy's marriage in June 1911, Wesley wrote and delivered a long "prayer for blessings to rest upon the family and upon the bride and groom."[28]

When Mollie's husband, Albert, was terminally ill, Wesley wrote: "I know your trust is in God and you submit your will to his Holy Will, for He knows what is best for Albert and for you, and for each of us. All that I can do is to pray that if it is His Holy will to take him from his suffering here to his heavenly home . . . that His Holy Spirit may be your comforter and heaven your hope where there is no parting, nor sorrow. You have the deepest sympathy of myself and Mama, but nothing but the gracious love of our heavenly father can give you comfort, and I pray He will comfort your heart and mind in Christ Jesus and keep you in perfect peace. . . . Please tell Albert of my sorrow for him in his sufferings. In love from Pa."[29]

In the spring of 1914, Wesley made plans for Mollie Bet and Lucy to attend his family birthday party in Waco. "I trust neither you nor I will be disappointed by anything occurring to hinder my seeing you on my birthday, for I anticipate with so much pleasure the happiness it will give to have you with me. Anna wants to be here too; and maybe Bessie. . . . And indications are that it will be the last one I will see in this life, but the hope remains that in the next one we will be together forever."[30]

At the time he wrote this letter, Wesley's health was failing, and his usual strong, clear handwriting had become shaky. He told Mollie Bet, "My hip and leg hurt so badly and I am so weak in them that I can hardly get out of the house; and I have to sit in my chair day and night, as I can lie down but little on account of shortness of breath." He longed to get outside and go for a buggy ride. “I sit and think about the relief it would be if you and I could ride about in the buggy and see everything and visit the grave yard and take my mind off my troubles.” Mollie Bet had offered to come to Waco and take her father to Bryan for a visit. “If it is your wish and would be agreeable to the children to have me to go with my bodily infirmities—it would be a great pleasure to me to go and be with you.”[31]

He closed one letter, “My love to you all, and to you especially. Your devoted father W. C. Dodson.” Another time he closed, “All send love to all. Accept the love of your affectionate father, W. C. Dodson.”[32] And another time he closed his letter: “My love and a kiss to the dear children, including Sam [Mabel’s son], and tell him grandpa is proud of his manly little fourth degree boy. With love and a kiss from Pa.”[33]

Wesley enjoyed sharing poetry with his grandchildren. In 1911, he read a poem in *Christian Magazine* by Gertrude Morton Cannon with a message that resonated with him. Modifying it to include his grandson’s dog Jack, he copied it on one of the yellow legal pads that he always used for writing. On the outside of the folds, he wrote, “From Grandpa to Chas. Henry.”

“GRANDPA AND ME”

My grandpa says that he was once
A little boy like me;
I ‘spose he was, and yet it does
Seem queer to think that he
Could ever get my jacket on,
Or shoes, or like to play
With games and toys, or race with Jack,
As I do every day.
He’s come to visit us, you see,
And Mama says I must be good
And mind my manners, as a child
With such a grandpa should; For grandpa’s very old and straight
And very dignified,
He knows most all there is to know,
And other things beside.
So, though my grandpa knows so much
I thought that maybe boys
Were things he hadn’t touched,
They make such awful noise;
But when at dinner I asked mama
For another piece of pie

I thought I saw a twinkle
In the corner of grandpa's eye.
So yesterday when they went out
And left us two alone,
I was not quite so much surprised
To find how nice he'd grown;
You should have seen us romp and run
My! Now I almost see
That p'r'haps he was, long, long, ago,
A little boy like me.

When Wesley went to Nashville in 1897 to attend the Confederate Veterans Reunion, he found some schoolmates whom, he noted, "God had spared that we might meet again." They had attended the old-field school taught by his uncle, James Blackwell. He also visited his father's farm in Marshall County and the cemetery where his father and sister Caroline were buried on the old Murdock place. Going back to his "old boyhood home," he wrote, was "indeed like the renewing of my youth."[34]

On that trip, Wesley reunited with his cousin John Blackwell, son of his Aunt Betsy and Uncle Tommy Blackwell, whom he had not seen in over fifty years. He wrote his cousin beforehand that he hoped to "hold sweet communion with you once again on earth, before we both go hence to hold sweet and eternal communion with our loved ones who have gone before, and with our blessed Lord and Saviour Jesus Christ." He admitted to his cousin: "You don't know how sweet to me is the memory of those old names and those old places, where I was taught by a sainted father and mother to love and fear God and work righteousness." He finished the letter with the old poem,

How dear to my heart are the scenes of my childhood,
when fond recollection recalls them to view.
The orchard, the meadow, the deep tangled wildwood,
and every loved spot which my infancy knew.[35]

Toward the end of his life, while reminiscing with his cousin Dillingham, Wesley commented that his parents, brothers, and sisters were all gone. "I am left alone like an old limb, the only one on an old tree."[36]

On the morning of August 1, 1914, Charles Henry Dodson, Wesley's nine-year-old grandson, peddled his bicycle over to the McLennan County Courthouse. He went to tell his father, Cavitt Watson Dodson, the assistant county auditor, that Wesley had died.

Charles Henry Dodson, about nine years of age. Credit: Provided by author.

Assistant County Auditor C. W. Dodson, on left, with County Auditor W. C. Lockwood in McLennan County Courthouse, ca. 1915. Credit: Provided by author.

The *Waco Morning News* reported the loss of a "pioneer citizen of Waco and one of the pioneer architects of Texas."[37] The *Fort Worth Star-Telegram* reported: "Waco—WC Dodson, one of the oldest architects in the state, who came here in 1876, died early this morning, after an illness of several years. Dodson designed many prominent buildings in this city and drew the plans for the second courthouse built here since he came to Waco. He was born in Alabama and served in the Fifth Alabama Regiment. He is survived by his widow and seven children. He was in his eighty-sixth year."[38]

The *Waco Times-Herald* mourned the loss of one of the city's "pioneer citizens," a man whose "indomitable courage and valor on the battlefield were matter of common knowledge with his old comrades in action. . . . Mr. Dodson drew the plans for the old courthouse, located at Second and Franklin streets and for the Fifth Street Methodist Church at Fifth and Jackson Streets, supervising the erection of both these buildings. Many of the other prominent buildings erected here, in days gone by, stand as monuments to his architectural genius. . . . For years there was no architect in the south with a wider reputation than Mr. Dodson, neither was there one considered more capable. His faithfulness in all things, even the minor details of life, had endeared him to hundreds, and his word was accepted implicitly in all things."[39]

On its editorial page, the *Waco Times-Herald*'s president and one of Wesley's pallbearers, George C. Roberts, penned the following tribute: "Wesley Clarke Dodson was a man of the highest integrity and the sincerest purposes. He believed in God and he never wavered. He was a Democrat of the old school. He had little or no patience with new contrivances for the conduct of government. To him Federalism meant death to Freedom. He lived the simple life. He found no delight in the blare of trumpets. Pretense he could not abide. He leaves to his children and to his grandchildren that greatest of all legacies, a good name."[40]

At the September 1914 meeting of the First Presbyterian Church Ruling Session, the elders appointed R. H. Rogers and G. W. Davis to prepare a resolution on the death of Elder W. C. Dodson. At the following meeting, "in remembrance of his worth," they presented "the last record of his life and work." Wesley served the church as a ruling elder for over two decades. "During the years of his service in this capacity he proved himself to be a profound church lawyer, sound in the faith once delivered to the Saints, and of consecrated loyalty to his Lord and to his word. He was a deep thinker and a careful student of the word of God, and well-grounded in the doctrines and polity of the denomination of his choice. In the Session, in Presbytery, in Synod, and in General Assembly he was ever found, and eminently safe and sane. . . . He is gone. Gone to meet his Lord. . . . His strong and rugged face will shine no more among us, his rich deep voice be heard no more in council,

Wesley was buried in the cemetery he designed, Waco's Oakwood Cemetery. Credit: Provided by author.

but in the life beyond . . . may we meet him, may we greet him, in that day that has no end."[41]

By the end of his long architectural career, Wesley Clark Dodson had designed courthouses for eighteen Texas counties.[42] Today, all but seven of his courthouses have fallen victim to fire or modernization. The seven that are still standing have been completely restored, and currently six are listed in the National Register of Historic Places. The Williamson County Jail, the Hill County Jail, and the Palestine First Presbyterian Church also are listed in the National Register for Historic Places. One judge of his work said that he was "one of the more famous and prolific courthouse architects of the age"[43] and that he "ranks among the most important architects in nineteenth-century Texas."[44]

As one of the "pioneer architects of Texas," Wesley built courthouses, schools, and churches that were important in the creation of a civilized society. His imposing brick and stone buildings that towered over the Texas prairies represented stability, order, and the rule of law and gave citizens a sense of community. While his buildings had a commanding presence, they were also beautiful, with architectural elements that made them elegant and refined, something in which the people could take pride. His buildings remain as part of his legacy.

Wesley's well-lived life was also his legacy. He was a deeply religious man who always believed God had a purpose for him. He was a moral man, an honorable man, and a man of principles. He was devoted to his family, thought it was his duty to help and comfort them, and was generous and charitable in his support of them all. Civic-minded, he felt an obligation to participate in and better his community. A patriot, he willingly fought, like his father and grandfathers before him, to maintain the freedom and rights of his homeland as he saw them. A Romantic, he adored all that was beautiful in nature, and he was not afraid of expressing his emotions, particularly his love for his family. He was an educated and cultured man, who studied the Bible and enjoyed literature, history, and poetry. He had an indomitable spirit. Although he never fully recovered from his Civil War injuries, he bore his suffering without complaint "as became a man of God," as one friend said.[45] Despite the many misfortunes he endured, he always praised God for blessing him and keeping him safe. As he said at an earlier time, his intention was "to take the world as I find it, but never to be driven from my highest design, that of making myself useful to my friends and my country."[46]

In his memoirs, Wesley wrote that he wanted his children to know "something of my ancestors, whose characters and worth are their heritage." He believed that "those that can revert with thankfulness and with commendable pride to an honest and godly ancestry are in possession of an heritage above the price of rubies."[47] Wesley would have agreed that by leaving to his children and their posterity a good name, he had given them that greatest of all legacies.

Texas Odd Fellow's Home for Widows and Orphans. Credit: El Paso Daily Herald, April 25, 1899, p.7, Newspapers.com, 25 Apr 1899, Page 7—El Paso Herald at Newspapers.com

# Appendix 1

## My Heritage

Wesley knew a great deal about his ancestors and took pride in his ancestry. "None of my ancestors were nobles or peasants, that I know of, but were of what was called the upper middle class—the class that is the bone and sinew, and the body and soul of all nations and peoples who have made history. My grandparents, on both sides, were well off in the world's goods, as it was considered in their time, and they and their children were slave holders; but this counted but little with them as their chief pride was the nobility of character, the honesty of their lives, and the independence of their spirit and the honor maintained by their ancestors for generations before them as a liberty loving and life defending people."[1]

Wesley was only thirteen when his father, Elisha Jefferson Dodson, died. Most of the Dodson family history that he knew he had learned before then, and most of the names, dates, and locations of relatives have shown to be correct. But he didn't learn it all; as he told his cousin Dillingham in 1902, he did not know who his father's sisters were. While his father talked of them, Wesley could not remember their names, with the exception of Millie Stamps, the only aunt that he knew. In his memoirs, Wesley gets his distant ancestry confused. He knew nothing about several generations between him and his third great-grandfather Charles Dodson. He confused his grandfather Charles with his grandfather's brother, Elisha Joel, the relative killed by a Native American.

Perhaps his memory was failing him when he was eighty-three. More likely, though, the stories he learned had been jumbled in the telling. Even with access to census records, it is difficult to keep Dodson family history straight. Names were repeated, generation after generation. As was the custom in southern colonial America, where most people were members of large family groups, families often named their older sons after the boys' grandfathers or father, with the younger boys named for uncles.[2] There were, for example, two Charleses in Wesley's direct family line: his grandfather and his third great-grandfather. There are also many other Charles Dodsons. The 1800 Census alone records Wesley's grandfather Charles Dodson living in the Pendleton District of South Carolina; another Charles Dodson living in Pulaski, Kentucky; another Charles Dodson living in Granville, North Carolina (and marrying Lucy Dodson in 1801); and another Charles Dodson living in Abbeville, South Carolina.[3]

### WESLEY'S THIRD GREAT-GRANDFATHER CHARLES DODSON

Wesley had been told that his first Dodson ancestor in the Americas, Charles Dodson (1649–1704), left England because of the political and religious persecution many people suffered at the time. Charles may have been a member of the Anglican Church fleeing persecution by the Catholic monarchs, or a Dissenter or Separatist escaping discrimination by the Anglican Parliament. No known records exist that indicate exactly when Charles arrived in the American colonies. Wesley's understanding that this occurred around 1680 is supported by existing records that show Charles in Old Rappahannock County, Virginia, in 1680, buying land that he and his sons worked and improved.[4]

Charles's parentage has been the topic of much speculation. Some researchers have suggested that this was the same Charles Dodson who was born on November 25, 1659, in Lewes, Sussex, England, to Richard and Elinor Dodson.[5] Others have suggested that he is the son of Thomas Dodson, who was listed as an immigrant to Virginia in 1645. No

North Farnham Parish was in Richmond County, north of the Rappahannock River. Credit: Map courtesy of Nathan Shapard. Marked by author.

records supporting either of these ideas have been found. Other researchers have supported the theory that Charles Dodson was the grandson of John Dods and the son of either William or Jesse Dodson. Records do indicate that John Dods was one of the original settlers who founded Jamestown in 1609 and that he married a woman named Jane. According to this theory, this woman was either Jane Dier (1584–1655), who arrived in Jamestown on a "bride ship," or Jane Eagle Plume, daughter of a Powhatan chief and a cousin of Pocahontas. But no existing records support either of these connections. On lists of colonists, no notation has been found that Jane was "Native," as was indicated for other women. Furthermore, no children are listed in the household of John and Jane Dods although children are included in other households.[6] In the 1624 muster list of inhabitants, no other Dods (or Dodds, or Dodsons) are listed. The parentage of Charles Dodson of Old Rappahannock County, Virginia, is simply unknown.

What is known is that Charles was born about 1649. In a sworn court deposition from March 6, 1699 or 1700, Charles states he is "aged fifty years or thereabouts."[7] He lived in what was then known as Old Rappahannock County, which was divided into Richmond and Essex Counties in 1692. Although he owned land in both areas, his home was in Richmond County, on the north side of the York River in North Farnham Parish. He married Ann, whose surname is not definitively known, between 1678 and 1680.[8]

Charles was a successful tobacco planter who accumulated over one thousand acres of land. In July 1679, records show that he leased land from Peter Elmore for nineteen years. The amount of land involved was "as much land as three titheables can tend in corn and tobacco."[9] In colonial Virginia, a "titheable" was a person over sixteen subject to the tax levied annually by the general assembly to support the parish, the county, and the colonial government. In 1623, for example, the general assembly imposed a tax of ten pounds of tobacco "upon every male head above sixteen years of adge now living."[10] Land and personal property were not taxed, so the only records of land ownership involve the lease, purchase, or sale of the land. In colonial Virginia, land was usually bought and sold in tobacco. The terms of Charles Dodson's lease indicated that he would pay Elmore fifty pounds of tobacco yearly, that Elmore would supply enough peach and apple trees to constitute an orchard, that Dodson could cut any timber needed for use on the land, and that at the end of the lease he would leave a thirty-foot dwelling house, a fifty-foot tobacco house, and fencing, all in good repair.[11]

Before the lease on his land expired, Charles had sufficient resources to be able to buy his own land. On December 20, 1685, he bought one hundred acres in North Farnham Parish of Richmond County from William Thacker and his wife, Alice, "for a valuable consideration to them paid."[12] On October 21, 1687, Charles purchased three hundred acres from Samuel Travis (or Travers). On January 2, 1693, Charles purchased five hundred acres on Totusky Creek, also in North Farnham Parish, for ten thousand pounds of tobacco, or twenty pounds of tobacco per acre. The land seems to have been a bargain. In his 1711 will, Thomas Durham required his son Thomas Jr. to give his brother John either fifty acres of his plantation or eight thousand pounds of tobacco—160 pounds of tobacco per acre.[13]

Charles was well respected in the community. Besides being a large landowner, he was a man who could read and write. Several documents survive that show him as a witness to a legal document or as the executor for another man's will. In 1686, he was the executor for both Edward Johnson and John Lincoln. In Lincoln's will, dictated December 18, 1686, a comment in the affidavit of witnesses stated that the maker of the will "would have no other but Charles Dodson as his executor."[14] That same year, the court appointed Charles to audit the accounts of two men who were disputing money each maintained the other owed.[15]

Charles died in 1704 or 1705, leaving a will that named his eight children as heirs: Charles Jr., Thomas, Bartholomew Richard, William, John, Lambeth, Anne, and Elizabeth. Charles divided his land among his six sons. He stipulated, however, that the land not be sold "except that one Brother selleth to another and if no male heir appeareth by none of my sons that then my Daughters may Inherrit the Land."[16] This restriction caused problems when one of the brothers wished to move. Some sold to other brothers. Others leased the land to other men for "three natural lifetimes."

When Ann Dodson, Charles's wife, died in 1718, she bequeathed household goods that indicated she still had considerable wealth. Her son Charles Jr. was given "my Riding hors and one feather bed and fournitire and one frying pan." William received "one Iarn Pott and pott huks and one Cowe." The remainder of the estate, including "2 cows and calfs, 2 barren cows, 1 heifer & 3 yearlings, 1 cow and calf, 5 pidgs, 7 shotes, 2 old sows, 16 sheep," and additional household goods were to be equally divided.[17]

**WESLEY'S SECOND GREAT-GRANDFATHER THOMAS DODSON**

Thomas Dodson was born to Charles and Ann Dodson on May 15, 1681, in Old Rappahannock County, Virginia.[18] In August 1701, Thomas married Mary Durham, the fifteen-year-old daughter of Thomas and Dorothy Durham, prosperous neighbors of the Dodsons in North Farnham Parish. When his father died, Thomas inherited a plantation "seated in a neck formerly called the Rich neck with a hundred and fifty acres of Land."[19] All of his brothers inherited similar parcels of land, between one hundred and two hundred acres each.[20] One son inherited the contract of an indentured servant who had "three years eight months to serve."[21] With the exception of John and Bartholomew Richard, Thomas's brothers all remained in the Richmond County area where they raised their families.

When Thomas died in 1744, he left bequests to his nine children: George, Thomas Jr., Greenham, Mary, Elisha, David, Alice, Abraham, and Wesley's great-grandfather, Joshua. To his wife, Thomas left for her lifetime use the 150-acre plantation on Rich Neck where they were living. Upon her death, the property would pass to Elisha. Thomas gave both George and Greenham tracts of about 150 acres. He also willed his seven slaves to some of his children. As the youngest son, nineteen-year-old Joshua inherited no land but was given "a feather bed and furniture" as well as "one negro woman named Sue and one negro boy named Dick."[22]

**WESLEY'S GREAT-GRANDFATHER JOSHUA DODSON**

Joshua Dodson was born in Richmond County on May 25, 1725. He married Ruth, whose family name is unknown. In about 1734, Joshua's older brother Thomas sold his land in Richmond County and moved to Prince William County, Virginia, settling on Broad Run of Occoquan Creek.[23] His uncle Lambeth also left, and poll tax records indicate that he went to Halifax County, Virginia, in 1753, before the French and Indian War, and before the area was opened for settlement. At some point, Joshua followed his older brother Thomas up the Rappahannock to Prince William County. He is found on a list of titheables from 1751 for Hamilton Parish, Elk Run and vicinity, in Prince William County, in the area that became Fauquier County in 1759.[24]

The Church of England was the established church in colonial Virginia. Not only were people taxed to support the church, they were routinely fined for failure to attend church services, as was the case with brothers Thomas and Charles Dodson Jr. in 1707.[25] In the eighteenth century, the church's authority was challenged by a series of religious revivals known as the Great Awakening. The revivals called for religious freedom and a break from the ritual, ceremony, and authority of the established church. The revivals swept across the northern colonies in the 1730s and 1740s and reached the southern colonies and the backcountry in the 1750s and 1760s. The movement strengthened the Presbyterian, Baptist, and Methodist Churches. All were evangelical religions that supported itinerant ministers who traveled in the frontier regions preaching the need for salvation by a personal conversion experience.[26]

Virginia map showing Richmond and Fauquier Counties. Credit: Courtesy of the New York Public Library. Cropped and marked by author.

In 1762, Joshua Dodson was a founding member of the Broad Run Baptist Church in Fauquier County, Virginia.[27] Among the other nine founding members were his wife Ruth, his brother Thomas, and Thomas' wife, Elizabeth Rose Dodson. A number of Dodsons and other family members, including Thomas's daughter Rhoda Dodson Creel and her husband, John, were members of the church. Joshua's slave Dick was also a member. The church taught the Calvinist doctrine that a vengeful God meted out justice in the form of fire and brimstone but that He chose some, "the elect," for salvation. It expected and enforced among its members a commitment to moral behavior. The Broad Run Baptist Church was not afraid to censor a member's conduct, as it did with trustee Lazarus

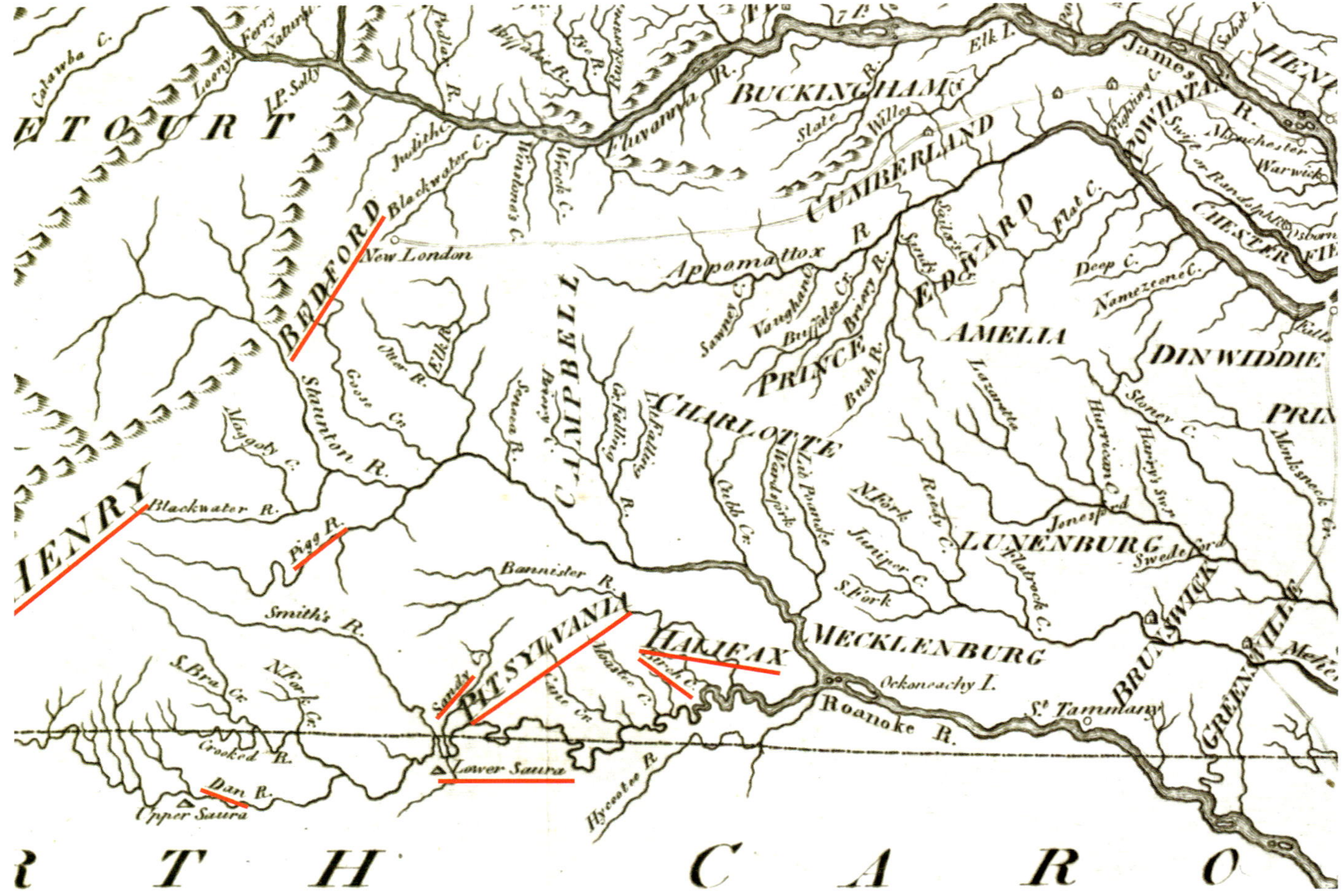


Map of Halifax-Pittsylvania area of Virginia. Dodson family members settled on Birches Creek, Sandy Creek, and Pigg River, and in Henry County, Virginia, and Surry County, North Carolina. Credit: Courtesy of the New York Public Library. Cropped and marked by author.

Dodson's wife, Barbary, in June 1775, or to ex-communicate a member, as it did with William Dodson in 1769. Their offenses were not recorded in the church minutes.[28]

The Baptists did not have theological schools for training their ministers. Instead, their pastors were selected from the congregation—men who had taught themselves the scriptures, had a gift for preaching, and were faithful to the church and its principles. The Broad Run Baptist Church produced a number of ministers, including Joshua, his brothers George and Thomas, and their sons Charles, William, George, and Lazarus. The ministry remained the calling of Dodson descendants for several generations.

The third generation of Dodsons in colonial America started leaving northern Virginia in the 1760s. With the French and Indian War concluded and the Cherokee no longer a constant threat to white settlers, new land was opening up for settlement in the back-country wilderness. In 1766, a contingent of over thirty people—Dodson families and other members of the Broad Run Baptist Church—left Fauquier County and went south to Halifax County, Virginia, part of which later became Pittsylvania County. The Piedmont region of southwestern Virginia, with its gently rolling countryside on the North Carolina border, was ideal for cultivating tobacco.

The migration of the Dodsons, undertaken as a group of family members and friends, was typical of the early American migration pattern. In the colonial era and the early days of the republic, family groups often lived near one another. They tended to sell their land and migrate to new areas together so that they could provide a support system for one another. Grown children felt an obligation to take care of their elderly parents and their younger brothers and sisters. Unmarried women continued to live at home or with married siblings and their families. When one elderly parent died, the surviving parent commonly moved in with one of the children, typically a daughter. And when a young mother died, often in childbirth, family members took her children into their homes and raised them. They knew and cared for one another.

Thomas Dodson, Joshua's older brother, sold his land and moved to Halifax County with his wife, Elizabeth Rose, and their children. There, in December 1766, he bought 440 acres on "Burches" (or Birches) Creek, on the line of Halifax and Pittsylvania Counties, from Joseph Terry for fifty pounds.[29] Joshua's brothers George and Elisha also settled in Halifax with their extended families.[30] Joshua's brother Abraham made plans to move to Halifax with the family. In March 1766, he had a survey made of "four hundred acres on the south side of Birches creek adjoining Cap. Joseph Terry and a new survey on the road near the pulpit spring then down, not to exceed four hundred acres." Probably because of poor health, Abraham did not leave Fauquier County as planned. He died there in 1768.[31]

The Reverend Joshua Dodson was also in the contingent of family and church members who, according to the Broad Run Baptist Church minutes, left for Halifax. With Joshua and his wife, Ruth, were their children, Joshua Jr., Charles, Isaac, Elisha, Elijah Joel, Daniel, Dorcas, and Pheby. Although no records have been found of Joshua buying land in Halifax or Pittsylvania Counties, it is possible that he lived on the property of one of his brothers—perhaps Lambeth, who had settled in Halifax much earlier. The Reverend Elias Dodson, author of the *Genealogy of the Dodson Families of Pittsylvania and Halifax Counties in the State of Virginia*, indicated that Joshua was in those counties and commented that "Joshua Dodson . . . was considered one of the best men in the world."[32] At some point, Joshua crossed over the border into Surry County, in the Piedmont region of Western North Carolina.

### WESLEY'S GRANDFATHER CHARLES DODSON

Charles Dodson was born on February 2, 1747, in Prince William County, Virginia. He left for Halifax County with his father and other relatives in 1767. In 1771, he appeared on the tax rolls in neighboring Surry County, North Carolina. Appearing on the same tax rolls were his cousins Reuben and John Dodson, sons of Lambeth, which suggests that the cousins left Halifax together to lay the groundwork for a new Dodson settlement.[33]

By 1774, Charles had married Lucy Morgan, a woman of Welsh descent often referred to as "Carolina Lucy." Her family background is not known. Since almost no Welsh migrated directly to the Carolinas at that time,[34] the Morgans probably came to the Carolinas from the Welsh tracts in Delaware and Pennsylvania. Those large Welsh communities were primarily Baptists with strong Calvinist beliefs. Charles and Lucy's neighbors,

In 1777, this area was still Indian Territory. In 1789, it would become the Pendleton District. The Keowee River is marked. Credit: Courtesy of the South Carolina Archives.

according to the 1784 North Carolina Census, were the households of Valentine, Reuben, and John Morgan, possibly Lucy's father and brothers.[35] Charles and Lucy's daughter Millicent was born in Surry County on February 6, 1775.

Sometime in the 1770s, Charles and Lucy went to live in Keowee Town, in the far northwest corner of South Carolina, at the foot of the Allegheny Mountains. Keowee was in Indian Territory, land held by the Cherokee people. Earlier in the 1700s, the British colonists in South Carolina had established important trade with the Cherokee Nation, exchanging guns, blankets, and other supplies for furs, antlers, and even human scalps. In 1753, to protect their trade routes and themselves from their Creek and Choctaw enemies, who were aligned with the French, the Cherokee signed a treaty with the royal governor of South Carolina. This treaty, signed just before the outbreak of the French and Indian War, called for a fort to be built on the Keowee River. Fort Prince George was built across the river from Keowee Town.[36]

Charles was a Baptist minister in Keowee. He may have gone there to minister to a congregation of white settlers and traders, or he may have been sent by the Baptist Church to evangelize the Cherokee. Since the early 1700s, the Baptist movement had sought to convert Native Americans to Christianity and had helped establish Native American Baptist Churches.[37] Charles and Lucy's son Dillingham was born in Keowee in 1777.

During the 1770s, the British tried to raise revenues in the colonies to pay the costs incurred in waging the French and Indian War. Their efforts were met with increasing resistance that eventually resulted in violent confrontations and the issuance of the Declaration of Independence in 1776. When the Revolutionary War broke out, Charles returned to North Carolina, where, on May 15, 1777, he enlisted in the 4th North Carolina Regiment, commanded by Col. Thomas Polk. Serving with him was his neighbor and possible brother-in-law, John Morgan. He served in Capt. Joseph Phillips's company until 1881.[38] The regiment was reassigned from the Southern Department, where it had expected to confront the British in South Carolina, to the Northern Department and was sent to Pennsylvania where it was needed to buttress General Washington's hard-pressed forces. The regiment participated in heavy fighting at the Battles of Brandywine and Germantown in the autumn of 1777, in a vain attempt to keep the British from occupying Philadelphia. Although the regiment wintered at Valley Forge, it had suffered such heavy losses that, in June 1778, it was sent home to recruit replacements for its depleted ranks. In North Carolina, the companies were reorganized with mostly "New Levies," men who were obligated to serve nine months, but who then could go home for the winter. When the British invaded Georgia in 1778, the 4th North Carolina Regiment was reassigned to the Southern Department and engaged in fighting in Georgia and North Carolina.[39]

The American Revolution was a civil war. While approximately one-third of the colonists were Patriots and another third were neutral, one-third were Loyalists. Some of the Loyalists had businesses that were dependent on connections and good relations with the British. Others were colonists with ties to the King. In North Carolina, many colonists had come from Scotland, where, before emigrating, they had been required to sign an oath that they would never take up arms against the King. Many of these Scots honored that oath.

As the war progressed, the British recruited large numbers of Loyalists to fight against the Patriots. In March 1779, at the Battle of Brier Creek near the Savannah River in eastern Georgia, the 4th North Carolina Regiment surprised a Loyalist force consisting of militia from North Carolina and Georgia and soundly defeated it.[40] In the summer of 1780, at the Battles of Ramseur's Mill and at Colson's Mill in North Carolina, the 4th North Carolina Regiment joined Patriot militias to defeat a Loyalist militia.[41] And a few months later, at the Battle of King's Mountain, South Carolina, in October 1780, the 4th North Carolina Regiment and Patriot militias crushed a larger force of Loyalists.[42] These were important, decisive Patriot victories that hurt the British efforts to enlist Loyalist fighters and to control the rebellious colony.

As the war was coming to an end in 1781, Charles left the regiment and returned to his family in Surry County. His father, Joshua, was living on three hundred acres along Reed Creek with a household that included his wife, Ruth; his sons Isaac, Daniel, and Elijah Joel; and his daughters Sarah and Dorcas. Joshua's daughter Pheby and her husband, Thomas Kreel, were living nearby, as were Charles' daughter Millicent and her husband, Timothy Stamps. Samuel Warnock, whose daughter Sarah married Joshua Dodson Jr., lived in the area as well. By this time, Joshua Dodson and Samuel Warnock were in their sixties and, as such, were declared "aged and infirm men" who were exempted from the poll tax that required men to work maintaining the local roads.[43] On December 8, 1782, Charles and Lucy's son Armstead was born and in 1785, their daughter Rebecca. Wesley's father, Elisha Jefferson, was born on March 31, 1788. Charles's last child, Rutha, was born in 1790.

State Census of North Carolina, 1784–1787. Credit: State Census of North Carolina, 1784–1787 (Baltimore: Genealogical, 1987), 148.

STATE CENSUS OF NORTH CAROLINA 1784-1787

| Head of Household | WM 21-60 yrs. | WM under 21 & above 60 | WF all ages | Blacks 12-50 | Blacks under 12 & above 50 |
|---|---|---|---|---|---|
| Valintine Morgin | 1 | . | 3 | . | . |
| Samuel McChesney | . | 1 | 2 | . | . |
| Anthoney Dearing | 1 | 3 | 3 | 3 | 2 |
| Nimrod Siras | . | 2 | 3 | . | . |
| John Golahorn | 1 | 4 | 4 | . | . |
| Rubin Morgin | 1 | . | . | . | . |
| John Webstor | 1 | 1 | 4 | . | . |
| Jonathin Varnom Sr. | 1 | 1 | 2 | . | . |
| James Dunlap | 2 | 1 | 6 | . | . |
| Drury Williams | 1 | 1 | 2 | 3 | 2 |
| Major Wilkerson | 1 | 4 | 4 | . | . |
| Thomas Stamps | 1 | 3 | 4 | . | . |
| Jonathin Jarmon Sr. | . | 2 | 3 | . | . |
| Gibson Sothern | 1 | . | 2 | . | . |
| Michal Gilbert | 1 | 1 | 9 | . | . |
| Edward Thompson | 1 | 1 | 2 | . | . |
| Elisha Parker | 1 | 1 | 3 | . | . |
| Thomas Creel | 1 | . | 4 | . | . |
| Richard Taylor | 2 | 2 | 4 | . | . |
| | 46 | 78 | 116 | 31 | 25 |
| Pg. 2 | | | | | |
| Samuel Warnock | . | 2 | . | . | . |
| Richard Webstor | . | 1 | 5 | . | . |
| Jacob Camplin | 1 | 1 | 3 | . | . |
| Joseph Read | 1 | 4 | 2 | . | . |
| Joshua Dodson | 2 | 2 | 3 | . | . |
| Adam Craford | 1 | . | 2 | . | . |
| Charles Dodson | 1 | 2 | 4 | . | . |
| Joseph Vaughn | 1 | 2 | 4 | . | . |
| Rubin Sothern | 1 | 2 | 3 | . | . |
| Joshua Dodson Jr. | 1 | 1 | 1 | . | . |
| Charles Angill | 1 | 2 | 4 | . | . |
| John Dunlap | 2 | 1 | 1 | . | . |
| William Kinmon | 1 | 2 | 3 | . | . |
| John Davis | 1 | 2 | 2 | . | . |
| George Ray | 1 | 1 | 3 | . | . |
| Joseph King | 1 | . | 1 | . | . |
| John Thompson | 1 | 2 | 3 | . | . |
| Partrick Bair | 1 | 2 | 1 | . | . |
| Thomas Gunn | 1 | 3 | 6 | . | . |
| John Morgin | 1 | 4 | 3 | . | . |
| John Bair | 1 | . | . | . | . |
| Ann Ladd for Wm. Ladd | . | 1 | . | 2 | . |
| Ambros May | 1 | 4 | 2 | . | . |
| Thomas Eason | 1 | . | 1 | . | . |
| Mary Eason | 1 | . | 2 | . | . |
| Robin Majors | 1 | . | 2 | . | . |
| James Eason | 1 | . | 2 | . | . |
| John Majors | 1 | 2 | 4 | . | . |
| Harry Terril | 3 | 5 | 9 | 6 | 10 |

| Head of Household | WM 21-60 yrs. | WM under 21 & above 60 | WF all ages | Blacks 12-50 | Blacks under 12 & above 50 | |
|---|---|---|---|---|---|---|
| Judah Ladd | . | . | 2 | 1 | 2 | |
| Martin Burrus | 1 | 2 | 4 | 7 | 5 | |
| Mary Grinder | . | 1 | 5 | . | . | |
| Peter Harston | 1 | 1 | 2 | 6 | 13 | |
| Meridith Smith | 1 | . | 2 | . | . | |
| James Bools | 1 | 3 | 2 | . | . | |
| Peter Eason | 1 | . | . | . | . | |
| Jesse Standley | 1 | 1 | 4 | . | . | |
| Benjamin Bennit | 1 | 4 | 3 | . | . | |
| Elias Smith | 1 | . | 3 | . | . | |
| John Wood or Ward | 1 | 1 | 4 | . | . | |
| Joseph Ladd | 1 | . | 2 | 2 | . | |
| Robin Crump | 1 | 6 | 4 | 1 | . | |
| | 41 | 66 | 113 | 25 | 30 | |
| By: Absalom Bostick | | | | | | |
| Pg. 1 | | | | | | |
| Henry Banner | . | 1 | 2 | 7 | 8 | 18 |
| Henry Fry | 1 | 3 | 2 | . | . | 6 |
| Abel Wakefield | 1 | 1 | 2 | . | . | 4 |
| Hammon Morriss | 1 | 4 | 1 | 1 | . | 7 |
| William Morriss | 1 | . | 4 | . | . | 5 |
| Traviss Morriss | 1 | . | 5 | . | . | 6 |
| Thos. Morriss | 1 | . | 1 | . | . | 2 |
| John Appleton | 1 | 2 | 6 | 1 | . | 10 |
| John Cooley | 1 | 6 | 3 | . | . | 10 |
| Isaac Garrison | 1 | 4 | 7 | . | . | 12 |
| John Goode | 1 | 1 | 2 | . | . | 4 |
| John Scott | 1 | 6 | 5 | . | . | 12 |
| Delany ? Hearin | 1 | 3 | 3 | . | . | 7 |
| Thos. Bolkum | 1 | . | 1 | . | . | 2 |
| Gabriel Waggoner | 1 | . | 5 | . | . | 6 |
| Thos. Flynt | 1 | 4 | 2 | 2 | 3 | 12 |
| Saml. Waggoner | . | 1 | 4 | . | 1 | 6 |
| Joseph Waggoner | 1 | 1 | 4 | . | . | 6 |
| John Clayton | 1 | 1 | 3 | 1 | . | 6 |
| Thos. Smithermon | 1 | 2 | 4 | . | . | 7 |
| Jas. Day | 1 | 2 | 2 | . | . | 5 |
| Thos. Day | 1 | 2 | 2 | . | . | 5 |
| John Snow | 1 | . | 1 | . | . | 2 |
| Usly Ray | . | 2 | 1 | . | 1 | 4 |
| Thos. Ring | . | 2 | 1 | . | . | 3 |
| Thos. Wilson | 1 | 1 | 3 | . | . | 5 |
| John Wells | . | 7 | 3 | . | . | 10 |
| William Wells | 1 | . | 2 | . | . | 3 |
| Mary Wakefield | . | 7 | 2 | . | . | 9 |
| John Martin | 1 | 2 | 2 | . | . | 5 |
| Johnson Heath | 1 | 1 | 4 | . | . | 6 |
| | 25 | 64 | 103 | 12 | 14 | 218 |

In about 1790, this entire group of Dodson families moved back to South Carolina where new lands had just opened for settlement in the Pendleton District. This district was created in 1789 from former Cherokee lands and abutted the lands still held by Native Americans. It eventually became Anderson, Pickens, and Oconee Counties. Charles became the minister of the Keowee River Church organized in 1791.[44] The small church was built near Fort Prince George and Crow Creek. In 1800, Charles reported to the Bethel Association, which the Keowee River Church joined in 1793, that it had seventeen communicants.[45]

The new Keowee River Church was closely connected to another, larger Baptist congregation, the Shoal Creek Church, that reported 108 members. This church was located across the Tugaloo River in Franklin County, Georgia.[46] In 1789, Charles's father, Joshua, was listed in the Annual Register of the Baptist Denomination as a minister serving in Georgia. Since no record has been found of Joshua living in Georgia, it is probable that sixty-five-year-old Joshua lived in the Pendleton District with or near family members and traveled to serve the nearby Shoal Creek Church in Georgia.[47]

In the early 1790s, Charles and Joshua Dodson each bought about one hundred acres of land on the Keowee River.[48] Timothy Stamps purchased land on the nearby Little River of the Keowee. The group of families all appeared on the 1800 Census as living in the Pendleton District with the exception of Joshua Sr., who had died sometime in the 1790s.

After the Revolutionary War, the government gave land grants to the Revolutionary soldiers, an act that facilitated a new wave of migration. Charles's brother Elijah Joel secured a land grant in the wilderness of Lincoln County, Tennessee, and moved his family there in 1785. One day, while clearing a field, Elijah Joel was killed by a Native American. His wife, Martha, escaped with their three children, Joel, Nancy, and Joshua, and returned to North Carolina to be near her family.[49]

Although Elijah Joel Dodson had migrated alone, the majority of his family moved together from South Carolina to Allen County, Kentucky, sometime before 1804. Charles received land grants totaling 640 acres in 1783 and another land grant totaling 640 acres in 1796. Charles claimed land on John's Creek, near Trammel Creek, about seven miles west of Scottsville, the county seat of Allen County. He made his home there for the next twenty-seven years. His family members all acquired land near Trammel Creek. His son Elisha Jefferson, Wesley's father, obtained two hundred acres on Trammel Creek in 1799 and an additional two hundred acres elsewhere in the county in 1807.[50] Charles's sons Dillingham and Armstead, his daughters Millicent Dodson Stamps and Rutha Dodson Holloway, and his sister Pheby Dodson Creel all settled nearby with their families.[51] Charles's younger brothers Daniel and Isaac Dodson decided against moving to Kentucky and instead went to Georgia, to territory that had just been ceded by the Creeks. There, in 1805, they entered the land lottery.[52]

Wesley's grandmother, Lucy Morgan Dodson, died in Allen County, Kentucky, in 1823. His grandfather, Charles Dodson, died there in 1831. They are buried in the Dodson family cemetery, a wooded area on private property in an area that is still largely rural. In 1940, the Daughters of the American Revolution procured grave markers for Revolutionary War soldiers whose graves were unmarked. The Reverend Charles Dodson had been a private in the 4th North Carolina Regiment under Capt. Joseph Phillips and Col.

The Dodson Cemetery sign, provided by the Simpson County Historical Society, marks the cemetery in Allen County. Credit: Courtesy of Debbie Walden, Allen County Historical Society.

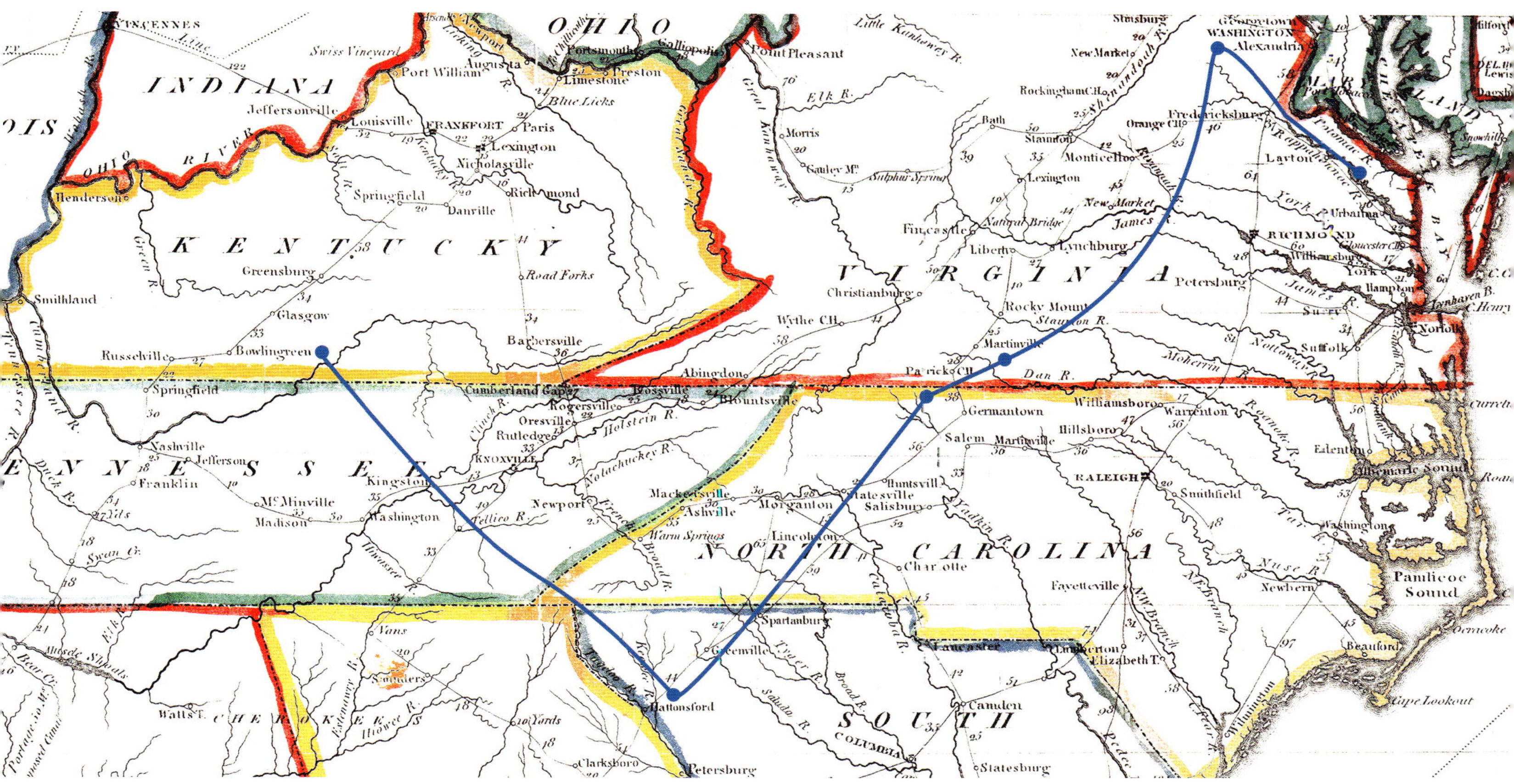


The blue line indicates Dodson family moves in Virginia from Richmond County to Fauquier County to Halifax County, then to Surry/Stokes County, North Carolina, to Pendleton District, South Carolina, and finally to Allen County, Kentucky. Credit: Courtesy of Map & Imagery Library, Special and Area Studies Collections, George A. Smathers Libraries, University of Florida.

Thomas Polk. The tombstone states that he was in the Virginia Troops and that he had been born in England. This incorrect information was provided by Dodson relatives in the 1930s, who seem to have confused the Charles Dodson who served in the Revolutionary War with his great-grandfather—the Charles Dodson who was in Rappahannock County, Virginia, in the 1600s.

**Wesley Clark Dodson**
b: 28 May 1829 in Morgan County, Alabama
m:
d: 01 Aug 1914 in Waco Texas; Age 85

**Rev Elisha Jefferson Dodson**
b: 31 Mar 1788 in Stokes County, North Carolina
m: 14 May 1814 in Warren County, Kentucky
d: 29 Jul 1942 in Marshall, Tennessee; Age 54

**Rev Charles Dodson**
b: 02 Feb 1747 in Richmond, Virginia
m:
d: 02 May 1831 in Allen, Kentucky; Age 84

**Rev Joshua Dodson**
b: 25 May 1725 in North Farnham Parish, Richmond County, Virginia
m: 1745 in North Farnham Parish, Richmond County, Virginia
d: 1790s in Pendelton District, South Carolina or Stokes County, North Carolina

**Ruth**
b: 21 Sept 1727 in North Farnham, Virginia
d: 15 Jan 1803 in Surry County, North Carolina; Age 76

**Lucy Morgan**
b: 1755 in South Carolina
d: 1823 in Allen, Kentucky; Age 67

**Jane Elizabeth Blackwell**
b: 05 May 1788 in Halifax County, Virginia
d: 23 Aug 1861 in Livingston, Alabama; Age 73

**James Benjamin Blackwell**
b:1750 in King William County, Virginia
m: 1783 in Virginia
d: 1801 in Halifax County, Virginia; Age 51

**James Josia Blackwell**
b:1730 in Culpeper, Virginia
m:
d: 1783 in Culpeper, Virginia; Age 53

**Elizabeth Ann Crenshaw**
b: 1763 in Westmoreland, Virginia
d: 1800 in Halifax County, Virginia; Age 37

Ancestors of Wesley Clark Dodson.
Credit: Provided by author.

**Thomas Dodson I**
b: 15 May 1681 in North Farnham Parish, Old Rappahannock County, Virginia; later became Richmond County
m: 29 Aug 1701 in Richmond County Virginia
d: 21 Nov 1740 in Farnham, Richmond, (Was Rappahannock County), Virginia; Age 59

**Charles Dodson Sr.**
b: 1649
m: 1679 in Richmond, Virginia
d: Before 06 Febr 1705 in North Farnham Parish, Richmond County, Virginia; Age 56

**Anne**
b: 1654 in Old Rappahannock County, Virginia
d: 01 Aug 1715 in North Farnham Parish, Richmond County, Virginia; Age 61

**Rev Joshua Dodson**
b: 25 May 1725 in North Farnham Parish, Richmond County, Virginia
m: 1745 in North Farnham Parish, Richmond County, Virginia
d: 1790s in Pendelton District, South Carolina or Stokes County, North Carolina

**Mary Durham**
b: 05 Jun 1686 in North Farnham Parish, Richmond County, Virginia
d: After 1743; Age 57

**Thomas Durham**
b: 06 Mar 1661 in North Farnham Parish, Rappahannock County (later Richmond), Virginia
m: 1691 in North Farnham, Richmond County, Virginia
d: 30 May 1715 in North Farnham Parish, Richmond County, Virginia; Age 54

**Dorothy**
b: 1663 in North Farnham Parish, Rappahannock County, Virginia
d: 21 Nov 1740 in North Farnham Parish, Richmond County, Virginia; Age 77

Early Postcard of the Waco Presbyterian Church. Credit: Waco Presbyterian Church, University of North Texas Libraries, The Portal to Texas History

# Appendix 2

## Family

Wesley's daughter Mollie Bet married Albert Gallatin Board, a Brazos County attorney and county judge. She died February 7, 1925, and was buried in the Bryan City Cemetery with her husband, who had died in 1912. Their children were:

Mabel, who married Samuel Cooke Hoyle. They had a son, Sam, who died in 1992. Mabel died in 1949.

Ada, who married Roscoe Bates and died in 1957.

Charles Frost Board, who died in 1918.

Lucy, who married Thomas Brawley Sammons Sr. and had a daughter, Quita. Lucy died in 1967.

Guy Milton Board, who died in 1947.

Irene, who married Harold Arnold Saunders and had a daughter, Mary Alice Saunders (Hall). Mary Alice carefully kept all of the family records that her grandmother had treasured. She typed them, so they would be preserved, and donated the papers to the Texas Collection at Baylor University in Waco. She died in 2015.

Wesley's daughter Anna married Robert N. Useiton and moved to Lampasas and later to Temple, Texas. They had three children: Robert, who died in 1972; Lawrence, who died in 1988; and Clarence, who died in 1978. Anna died in 1954.

Wesley's son Lee Jefferson married Davie Quaite and had a son, Quaite, who died in 1970. Lee started a real estate company in Waco in 1913 and, with his brothers Cavitt and Willie, engaged in buying and selling building lots.[1] He later moved to Tucson, Arizona, where he died in 1953.

Wesley's son Cavitt Watson married Ellen Elizabeth Blake, whom he met in Granbury, Texas, when he accompanied his father to the Hood County Courthouse construction site. Cavitt's son, Charles Henry, died in 1972. Cavitt partnered with his younger brother Sam in a real estate firm and also invested in land and mineral rights. In 1911, he became the assistant auditor for McLennan County. Until he retired, Cavitt worked in the courthouse that his father, as supervising architect, had helped build. He died in 1964.

Wesley's son James William, or Willie, married Florence Jefferson and had three daughters: Lallie Dodson (Gibson), who typed and preserved Wesley's *Memoirs of Civil War Battles*, and who died in 1977; Elizabeth Dodson (Rawls), who died in 1961; and Mary Dodson (Hamilton), who died in 1971. In 1911, Willie was a partner in a real estate company and with the First National Bank of Waco.[2] He died in 1946.

Wesley's daughter Martha Juliett (Mattie) married William Dougherty and moved to Victoria County, Texas. They had a son, John. Mattie died in 1949.

Wesley's daughter Bessie married Marcellus Dodson, a great-grandson of Charles and Lucy Dodson, and moved to Jonesboro, Arkansas. They had three children: Herndon Marcellus, Ruby Boyd, and Gladys Gray. Bessie died in 1937.

Wesley's son Samuel Byars married Belle Taylor and had a son, Lee Eric. Sam formed a real estate company, Dodson and Dodson, with his brother Cavitt and worked as a realtor in Waco until his untimely death from pneumonia at age thirty-eight in 1916.[3]

Front doors to the Denton County Courthouse. Photo by author.

# Appendix 3

## W. C. Dodson Buildings with Recorded Texas Historic Landmark (RTHL) and National Register of Historic Places (NRHP) Designations

**COURTHOUSES**

Coryell County Courthouse RTHL 1977 NRHP 1977

Texas SP Coryell County Courthouse, National Register of Historic Places Inventory Nomination Form, 1977, NAID 40971593, National Archives Catalog, accessed March 8, 2021, https://catalog.archives.gov/id/40971593.

Denton County Courthouse RTHL 1970 NRHP 1977

Texas SP Denton County Courthouse, National Register of Historic Places Inventory Nomination Form, 1977, NAID 40971803, National Archives Catalog, accessed March 8, 2021, https://catalog.archives.gov/id/40971803.

Fannin County Courthouse RTHL 1974

Fannin County Courthouse, Historical Marker Database, accessed January 20, 2025, https://www.hmdb.org/m.asp?m=128644

Hill County Courthouse RTHL 1971 NRHP 1971

Texas SP Hill County Courthouse, National Register of Historic Places Inventory Nomination Form, 1971, NAID 40972595, National Archives Catalog, accessed March 8, 2021, https://catalog.archives.gov/id/40972595.

Hood County Courthouse RTHL 1970 NRHP 1974

Texas SP Hood County Courthouse, National Register of Historic Places Inventory Nomination Form, 1974, NAID 40972605, National Archives Catalog, accessed March 9, 2021, https://catalog.archives.gov/id/40972605.

Lampasas County Courthouse RTHL 1965 NRHP 1971

Texas SP Lampasas County Courthouse, National Register of Historic Places Inventory Nomination Form, 1971, NAID 40972811, National Archives Catalog, accessed March 8, 2021, https://catalog.archives.gov/id/40972811.

Parker County Courthouse RTHL 1965 NRHP 1971

Texas SP Parker County Courthouse, National Register of Historic Places Inventory Nomination Form, 1971, NAID 40973160, National Archives Catalog, accessed March 8, 2021, https://catalog.archives.gov/id/40973160.

**OTHER PUBLIC BUILDINGS**

Hill County Jail RTHL 1981 NRHP 1981

Texas SP Hill County Courthouse, National Register of Historic Places Inventory Nomination Form, 1971, NAID 40972595, National Archives Catalog, accessed March 14, 2021, https://catalog.archives.gov/id/40972595.

McLennan County Courthouse (1900) RTHL 1970 NRHP 1978
Advising and supervising architect

Texas SP McLennan County Courthouse, National Register of Historic Places Inventory Nomination Form, 1978, NAID 40972997, National Archives Catalog, accessed March 4, 2021, https://catalog.archives.gov/id/40972997.

Old Main, Texas Woman's University RTHL 1974

The First Building of Texas Woman's University, Historical Marker Database, accessed January 20, 2025, https://www.hmdb.org/m.asp?m=178877.

Palestine First Presbyterian Church RTHL 1998 NRHP 1998
Texas MSP First Presbyterian Church, National Register of Historic Places Continuation Sheet, 1998, NAID 40967866, National Archives Catalog, accessed March 3, 2021, https://catalog.archives.gov/id/40967866.

Williamson County Jail RTHL 1965 NRHP 1977
Texas SP Williamson County Courthouse District, National Register of Historic Places Inventory Nomination Form, 1977, NAID 40973996, National Archives Catalog, accessed March 8, 2021, https://catalog.archives.gov/id/40973996.

# Notes

**INTRODUCTION**

1. W. C. Dodson, "Memoirs of W. C. Dodson" (1913). The author is in possession of an original thirteen-page handwritten copy. "Memoirs" is included in the Papers of W. C. Dodson, housed at Baylor University Libraries' Texas Collection in Waco. Dodson's words are quoted throughout this book as he wrote them, without the use of *sic* to identify writing errors or words whose spellings have changed. Other early documents with antiquated spellings also are quoted without the use of *sic*.

**CHAPTER 1**

1. Dodson, "Memoirs."
2. Sherman Williams and Silas Emmett Lucas Jr., *The Dodson (Dotson) Family of North Farnham Parish, Richmond County, Virginia: A History and Genealogy of their Descendants* (Easley, SC: Southern Historical Press, 1989), 160.
3. Dee E. Andrews, *The Methodists and Revolutionary America, 1760–1800: The Shaping of an Evangelical Culture* (Princeton: Princeton University Press, 2000). In the early 1800s, Southern Methodists moved away from their anti-slavery positions and by the 1830s were embracing pro-slavery arguments. This would lead to a split in 1844 between the abolitionist Northern Wesleyan Methodist Church and the Methodist Episcopal Church (South), which remained committed to slavery. See also Christine Leigh Heyrman, *Southern Cross: The Beginnings of the Bible Belt* (Chapel Hill: University of North Carolina Press, 1998).
4. Neither the Methodists nor the Baptists had theological seminaries until later in the nineteenth century.
5. John B. McFerrin, *History of Methodism in Tennessee*, vol. 3, 1818–1840 (Nashville: Southern Methodist Publishing House, 1879), 357, accessed August 9, 2020, https://catalog.hathitrust.org/Record/100106774. The church had a number of missionaries among the Cherokee and, in 1823, reported 675 members from the Cherokee Nation, including the minister Turtle Fields. Later, in 1838, the Methodists would send missionaries, such as Young Wolf, to accompany the Cherokee on the Trail of Tears to Oklahoma, preaching and seeking converts on the way.
6. McFerrin, *History of Methodism in Tennessee*, vol. 2, 320; Dodson, "Memoirs."
7. Dodson, "Memoirs."
8. Ibid.
9. Ibid.
10. Ibid.
11. Ibid.
12. Ibid.
13. Ibid.
14. Ibid.
15. Ibid.
16. Ibid.
17. Elisha Dodson's farm was some distance from the large plantations. Farmers closer to the plantations tended to sell more and varied farm products to planters.
18. Dodson, "Memoirs."

19. Dodson, "Memoirs"; United States Revolutionary War Rolls, 1775–1783, accessed May 5, 2020, https://www.familysearch.org/search/collection/2068326.

20. Dodson, "Memoirs."

21. Paul Kankula, "Baptist Church Associations and Conventions," US Gen Web Project, accessed June 30, 2020, https://sites.rootsweb.com/~scoconee/church-bapt.html.

22. Grants South of Green River, 1797–1866, vol. 1, part 1, Kentucky Land Grants, 301, https://sites.rootsweb.com/~kygrant/land.html.

23. Dodson, "Memoirs."

24. Ibid.

25. Ibid.

26. McFerrin, *History of Methodism in Tennessee*, vol. 3, 349.

27. Dodson, "Memoirs."

### CHAPTER 2

1. Dodson, "Memoirs."

2. 1830 Treaty of Dancing Rabbit Creek, September 27, 1830, NAID 176532909, General Records of the United States Government, RG 11, National Archives, Washington, DC. The Choctaws had been pressured to surrender their lands. Many were opposed to the agreement, but federal troops enforced their removal to Oklahoma on what was called the Trail of Tears.

3. Dodson, "Memoirs."

4. Noted historian C. Vann Woodward argued that in the antebellum period, the South's class system was comprised of the planter class, the slaves, and the yeoman farmer, with the middle class not emerging until after the Civil War. Today there is a growing body of scholarship on the earlier emergence of the Southern middle class. See Jonathan Daniel Wells, *The Origins of the Southern Middle Class, 1800–1861* (Chapel Hill: University of North Carolina Press, 2004).

5. Dodson, "Memoirs."

6. Modern historians might not agree with Dodson's assertion. See James Oakes, *The Ruling Race: A History of American Slaveholders* (New York: Alfred A. Knopf, 2013).

7. Dodson, "Memoirs."

8. Ibid.

9. Ibid.

10. Ibid.

11. Ibid.

12. Elizabeth Blackwell Dodson to Thomas Blackwell, February 9, 1846. The author is in possession of a copy of the letter.

13. Ibid.

14. Stephen B. Weeks, "History of Public Education in Alabama," 1915, United States Bureau of Education, Bulletin 12, Library of Congress, Washington, DC, https://lccn.loc.gov/e15001123. Before then, children either had private tutors, attended private academies, or went to local subscription schools. The Alabama State Legislature began offering some funding for local schools, sometimes on a per-pupil basis and sometimes giving

schools a section of land that could be leased or sold, with the money then being invested with the state at 6 percent interest until it could be spent on the schools.

15. Dodson, "Memoirs."
16. Ibid.
17. Ibid.
18. Ibid.
19. Ibid.
20. Ibid.

**CHAPTER 3**

1. "Sumter County, Alabama Genealogical Trails, Town of Livingston," Genealogy Trails, accessed September 6, 2020, http://genealogytrails.com/ala/sumter/town_living.html. The school later became known as the Alabama Normal Female College and subsequently the University of West Alabama.
2. Sarah Moffitt, "Country Life," Texas Collection, Baylor University Libraries.
3. Sarah Moffitt to Wesley Dodson, December 26, 1852, Papers of W. C. Dodson, Texas Collection, Baylor University Libraries. Unless noted otherwise, this and subsequent letters are found in the same collection.
4. Wesley Dodson to Sarah Moffitt, January 19, 1853.
5. Sarah Moffitt to Wesley Dodson, December 26, 1852.
6. These stories are in the possession of Mary Alice Hall's family.
7. Wesley Dodson to Sarah Moffitt, December 26, 1852.
8. Sarah Moffitt to Wesley Dodson, December 12, 1852.
9. Sarah Moffitt to Wesley Dodson, February 20, 1853.
10. Wesley Dodson to Sarah Moffitt, November 9, 1852.
11. Ibid.
12. Wesley Dodson to Sarah Moffitt, November 25, 1852.
13. Ibid.
14. Wesley Dodson to Sarah Moffitt, December 2, 1852.
15. Wesley Dodson to Sarah Moffitt, December 21, 1852.
16. Sarah Moffitt to Wesley Dodson, December 26, 1852.
17. Wesley Dodson to Sarah Moffitt, December 12, 1852.
18. Wesley Dodson to Sarah Moffitt, February 5, 1853.
19. Wesley Dodson to Sarah Moffitt, January 11, 1853, February 5, 1853.
20. Wesley Dodson to Sarah Moffitt, December 21, 1852, February 11, 1853.
21. Wesley Dodson to Sarah Moffitt, December 12, 1852.
22. Wesley was not living at the Seeleys' but was boarding nearby at the Murleys'.
23. Wesley Dodson to Sarah Moffitt, February 11, 1853.
24. Sarah Moffitt to Wesley Dodson, December 5, 1852.
25. Sarah Moffitt to Wesley Dodson, February 20, 1853.
26. Ibid.
27. Wesley Dodson to Sarah Moffitt, March 6, 1853.
28. Wesley Dodson to Sarah Moffitt, April 1, 1853.

29. Sarah Moffitt to Wesley Dodson, March 19, 1853.
30. Wesley Dodson to Sarah Moffitt, February 11, 1853.
31. Wesley Dodson to Sarah Moffitt, April 1, 1853.
32. Ibid.
33. Wesley Dodson to Dillingham Dodson, June 21, 1903.
34. Wesley Dodson to Sarah Moffitt, November 9, 1852.
35. Wesley Dodson to Sarah Moffitt, January 11, 1853. Before he went to Texas in 1855, Chapin Frost sold his house to Amariah Seely.
36. Dodson, "Memoirs."
37. Ibid.
38. Ibid.
39. Ibid.
40. "Bored Well at Livingston, Alabama," Rural SW Alabama, accessed June 24, 2020, https://www.ruralswalabama.org/attraction/the-bored-well-at-livingston-al. When Wesley revisited the town in the 1890s, he found Livingston continued to be known as a health resort, and the Bored Well was still active. An historical marker later erected there indicated that "the Bored Well became one of Livingston's most treasured landmarks."
41. Michael Holt, *The Rise and Fall of the American Whig Party: Jacksonian Politics and the Onset of the Civil War* (New York: Oxford University Press, 1999), 80–3; Dodson, "Memoirs."
42. Dodson, "Memoirs."
43. Ibid.
44. Willard B. Robinson, *The People's Architecture: Texas Courthouses, Jails, and Municipal Buildings* (Texas State Historical Association, 1983), 29.
45. United States Census (Slave Schedule), 1860, Family Search, https://community.familysearch.org.
46. 1860 US Census, Livingston, Sumter County, https://www.archives.gov/research/census/1860; Dodson, "Memoirs."

## CHAPTER 4

1. Mamie Yeary, comp., *Reminiscences of the Boys in Gray, 1861–1865* (Dallas: Smith and Lamar, 1912), 189, accessed July 12, 2020, https://texashistory.unt.edu.
2. Dodson, "Memoirs."
3. Reid Mitchell, *Civil War Soldiers: Their Expectations and Their Experiences* (New York: Viking Adult, 1988). For more on what Civil War soldiers believed, see James M. McPherson, *What They Fought For, 1861–1865* (New York: Anchor Books, 1995).
4. Henry Semple to Emily Semple, Spring 1862, *Alabama Textual Materials Collection*, accessed July 2, 2020, http://digital.archives.alabama.gov/cdm/ref/collection/voices/id/4002.
5. Sarah Dodson to Wesley Dodson, June 29, 1862.
6. Wesley Dodson to Sarah Dodson, July 1, 1862.
7. Sarah Dodson to Wesley Dodson, July 2, 1862.
8. Joseph Wheeler, *Confederate Military History of Alabama*, ed. Clement A. Evans (Atlanta: Confederate, 1899), 373.

9. W. C. Dodson, "A Tribute to General (Stephen D.) Lee," *Waco Times-Herald*, June 5, 1908, accessed July 7, 2020, https://www.newspapers.com.

10. "Report of the Operations of the Command of Col. S. W. Ferguson in the Deer Creek Country" in *War of the Rebellion: Official Records of the Union and Confederate Armies*, rev. ed. (1900; repr., Gettysburg, PA: National Historical Society, 1971), https://archive.org/details/warrebellionaco17offigoog.

11. Ibid.

12. Dodson, "A Tribute to General (Stephen D.) Lee."

13. Wheeler, *Confederate Military History of Alabama*, 374.

14. Clement A. Evans, ed., *Confederate Military History of Georgia*, vol. 6 (Atlanta: Confederate, 1899), 256, accessed July 14, 2020, https://hdl.handle.net/2027/hvd.hx2n9w.

15. W. C. Dodson, "Events Leading Up to the Battles around Chattanooga," in "Memoirs of Civil War Battles," 5.

16. Dodson, "Events Leading Up to the Battles around Chattanooga," 6; Wikipedia, s.v., "Battle of Chickamauga," accessed July 20, 2020, https://en.wikipedia.org/wiki/Battle_of_Chickamauga.

17. Wikipedia, s.v., "Battle of Chickamauga."

18. W. C. Dodson, "Errors concerning Ector's Brigade," *Confederate Veteran* 13, no. 10 (October 1905): 457, https://archive.org/embed/confederateveter13conf; Oran M. Roberts, *Confederate Military History: Texas*, vol. 11 (Gulf Breeze, Florida: eBooksOnDisk.com, 2003), 109.

19. Wikipedia, s.v., "Battle of Chickamauga."

20. Steven E. Woodworth, *Six Armies in Tennessee* (Lincoln: University of Nebraska Press, 1998), 111; Wikipedia, s.v., "Battle of Chickamauga."

21. Dodson, "Events Leading Up to the Battles around Chattanooga."

22. Ibid.

23. Wikipedia, s.v., "Battle of Chickamauga." The number of casualties varies somewhat depending on the source.

24. Wesley Dodson to Sarah Dodson, December 2, 1863.

25. W. C. Dodson, "The Battle of Lookout Mountain, Fought November 24, 1863," in "Memoirs of Civil War Battles," 13.

26. Wesley Dodson to Sarah Dodson, December 2, 1863.

27. Dodson, "The Battle of Lookout Mountain," 15.

28. Wesley Dodson to Sarah Dodson, December 2, 1863.

29. Wikipedia, s.v., "Battle of Chickamauga"; Wesley Dodson to Sarah Dodson, September 10, 1864.

30. Wesley Dodson to Sarah Dodson, December 2, 1863.

31. Wesley Dodson to Sarah Dodson, April 24, 1864.

32. Ibid.

33. Ibid.

34. Ibid.

35. Wesley Dodson to Sarah Dodson, April 25, 1864

36. Wesley Dodson to Sarah Dodson, April 24, 1864.

37. Ibid.

38. Wheeler, *Confederate Military History of Alabama*, 374; Wikipedia, s.v., "Battle of Rocky Face Ridge," accessed June 21, 2020, https://en.wikipedia.org/wiki/Battle_of_Rocky_Face_Ridge.

39. W. C. Dodson, "One of the 'Fighting Parsons,'" *Confederate Veteran* (1911): 71.

40. W. C. Dodson, "Flag of the Fortieth Alabama Regiment," *Confederate Veteran* (1911): 71.

41. Dodson, "A Tribute to General (Stephen D.) Lee."

42. The brigade was no longer under Moore but was now under Baker.

43. Wheeler, *Confederate Military History of Alabama*, 374; "The Battle of Spanish Fort," ExploreSouthernHistory.com, accessed July 31, 2020, https://exploresouthernhistory.com/spanishfort.html.

44. Wesley Dodson to Sarah Dodson, September 10, 1864.

45. Yeary, *Reminiscences of the Boys in Gray*, 189; Wheeler, *Confederate Military History of Alabama*, 375.

46. Wesley mentions a letter that was not received in which he had diagramed a battle.

47. Sarah Dodson to Wesley Dodson, December 31, 1863.

48. Sarah Dodson to Wesley Dodson, January 3, 1864.

49. Sarah Dodson to Wesley Dodson, September 17, 1864.

50. Wesley Dodson to Sarah Dodson, April 24, 1864.

51. Wesley Dodson to Sarah Dodson, September 10, 1864.

52. Wesley Dodson to Sarah Dodson, December 25, 1864.

53. Roberts, *Confederate Military History: Texas*, 373–5.

54. Wesley Dodson to Sarah Dodson, December 25, 1864.

55. Sarah Dodson to Wesley Dodson, September 17, 1864.

56. Wesley Dodson to Sarah Dodson, December 25, 1864.

57. "Surrender at Citronelle," ExploreSouthernHistory.com, https://exploresouthernhistory.com/citronelle.html; Wheeler, *Confederate Military History of Alabama*, 375.

58. "Surrender at Citronelle"; Yeary, *Reminiscences of the Boys in Gray*, 189.

## CHAPTER 5

1. Wesley Dodson to Dillingham Dodson, June 21, 1902.

2. Richard Taylor, *Destruction and Reconstruction: Personal Experiences of the Late War* (New York: Appleton, 1879), 236, accessed May 28, 2020, https://docsouth.unc.edu/fpn/taylor/menu.html.

3. Wheeler, *Confederate Military History of Alabama*, 375. Baker was a mining engineer with stakes in both coal and gold mines, but he was most famously known for developing uses for cottonseed oil. He founded Selma's first cottonseed oil mill.

4. Wesley Dodson to Sarah Dodson, January 7, 1866.

5. Juliett Dodson to Wesley Dodson, April 25, 1866. She died in 1872 in Alabama before she could move to Texas.

6. Eliza Seely to Sarah Dodson, November 10, 1866.

7. Wesley Dodson to Sarah Dodson, May 4, 1867, March 31, 1867.

8. Wesley Dodson to Sarah Dodson, May 12, 1867.

9. Sarah Dodson to Addie Lockard, November 21, 1866.

10. Ibid.
11. Ibid.
12. Ibid.
13. Ibid.
14. Ibid.
15. Ibid.
16. Ibid.
17. Sarah Dodson to Fanny Jackson, October 15, 1866.
18. Sarah Dodson to Addie Lockard, November 21, 1866.
19. Sarah Dodson to Fanny Jackson, October 15, 1866.
20. Ibid.
21. Wesley Dodson to Sarah Dodson, September 19, 1866.
22. Sarah Dodson to Wesley Dodson, March 2, 1867.
23. Frank Dodson to Wesley Dodson, March 10, 1867.
24. Sarah Dodson to Addie Lockard, November 21, 1866.
25. Sarah Dodson to Fanny Jackson, October 15, 1866.
26. Sarah Dodson to Addie Lockard, November 21, 1866.
27. Ibid.
28. Wesley Dodson to Sarah Dodson, April 21, 1867.
29. Wesley Dodson to Sarah Dodson, February 24, 1867.
30. For example, see Mark L. Bradley, *The Army and Reconstruction, 1865–1877* (Washington, DC: US Army Center of Military History United States Army, 2015).
31. Wesley Dodson to Sarah Dodson, March 3, 1867. Greenbacks were paper currency issued by the United States during the Civil War.
32. Wesley Dodson to Sarah Dodson, March 10, 1867.
33. Wesley Dodson to Mollie Bet Dodson, April 7, 1867; Wesley Dodson to Sarah Dodson, February 24, 1867.
34. Wesley Dodson to Sarah Dodson, February 24, 1867, March 3, 1867.
35. Wesley Dodson to Sarah Dodson, March 17, 1867.
36. Wesley Dodson to Sarah Dodson, May 12, 1867.
37. Wesley Dodson to Sarah Dodson, February 24, 1867.
38. Wesley Dodson to Sarah Dodson, March 17, 1867, March 3, 1867.
39. Sarah Dodson to Wesley Dodson, March 17, 1867.
40. Sarah Dodson to Wesley Dodson, May 5, 1867.
41. Sarah Dodson to Wesley Dodson, March 31, 1867.
42. Sarah Dodson to Wesley Dodson, April 28, 1867.
43. Sarah Dodson to Wesley Dodson, May 5, 1867.
44. Wesley Dodson to Sarah Dodson, April 7, 1867.
45. Wesley Dodson to Sarah Dodson, May 12, 1867.
46. Wesley Dodson to Sarah Dodson, May 4, 1867.
47. Wesley Dodson to Sarah Dodson, May 12, 1867.
48. Wesley Dodson to Mollie Bet Dodson, March 15, 1867.
49. Tickets were given for correct lessons. The tickets could then be used to purchase small prizes.

50. Wesley Dodson to Mollie Bet Dodson, April 7, 1867.
51. Mollie Bet Dodson to Wesley Dodson, March 24, 1867.
52. Frank Dodson to Wesley Dodson, March 10, 1867.
53. Sarah Dodson to Wesley Dodson, March 24, 1867. Definitions were vocabulary words.
54. Mary E. Board, *Wild Flowers of Texas as I Know Them in Brazos, Robertson, Leon and Hidalgo Counties*, ca. 1920. This typed eight-page article shows Mollie Bet to be as capable a writer as her mother.
55. Frank Dodson to Wesley Dodson, March 31, 1867.
56. Sarah Dodson to Wesley Dodson, March 24, 1867.
57. Sarah Dodson to Wesley Dodson, March 17, 1867.
58. Sarah Dodson to Wesley Dodson, May 5, 1867.
59. Sarah Dodson to Wesley Dodson, March 2, 1867.
60. Sarah Dodson to Wesley Dodson, March 17, 1867.
61. Sarah Dodson to Wesley Dodson, March 24, 1867.
62. Sarah Dodson to Wesley Dodson, April 7, 1867.
63. Wesley Dodson to Sarah Dodson, April 14, 1867.
64. Wesley Dodson to Sarah Dodson, May 19, 1867.
65. Wesley Dodson to Sarah Dodson, March 31, 1867.
66. Wesley Dodson to Sarah Dodson, April 25, 1867.
67. Wesley Dodson to Sarah Dodson, April 21, 1867.
68. Wesley Dodson to Sarah Dodson, May 5, 1867.
69. Wesley Dodson to Sarah Dodson, April 14, 1867.
70. Wesley Dodson to Sarah Dodson, April 7, 1867.
71. Wesley Dodson to Sarah Dodson, April 21, 1867.
72. Ibid.
73. Ibid.
74. Wesley Dodson to Sarah Dodson, April 14, 1867.
75. Ibid.
76. Wesley Dodson to Sarah Dodson, May 19, 1867.
77. Wesley Dodson to Sarah Dodson, May 4, 1867.
78. Wesley Dodson to Sarah Dodson, May 5, 1867.
79. Wesley Dodson to Sarah Dodson, May 12, 1867.
80. Wesley Dodson to Sarah Dodson, May 19, 1867.
81. Wesley Dodson to Sarah Dodson, April 7, 1867.
82. Wesley Dodson to Sarah Dodson, April 21, 1867.
83. Sarah Dodson to Wesley Dodson, May 19, 1867.
84. Sarah Dodson to Wesley Dodson, May 12, 1867.
85. Wesley Dodson to Sarah Dodson, May 12, 1867.
86. Wesley Dodson to Sarah Dodson, May 19, 1867.
87. Wesley Dodson to Sarah Dodson, April 21, 1867. "You alone is 'Tay' to me, and 'Tay' alone is sum and substance of precious, darling wife."
88. Wesley Dodson to Sarah Dodson, March 10, 1867.
89. In June 1867, Wesley registered to vote in Bryan, Brazos County. He probably did

not vote in the ensuing election. In defiance of the newly drawn Texas Constitution, the military governor barred Confederate veterans from voting.

90. Carl H. Moneyhon, "Reconstruction," Texas State Historical Association, accessed September 4, 2023, https://www.tshaonline.org/handbook/entries/reconstruction. A yellow fever epidemic did break out in the summer and fall of 1867.

91. Wesley Dodson to Sarah Dodson, April 14, 1867.

92. Wesley Dodson to Sarah Dodson, September 19, 1866.

93. Sarah Dodson to Wesley Dodson, April 7, 1867.

94. 1870 US Census, Wheelock, Robertson County.

95. 1860 US Census, Wheelock, Robertson County. Eliza Ellis is listed as a farm tenant in precinct 2.

96. Wesley Dodson to Sarah Dodson, February 5, 1853.

97. Wesley Dodson to Mollie Bet Dodson, October 25, 1892.

98. Dodson, "Memoirs"; Wesley Dodson to Sarah Dodson, March 31, 1867.

99. "The Synod of Texas," *Galveston Daily News*, November 12, 1869, accessed July 13, 2022, https://www.newspapers.com; "The Presbytery of Brazos," *Galveston Daily News*, December 12, 1873, accessed July 12, 2022, https://www.newspapers.com.

100. "The Presbytery of Brazos," *Galveston Daily News*, December 12, 1873, accessed July 11, 2022, https://www.newspapers.com; "The Synod of Texas," *Austin American-Statesman*, November 4, 1875, accessed July 11, 2022, https://www.newspapers.com.

101. "Ecclesiastical," *Galveston Daily News*, November 7, 1874, accessed July 13, 2022, https://www.newspapers.com.

102. *Galveston Daily News*, November 6, 1875, accessed July 13, 2022, https://www.newspapers.com; J. D. Fuller, "Austin College," Texas State Historical Association, accessed July 14, 2022, https://www.tshaonline.org/handbook/entries/austin-college.

103. The Cavitts were early settlers in Wheelock and a prominent family. Perhaps the Cavitts owned the farm the Watsons rented or helped the struggling Watson family. Perhaps Wesley and Cavitt became friends while either dealing with civic affairs or attending the Presbyterian church. The connection between the families is simply unknown.

104. "Judge A. G. Board Dead," *Bryan Eagle*, December 14, 1912, accessed July 11, 2022, https://www.newspapers.com. Albert Board was born in Breckinridge County, Kentucky, where his father had at one time been the sheriff, then county clerk, and later county judge. Albert attended school in Kentucky and taught there. In 1875, he came to Texas, where he continued teaching for a while. He was elected an alderman in Bryan in 1887. Then in 1888, he was elected district clerk, then Brazos County attorney, and in 1898, he was elected county judge. He served as county judge until his death fourteen years later in 1912.

105. "Transfers of Real Estate," *Waco Morning News*, June 17, 1893, accessed July 18, 2022, https://www.newspapers.com; Dodson, "Memoirs."

106. *The Bryan Eagle*, July 3, 1902, accessed June 12, 2022, https://www.newspapers.com. Wesley continued to build in the Bryan area even after moving to Waco. In 1902, he sold two cottages he built near the public school and bought a lot on which he planned to build another cottage.

## CHAPTER 6

1. Roger Conger, *A Pictorial History of Waco with a Reprint of Highlights of Waco History*, 2nd ed. (Waco: Texian, 1998), 12; Wikipedia, s.v., "Waco, Texas," accessed June 24, 2020, https://en.wikipedia.org/wiki/Waco,_Texas.

2. "Churches," *Waco Daily Examiner*, September 1, 1878, accessed July 19, 2022, https://www.newspapers.com.

3. Vivian Elizabeth Smyrl, "McLennan County," Texas State Historical Association, accessed January 14, 2021, https://www.tshaonline.org/handbook/entries/mclennan-county.

4. Waco City Directories, 1876–1923, Texas Collection, Baylor University Libraries, accessed February 24, 2021, https://digitalcollections-baylor.quartexcollections.com/texas-collection-collections/waco-city-directories-1876-1923.

5. "The New Cemetery," *Waco Daily Examiner*, September 15, 1878, accessed July 7, 2020, https://www.newspapers.com; "Oakwood Cemetery," *Waco Daily Examiner*, September 17, 1878, accessed July 7, 2020, https://www.newspapers.com; "Our History," http://www.oakwoodwaco.com/history.

6. *San Saba News and Star*, May 10, 1889, accessed July 14, 2022, https://www.newspapers.com. The Karporama of Texas was held from May 29 to June 20, 1889.

7. Waco City Directories, 1876–1923, Texas Collection.

8. Minutes of the Session of the First Presbyterian Church of Waco, vol. 1, 99, accessed June 17, 2022, https://texashistory.unt.edu.

9. Ibid.; *Galveston Daily News*, November 6, 1875, accessed July 12, 2022, https://www.newspapers.com. By 1875, there were 74 ministers representing 133 churches at the synod.

10. "Presbyterians in Council," *Austin American-Statesman*, October 21, 1885, https://www.newspapers.com; "Avenue Hotel," *Austin American-Statesman*, April 16, 1886, https://www.newspapers.com; *Waco Daily Examiner*, May 7, 1889, https://www.newspapers.com; "Texas Synod," *Galveston Daily News*, October 23, 1892, accessed July 14, 2022, https://www.newspapers.com; "The Presbytery," *Austin Weekly Statesman*, May 16, 1889, accessed July 14, 2022, https://www.newspapers.com. On May 7, 1889, the *Waco Daily Examiner* reported that "Rev S A King and C W Dodson are at Austin in attendance on the Presbyterian synod, there." Dodson wrote Mollie Bet on October 25, 1892, that he was going to be at synod.

11. William A. McLeod, "Austin School of Theology," Texas State Historical Association, accessed July 13, 2022, https://www.tshaonline.org/handbook/entries/austin-school-of-theology.

12. Louise Kelly, "Texas Synodical Female College," Texas State Historical Association, accessed July 13, 2022, https://www.tshaonline.org/handbook/entries/texas-synodical-female-college. The school was closed in 1893.

13. "Presbyterian University," *Galveston Daily News*, March 4, 1893, accessed July 13, 2022, https://www.newspapers.com.

14. Both Austin College and the Austin Presbyterian Theological Seminary are still educating young people today.

15. Minutes of the Session of the First Presbyterian Church of Waco, vol. 1, January 1883, March 11, 1883, April 1, 1883. The church met temporarily at the Cumberland

Presbyterian Church and the chapel of the M. E. College while it moved forward with "procuring another house of worship."

16. C. T. Caldwell, "Historical Sketch of the First Presbyterian Church, Waco, Texas," (ca. 1938), 27, accessed April 23, 2020, https://www.genealogycenter.info/viewpage _tx-waco1stpres.php?realpage=140&display=028_Page_027.

17. Caldwell, "Historical Sketch," 36, 40.

18. Dodson's courthouses are discussed in chapter 7.

19. *Waco Daily Examiner*, August 30, 1878.

20. *Waco Daily Examiner*, September 7, 1878, October 2, 1878, October 24, 1878, November 1, 1878.

21. Waco City Directories, 1876–1923, Texas Collection. Dodson kept his office there for ten years until moving to 503½ Austin Avenue in 1888.

22. Waco City Directories, 1876–1923, Texas Collection.

23. *Waco Daily Examiner*, November 1, 1878.

24. Waco City Directories, 1876–1923, Texas Collection. Samuel B. and Cavitt W. Dodson formed Dodson and Dodson Real Estate. J. W. Dodson was with Dryden-Mosely-Cooper-Dodson Real Estate. Unfortunately, the Waco papers did not include news of new homes and businesses being constructed. The *Austin Weekly Statesman* regularly published lists of new buildings and their architects. See *Austin Weekly Statesman* issues from June 17, 1875, and August 5, 1883, at https://www.newspapers.com.

25. Kenneth Hafertepe, *Historic Homes of Waco* (College Station: Texas A&M University Press, 2019), 61; 1822–1905 Tax Rolls, McLennan County, Texas, accessed September 29, 2022, https://www.mclennan.gov/229/1882---1905-Tax-Rolls; Waco City Directories, 1876–1923, Texas Collection. The house is at 2325 Parrott Avenue.

26. *Memorial and Biographical History of McLennan, Falls, Bell and Coryell Counties, Texas* (Chicago: Lewis, 1893), 616–7, accessed August 25, 2022, https://texashistory.unt .edu/ark:/67531/metapth821501.

27. Waco City Directories, 1876–1923, Texas Collection. The partnership was dissolved sometime before 1890.

28. *Waco Daily Examiner*, November 6, 1885.

29. *Waco Daily Examiner*, July 30 1884, August 7, 1884, August 8, 1884.

30. *Waco Daily Examiner*, June 20, 1885. In the early 1880s, the city of Waco also lobbied to have the new state university located there. The city lost out to Austin, where the University of Texas was built.

31. "Notice to Contractors," *Waco Daily Examiner*, June 28, 1894, accessed July 20, 2022, https://www.newspapers.com.

32. T. Bradford Willis, "Austin Avenue United Methodist Church (Waco)," Texas State Historical Association, accessed August 20, 2020, https://www.tshaonline.org/handbook /entries/austin-avenue-united-methodist-church-waco.

33. "Churches," *Waco Daily Examiner*, September 1, 1878, accessed July 16, 2022, https://www.newspapers.com. William Pitt Wentworth was the architect of the church, whose cornerstone was laid on August 5, 1878.

34. St. Paul's Episcopal Church Archives; Randy Schormann, *The Story of St. Paul's Episcopal Church and its People, 1865–2021* (Waco: 2021); "Notice to Contractors,"

*Houston Post*, May 25, 1906, accessed July 17, 2022, https://www.newspapers.com.

35. *Waco Daily Examiner*, November 22, 1885, accessed June 3, 2020, https://www.newspapers.com.

36. "Convention of Architects," *Austin Weekly Statesman*, January 20, 1886, accessed July 12, 2022, https://www.newspapers.com.

37. Texas State Association of Architects Minutes and Proceedings, FromThePage, University of Texas Libraries, accessed December 29, 2020, https://fromthepage.lib.utexas.edu/katiepiercemeyer/james-riely-gordon-collection/texas-state-association-of-architects-minutes-and-proceedings.

38. Ibid.

39. Ibid.; "State Association of Architects," *Austin American-Statesman*, December 19, 1886, accessed July 13, 2022, https://www.newspapers.com.

40. Texas State Association of Architects Minutes and Proceedings; *Waco Morning News*, January 17, 1889, https://www.newspapers.com; "The Texas Architects," *Galveston Daily News*, January 17, 1889, accessed July 13, 2022, https://www.newspapers.com.

41. "Architects' Bill," *Fort Worth Daily Gazette*, January 18, 1889, accessed July 9, 2022, https://www.newspapers.com. The complete bill was printed in the *Fort Worth Daily Gazette*.

42. Hank Todd Smith, *Since 1886: A History of the Texas Society of Architects* (Austin: AIA, 1983), 4, 15.

43. The WAA members were W. C. Dodson, Nicholas J. Clayton, James Flanders, George E. King, W. H. Tyndall, A. J. Armstrong, W. S. Hull, and W. W. Larmour.

44. Architects seeking membership needed to be sponsored by two current members. Prospective members were then voted upon by the entire AIA membership. Three negative votes resulted in a rejection.

45. N. J. Clayton to J. W. Root, May 2, 1890, in Smith, *Since 1886*, 4.

46. J. Riely Gordon to Dankmar Adler, October 21, 1891, in Smith, *Since 1886*, 7.

47. Smith, *Since 1886*, 8. It was 1908 before the TSAA was reconstituted.

48. Texas State Association of Architects Minutes and Proceedings. Neither the secretary, W.W. Larmour (also an AIA member), nor the treasurer, Eugene Heiner, attended the 1900 meeting.

49. Ibid.

50. Ibid.

## CHAPTER 7

1. Sarah Dodson to Addie Lockard, November 21, 1866.

2. "Procedures of the Fourth Annual Meeting of the Texas Association of Architects, Waco, Texas, January 15, 1889," Texas State Association of Architects Minutes and Proceedings.

3. Mavis Kelsey and Donald H. Dyal, *The Courthouses of Texas*, 2nd ed. (College Station: Texas A&M University Press, 2007), 116. In 1881, for example, Gillespie County offered a fifty-dollar prize. Alfred Giles and F. E. Ruffini submitted the only two designs. Giles, who was awarded the prize, asked that the money be given to Ruffini.

4. "Notice to Contractors," *Fort Worth Daily Gazette*, April 25, 1890, accessed July 16,

2022, https://www.newspapers.com; "Notice to Contractors," *Galveston Daily News*, October 29, 1894, accessed July 17, 2022, https://www.newspapers.com. In 1890, for example, Armstrong County sought proposals directly from contractors for a small, two-story frame courthouse for $2,500. Bids had to be accompanied by plans and specifications. Likewise, Matagorda County asked contractors for plans, specifications, and bids for its courthouse.

5. Gillespie County, "Notice to Architects and Builders," *Austin American-Statesman*, August 17, 1881, accessed September 15, 2022, https://www.newspapers.com.

6. Houston County Commissioners Court Minutes, vol. 1, 29. In Houston County, for example, a number of people identified as "paupers" in 1882 were given sixty dollars per year in support.

7. Bandera County Commissioners Court Minutes, vol. 4, 24. In 1895, in Bandera County, for example, the commissioners granted use of the courtroom to the free public school.

8. Paul Goeldner, "Temples of Justice: Nineteenth Century County Courthouses in the Midwest and Texas" (PhD diss., Columbia University, 1970).

9. Mary Carolyn Hollers George, *Alfred Giles: An English Architect in Texas and Mexico* (San Antonio: Trinity University Press, 1972).

10. Stephen Fox, "Eugene T. Heiner, 1852–1901," Texas State Historical Association, accessed June 19, 2022, https://www.tshaonline.org/handbook/entries/heiner-eugene-t.

11. Sally S. Victor, "Jacob L. Larmour, 1822–1901," Texas State Historical Association, accessed February 17, 2021, https://www.tshaonline.org/handbook/entries/larmour-jacob-l; "Notice to Contractors and Builders," *Galveston Daily News*, May 12, 1874, https://www.newspapers.com.

12. "1888 Presidential Address," Texas State Association of Architects Minutes and Proceedings. In his 1888 presidential address to the Texas Association of Architects, J. J. Kane noted that the recent Second Empire Philadelphia public buildings "present a degree of architectural elegance for beauty in design [and] harmony in finish." He lauded the Second Empire War, Navy and State Department Building in Washington, DC, as "one of the most beautiful granite buildings on the American continent."

13. Robinson, *The People's Architecture*; Kelsey and Dyal, *The Courthouses of Texas*.

14. Chris Meister, *James Riely Gordon: His Courthouses and Other Public Architecture* (Lubbock: Texas Tech University Press, 2011).

15. W. C. Dodson, Report to the McLennan County Commissioners Court, McLennan County Commissioners Court Minutes, vol. F, September 6, 1900, 254–60.

16. Willard B. Robinson, *Texas Public Buildings of the Nineteenth Century* (Austin: University of Texas Press, 1974), 202; Robinson, *The People's Architecture*, 160–61; Meister, *James Riely Gordon*, 285. Dodson also presented a proposal for the Hopkins County Courthouse in Sulphur Springs.

**CHAPTER 8**

1. Architexas, "McLennan County Courthouse, Waco, Texas, Historic Structure Report and Restoration Master Plan," January 25, 2020.

2. Texas SP McLennan County Courthouse, National Register of Historic Places Inventory Nomination Form, 1978, NAID 40972997, National Archives Catalog, accessed

August 2, 2020, https://catalog.archives.gov/id/40972997; "McLennan County Courthouse, Waco, Texas," 254 Texas Courthouses, accessed August 2, 2020, http://254texascourthouses.com/courthouse-collection/mclennan-county-5.

3. County Court of McLennan Minutes, vol. A, May 25 and 27, 1874.

4. Ibid., vol. B, August 14, 1875, June 20, 1876; Architexas, "McLennan County Courthouse," 245.

5. Robinson, *The People's Architecture*, 336. Quoins (pronounced "coins") are the pronounced masonry blocks at the corners of a building that usually contrast with the adjacent masonry.

6. A mansard roof is a four-sided, steeply pitched roof with a shallow, flat top.

7. Robinson, *The People's Architecture*, 72.

8. McLennan County Commissioners Court Minutes, vol. B, June 20, 1876.

9. Architexas, "McLennan County Courthouse," 245.

10. McLennan County Commissioners Court Minutes, vol. B, June 20, 1876, August 1876, December 18, 1876.

11. "Annual Review," *Waco Daily Examiner*, September 1, 1878, accessed July 19, 2022, https://www.newspapers.com; Architexas, "McLennan County Courthouse," 245–6.

12. *Waco Daily Examiner*, August 2 and 3, 1884. https://www.newspapers.com.

13. Cecil Harper Jr., "Camp County," Texas State Historical Association, accessed September 19, 2022, https://www.tshaonline.org/handbook/entries/camp-county.

14. *Dallas Daily Herald*, June 10, 1881, accessed September 15, 2022, https://www.newspapers.com.

15. Ibid., August 13, 1881.

16. *Marshall Messenger*, December 30, 1881, accessed September 15, 2022, https://www.newspapers.com.

17. *Austin Weekly Statesman*, April 21, 1881, accessed July 29, 2022, https://www.newspapers.com.

18. Ibid., September 15, 1881; Brian Hart, "Greenville, TX, Hunt County," Texas State Historical Association, accessed May 23, 2022, https://www.tshaonline.org/handbook/entries/greenville-tx-hunt-county.

19. *Greenville Banner and Herald*, August 1884, https://www.newspapers.com; Hunt County History Timeline, Hunt County Texas Historical Society, accessed April 30, 2020, http://huntcohc.org/timeline.html.

20. *Dallas Daily Herald*, August 19, 1881, accessed July 29, 2022, https://www.newspapers.com; Carol C. Taylor, "Courthouse Burned One Year After Construction," *Carol C Taylor Blog*, April 12, 2021, accessed June 26, 2022, http://carolctaylor.com/wordpress/?p=1844; "National Register of Historic Places Registration Form, Hunt County Courthouse," Texas Historic Commission, May 1996, accessed May 20, 2022, https://www.thc.texas.gov/public/upload/preserve/survey/highway/Hunt%20Co%20Courthouse%20Greenville.pdf.

21. Pavilions are projecting sections of the building.

22. *Galveston Daily News*, January 20, 1882, accessed July 29, 2022, https://www.newspapers.com.

23. Ibid., November 18, 1882.
24. Ibid., March 24, 1884.
25. John Mark Dempsey, "Seven Hunt County Courthouses Have Stood on the Current Site," KETR, June 14, 2021, accessed June 24, 2022, https://www.ketr.org/news/2021-06-14/seven-hunt-county-courthouses-have-stood-on-the-current-site.
26. "The Crowning Calamity," *Galveston Daily News*, August 18, 1884, accessed November 20, 2022, https://www.newspapers.com.
27. *Austin American-Statesman*, October 1, 1884, accessed November 20, 2022, https://www.newspapers.com.
28. Taylor, "Courthouse Burned One Year After Construction."
29. "Notice to Contractors," *Fort Worth Daily Gazette*, October 2, 1884, accessed July 15, 2022, https://www.newspapers.com.
30. *Fort Worth Daily Gazette*, October 13, 1884, accessed September 17, 2022, https://www.newspapers.com.
31. "State News," *Austin American-Statesman*, October 6, 1884, accessed July 26, 2022, https://www.newspapers.com. Ellis and Graham's bid was $31,675.
32. *Fort Worth Daily Gazette*, October 22, 1885, accessed November 20, 2022, https://www.newspapers.com.
33. Ibid., May 3, 1884.
34. *Austin Weekly Statesman*, December 31, 1885, accessed November 20, 2022, https://www.newspapers.com.
35. "Notice to Architects," *Galveston Daily News*, March 14, 1882, accessed July 27, 2022, https://www.newspapers.com; Johnson County Commissioners Court Minutes, February 21, 1882; Richard Elam, "Johnson County," Texas State Historical Association, accessed June 24, 2022, https://www.tshaonline.org/handbook/entries/johnson-county.
36. Johnson County Commissioners Court Minutes, April 17–19, 1882, April 21, 1882.
37. "A Waco Architect's Triumph," *Waco Daily Examiner*, April 25, 1882, accessed April 15, 2020, https://www.newspapers.com.
38. Ibid.
39. Texas SP Johnson County Courthouse, National Register of Historic Places Inventory Nomination Form, 1988, NAID 40972724, National Archives Catalog, accessed March 8, 2021, https://catalog.archives.gov/id/40972724; "Johnson County Courthouse, Cleburne, Texas," 254 Texas Courthouses, accessed May 23, 2020, http://www.254texascourthouses.net/138-johnson-county.html.
40. Johnson County Commissioners Court Minutes, 1882, 370.
41. "Notice to Contractors," *Galveston Daily News*, May 20, 1882, accessed July 12, 2022, https://www.newspapers.com.
42. Johnson County Commissioners Court Minutes, 1882, 359–63.
43. Ibid., 377.
44. Ibid., June 19, 1882, August 16, 1882, November 6, 1882, February 14, 1883, August 18, 1883. In June 1882, the commissioners issued $26,000 in fifteen-year bonds at 8 percent interest. A year later, in August 1883, they issued another $7,000 in bonds. To handle the debt payments, they levied a special tax of 1.5 mills on each dollar of assessed

property in the county. Until the courthouse on the square was completed, the commissioners designated the Guggenheim and Merritt Building as the courthouse. The district court met in Brown's Opera House.

45. Ibid., October 1882, December 19, 1882, February 16, 1883, March 24, 1883, April 21, 1883, May 14, 1883, June 16, 1883.

46. *Galveston Daily News*, July 21, 1883, accessed July 27, 2022, https://www.newspapers.com; Johnson County Commissioners Court Minutes, July–December 1883, October 6, 1883. The nature of the adverse circumstances was not documented.

47. *Galveston Daily News*, May 30, 1884, accessed September 17, 2022, https://www.newspapers.com. Arson was an all-too-frequent tactic used by people seeking to destroy indictments. The Wilson County Courthouse was set ablaze in 1884 by a man facing murder and cattle-rustling charges.

48. Houston County Commissioners Court Minutes, vol. A, November 14, 1882; "Notice to Contractors and Builders," *Galveston Daily News*, December 3, 1882, accessed July 28, 2022, https://www.newspapers.com; Texas SP Houston County Courthouse, National Register of Historic Places Inventory Nomination Form, 2010, NAID 40972618, National Archives Catalog, accessed August 7, 2021, https://catalog.archives.gov/id/40972618; Armistead A. Aldrich, *The History of Houston County Texas* (San Antonio: Naylor, 1943).

49. Houston County Commissioners Court Minutes, vol. A, February 24, 1883, March 3, 1883. A tax on county residents of twenty-five cents for each one hundred dollars of assessed property was enacted to pay the interest on the loan and create a sinking fund to retire the bonds.

50. Specifications [for 1883 courthouse], Houston County Deed Records, vol. 5, 209–22; Houston County Commissioners Court Minutes, vol. 1, March 2, 1883.

51. Houston County Commissioners Court Minutes, vol. 1, March 2, 1883, November 14, 1883, January 4, 1884.

52. Ibid., July 2, 1884.

53. Lampasas County Commissioners Court Minutes, vol. 2, May 17, 1883.

54. Ibid.

55. *Wise County Messenger*, June 1, 1883, accessed August 5, 2022, https://www.newspapers.com.

56. Lampasas County Commissioners Court Minutes, vol. 2, June 1, August 13, and November 12, 1883; *Galveston Daily News*, October 6, 1883, accessed August 20, 2022, https://newspapers.com. To finance the project, the county authorized the issuance of $40,000 in fifteen-year bonds, paying eight percent interest. Commissioner A. J. Northington, who was charged with negotiating the bond's issuance, managed to sell a $30,000 bond bearing 6% interest to the Texas Board of Education, saving the county considerable interest money.

57. The ashlar, or rectangular stone block, was chiseled with wandering grooves to resemble worm tracks. The belt course is the slightly projecting horizontal molding.

58. Goeldner, "Temples of Justice: Nineteenth Century County Courthouses in the Midwest and Texas."

59. "Notice to Contractors," *Galveston Daily News*, June 22, 1883, accessed August 5, 2022, https://www.newspapers.com; Alice J. Rhoades, "Lampasas, TX," Texas State Historical Association, accessed July 26, 2020, https://www.tshaonline.org/handbook/entries/lampasas-tx; Texas SP Lampasas County Courthouse, National Register of Historic Places Inventory Nomination Form, 1971, NAID 40972811, National Archives Catalog, accessed March 8, 2021, https://catalog.archives.gov/id/40972811.

60. Paul J. Gately, "A Tale of Two Courthouses, Both Built by the Same Scottish Immigrant," KWTX, April 22, 2017, accessed July 25, 2020, https://www.kwtx.com/content/news/A-tale-of-two-courthouses-both-built-by-the-same-Scottish-immigrant-420158093.html; "Thomas Lovell," Texas Escapes, accessed July 7, 2022, http://texasescapes.com/TexasCourthouses/Thomas-Lovell.htm. Lovell also constructed courthouses in Hardeman, Brazoria, Runnels, Brown, Childress, Hamilton, and Brewster Counties. Additionally, he built three county jails, five post offices, and two federal buildings.

61. "Its New Court House Dedicated by the Sparkling Liquid," *Austin Weekly Statesman*, May 15, 1884, accessed September 14, 2022, https://www.newspapers.com; Lampasas County Commissioners Court Minutes, vol. 2, June 18, 1884, July 19, 1883; *Galveston Daily News*, July 24, 1883, September 7, 1883, https://www.newspapers.com.

62. *Austin American-Statesman*, October 5, 1883, accessed August 20, 2022, https://www.newspapers.com; Texas SP Lampasas County Courthouse, National Register of Historic Places Inventory Nomination Form; Lampasas County Commissioners Court Minutes, vol. 2, February 1884; *Galveston Daily News*, March 11, 1884, accessed September 15, 2022, https://www.newspapers.com.

63. Lampasas County Commissioners Court Minutes, vol. 2, May 12, 1884.

64. *Galveston Daily News*, May 13, 1884, accessed September 14, 2022, https://www.newspapers.com.

65. *Austin American-Statesman*, May 16, 1884, accessed September 14, 2022, https://www.newspapers.com.

66. "Its New Court House Dedicated by the Sparkling Liquid," *Austin Weekly Statesman*.

67. *Galveston Daily News*, March 11, 1884, https://www.newspapers.com; *Lampasas Leader*, August 7, 1914, https://www.newspapers.com.

**CHAPTER 9**

1. *Fort Worth Daily Gazette*, February 23, 1884, accessed July 20, 2022, https://www.newspapers.com; *Galveston Daily News*, April 13, 1884, April 23, 1884, accessed July 20, 2022, https://www.newspapers.com; *Fort Worth Daily Gazette*, April 29, 1884, accessed July 20, 2022, https://www.newspapers.com.

2. *Galveston Daily News*, February 26, 1884, accessed July 20, 2022, https://www.newspapers.com; *Dallas Weekly Herald*, February 21, 1884, accessed July 20, 2022, https://www.newspapers.com.

3. *Galveston Daily News*, February 26, 1884, accessed July 20, 2022, https://www.newspapers.com.

4. Ibid.

5. "A New Court House," *Wichita Falls Times*, April 14, 1915, accessed September 5, 2022, https://www.newspapers.com.

6. Wichita Falls Commissioners Court Minutes, vol. 1, 72; "Notice to Architects," *Fort Worth Daily Gazette*, March 3, 1884, accessed September 5, 2022, https://www.newspapers.com.

7. Wichita County Commissioners Court Minutes, vol. 1, March 29, 1884, September 3, 1884, December 16, 1885; *Galveston Daily News*, March 29, 1884, accessed July 20, 2022, https://www.newspapers.com.

8. Wichita County Commissioners Court Minutes, vol. 1, March 27, 1884.

9. Ibid., April 12, 1884, May 12, 1884; *Galveston Daily News*, March 13,1844, April 13, 1884, accessed July 20, 2022, https://www.newspapers.com.

10. Wichita County Commissioners Court Minutes, vol. 1, August 11, 1884; *Fort Worth Daily Gazette*, August 22, 1884, accessed September 4, 2022, https://www.newspapers.com.

11. Wichita County Commissioners Court Minutes, vol. 1, September 3, 1884.

12. *Dallas Daily Herald*, September 18, 1884, accessed July 20, 2022, https://www.newspapers.com.

13. Wichita Falls Commissioners Court Minutes, vol. 1, January 17, 1885, February 10, 1885.

14. Ibid., August 11, 1884; *Galveston Daily News*, April 12, 1884, accessed July 21 2022, https://www.newspapers.com.

15. Wichita Falls Commissioners Court Minutes, vol. 1, November 11, 1884, January 23, 1886.

16. Ibid., May 14, 1885, July 15, 1885, August 29, 1885, October 19, 1885, January 23, 1886, February 26, 1886; *Dallas Daily Herald*, May 24, 1885, accessed July 21, 2022, https://www.newspapers.com.

17. Wichita Falls Commissioners Court Minutes, vol. 1, February 26, 1886.

18. *Dallas Daily Herald*, May 24, 1885, accessed September 14, 2022, https://www.newspapers.com.

19. Wichita Falls Commissioners Court Minutes, vol. 1, February 26, 1886.

20. *Galveston Daily News*, February 28, 1884, accessed September 15, 2022, https://www.newspapers.com. The existing Methodist and Presbyterian buildings would soon be joined by Baptist and Episcopal buildings.

21. Young County Commissioners Court Minutes, vol. 3, February 13, 1884; *Fort Worth Daily Gazette*, February 4, 1884, accessed September 15, 2022, https://www.newspapers.com.

22. Young County Commissioners Court Minutes, vol. 3, February 13, 1884, March 31, 1884; *Galveston Daily News*, March 5, 1884, accessed September 15, 2022, https://www.newspapers.com.

23. Young County Commissioners Court Minutes, vol. 3, March 31, 1884; *Galveston Daily News*, April 6, 1884, accessed September 18, 2022, https://www.newspapers.com.

24. Young County Commissioners Court Minutes, vol. 3, May 16, 1884.

25. Ibid., March 31, 1884; *Fort Worth Daily Gazette*, March 5, 1884, accessed September 18, 2022, https://www.newspapers.com.

26. Young County Commissioners Court Minutes, vol. 3, March 31, 1884.

27. Ibid.; *Galveston Daily News*, April 6, 1884, accessed September 15, 2022, https://www.newspapers.com.

28. Young County Commissioners Court Minutes, vol. 3, April 26, 1884.

29. Ibid., May 12, 1884; *Fort Worth Daily Gazette*, May 24, 1884, https://www.newspapers.com; Carrie Johnson Crouch, *A History of Young County*, rev. ed. (Austin: Texas State Historical Association, 1956), 62. Crouch says the bid was $28,000.

30. Young County Commissioners Court Minutes, vol. 3, May 12, 1884.

31. Ibid., May 16, 1884, September 9, 1884, March 20, 1885, May 13, 1885. In March 1885, Solon and Aubrey were paid $3,470, and on May 13, 1885, they were paid $7,181, the final payment due on completion of the building.

32. Ibid., November 7, 1884. The commissioners agreed to pay Solon and Aubrey for the additional foundation work.

33. Ibid., December 17, 1884.

34. Ibid., May 13, 1885; *Galveston Daily News*, April 28, 1885, accessed September 20, 2022, https://www.newspapers.com.

35. Crouch, *A History of Young County*, 62.

36. *Austin Weekly Statesman*, May 22, 1884, accessed September 15, 2022, https://www.newspapers.com.

37. Ibid., April 4, 1880.

38. Ibid., March 22, 1884.

39. Ibid., May 16, 1884.

40. *Galveston Daily News*, July 10, 1884, accessed September 15, 2022, https://www.newspapers.com.

41. Ibid., August 18, 1884, October 25, 1884.

42. "A New Court-house Wanted," *Galveston Daily News*, December 14, 1884, accessed August 16, 2022, https://www.newspapers.com.

43. "Special Notice," *Galveston Daily News*, January 20, 1885, accessed July 25, 2022, https://www.newspapers.com.

44. Texas SP Anderson County Courthouse, National Register of Historic Places Inventory Nomination Form, 1992, NAID 40970979, National Archives Catalog, accessed March 8, 2021, https://catalog.archives.gov/id/40970979.

45. *Fort Worth Daily Gazette*, March 30, 1885, accessed October 16, 2022, https://www.newspapers.com.

46. Robinson, *The People's Architecture*, 129.

47. W. C. Dodson, Report to the McLennan County Commissioners Court, McLennan County Commissioners Court Minutes, vol. F, September 6, 1900, 254–60.

48. "Notice to Contractors," *Galveston Daily News*, March 31, 1885, accessed July 25, 2022, https://www.newspapers.com.

49. "Palestine," *Fort Worth Daily Gazette*, May 19, 1885, accessed July 25, 2022, https://www.newspapers.com; *Galveston Daily News*, August 11, 1885, January 5, 1886, accessed October 16, 2022, https://www.newspapers.com.

50. Parker County Commissioners Court Minutes, vol. 1, part 1, April 2, 1878.

51. *Austin Weekly Statesman*, March 6, 1884, accessed September 15, 2022, https://

www.newspapers.com; Parker County Commissioners Court Minutes, vol. 1, part 2, March 3, 1884.

52. *Fort Worth Daily Gazette*, April 1, 1884, accessed September 18, 2022, https://www.newspapers.com.

53. Parker County Commissioners Court Minutes, vol. 1, part 2, April 15, 1884.

54. "State Items," *Waco Daily Examiner*, June 1, 1884, accessed March 8, 2021, https://www.newspapers.com; "Weatherford," *Fort Worth Daily Gazette*, May 31, 1884, accessed July 24, 2022, https://www.newspapers.com.

55. Texas SP Parker County Courthouse, National Register of Historic Places Inventory Nomination Form, 1971, NAID 40973160, National Archives Catalog, accessed March 8, 2021, https://catalog.archives.gov/id/40973160; *Galveston Daily News*, June 30, 1884, accessed September 17, 2022, https://www.newspapers.com.

56. Parker County Commissioners Court Minutes, vol. 1, part 2, May 12, 1884; "Notice to Contractors," *Fort Worth Daily Gazette*, May 20, 1884, accessed August 31, 2022, https://www.newspapers.com; "Proposals. Notice to Contractors," *Galveston Daily News*, May 23, 1884, accessed July 15, 2022, https://www.newspapers.com.

57. *Galveston Daily News*, June 30, 1884, accessed July 15, 2022, https://www.newspapers.com.

58. *Corpus Christi Weekly Caller*, April 27, 1884, accessed July 24, 2022, https://www.newspapers.com; "County Treasurer's Report," *Dallas Daily Herald*, January 17, 1885, accessed July 24, 2022, https://www.newspapers.com.

59. "Laying of the Cornerstone," *Dallas Daily Herald*, April 4, 1885, accessed July 24, 2022, https://www.newspapers.com.

60. Parker County Commissioners Court Minutes, vol. 1, November 13, 1884; *Dallas Weekly Herald*, June 18, 1885, accessed August 31, 2022, https://www.newspapers.com; *Galveston Daily News*, September 5, 1885, September 27, 1885, March 25, 1887, accessed August 31, 2022, https://www.newspapers.com; *Taylor County News*, October 9, 1885, January 15, 1886, accessed August 31, 2022, https://www.newspapers.com; *Dallas Daily Herald*, April 2, 1887, accessed August 31, 2022, https://www.newspapers.com; *Fort Worth Daily Gazette*, April 30, 1887, accessed August 31, 2022, https://www.newspapers.com.

61. Parker County Commissioners Court Minutes, vol 1, part 3, June 29, 1886; *Wise County Messenger*, July 10, 1886, accessed July 25, 2022, https://www.newspapers.com.

62. "History of Kaufman County," *Austin American-Statesman*, February 12, 1884, accessed July 23, 2022, https://www.newspapers.com; Brian Hart, "Kaufman County," Texas State Historical Association, accessed June 26, 2022, https://www.tshaonline.org/handbook/entries/kaufman-county; McCoy Collaborative, Kaufman County Courthouse Master Plan, Final Draft, September 8, 2019.

63. *Dallas Daily Herald*, July 9, 1885, accessed July 24, 2022, https://www.newspapers.com.

64. "Kaufman vs. Terrell," *Dallas Daily Herald*, August 28, 1885, accessed July 24, 2022, https://www.newspapers.com; "The Contest in Kaufman County," *Dallas Daily Herald*, September 4, 1885, accessed July 25, 2022, https://www.newspapers.com.

65. *Fort Worth Daily Gazette*, December 25, 1885, accessed July 24, 2022, https://www.newspapers.com.

66. Kaufman County Commissioners Court Minutes, vol. 3, 136; Kaufman County Courthouse Master Plan, 15.

67. Kaufman County Commissioners Court Minutes, vol. 3, 137–8.

68. Ibid., December 31, 1885, January 1, 1886, February 2, 1886; *Fort Worth Daily Gazette*, January 25, 1886, accessed July 24, 2022, https://www.newspapers.com; "County Seats of Kaufman County," Kaufman County Courthouse Master Plan.

69. Kaufman County Commissioners Court Minutes, vol. 3, March 3, 1886; "Kaufman," *Galveston Daily News*, March 5, 1886, accessed July 24, 2022, https://www.newspapers.com.

70. Mabel Covington Keller, "History of Kaufman County, Texas" (master's thesis, North Texas State College, 1950), 50.

71. *Fort Worth Daily Gazette*, March 1, 1890, accessed August 2, 2022, https://www.newspapers.com.

72. "Want a New Courthouse," *Fort Worth Daily Gazette*, March 4, 1887, accessed July 23, 2022, https://www.newspapers.com; "Fannin County to Have a New Courthouse," *Fort Worth Daily Gazette*, March 12, 1887, accessed July 23, 2022, https://www.newspapers.com.

73. Fannin County Commissioners Court Minutes, vol. F, March 9, 1887, May 14, 1887, August 8, 1887, August 13, 1887; "Notice to Builders," *Austin American-Statesman*, June 23, 1887, accessed July 23, 2022, https://www.newspapers.com; Tom Scott, "Fannin County Courthouse History," Fannin County Historical Commission, 1984, accessed July 19, 2020, https://www.fannincountyhistory.org/history-of-the-courthouse. In August, the commissioners paid the Dodson and Dudley firm $2,401, a partial payment for the designs and specifications plus reimbursement for two train trips to Bonham.

74. W. C. Dodson, Report to the McLennan County Commissioners Court, McLennan County Commissioners Court Minutes, vol. F, September 6, 1900, 254–60.

75. "Fannin County Courthouse," *Fort Worth Daily Gazette*, May 17, 1888, accessed July 23, 2022, https://www.newspapers.com.

76. Fannin County Commissioners Court Minutes, vol. F, July 6, 1887; Willard B. Robinson, "Temples of Knowledge: Historic Mains of Texas Colleges and Universities," *Southwestern Historical Quarterly* 77, no. 4 (April 1974): 474.

77. Dodson took his son Cavitt Watson, then nineteen years old, to Granbury when he was overseeing the construction of the Hood County Courthouse.

78. *Bonham Daily Favorite*, June 27, 1924, Fannin County Historical Commission.

79. *Bonham Daily Favorite*, 1887, Fannin County Historical Commission.

80. Ibid.; "Fannin County Courthouse," *Fort Worth Daily Gazette*, May 18, 1888, accessed July 23, 2022, https://www.newspapers.com.

81. "Jubilant Bonham Claims Handsomest Courthouse in the State," *Austin American-Statesman*, June 6, 1889, accessed July 23, 2022, https://www.newspapers.com.

## CHAPTER 10

1. Francis White Johnson, *A History of Texas and Texans*, vol. 2 (Washington, DC: American Historical Society, 1914); "Hill County, Texas, County History," Texas Genealogy Trails, accessed June 7, 2022, https://genealogytrails.com/tex/prairieslakes/hill/history_county.html.

2. Hill County Commissioners Court Minutes, vol. D, August 14, 1889.

3. Ibid., September 11, 1889; "Plans Adopted for an $85,000 Courthouse," *Fort Worth Daily Gazette*, September 12, 1889, accessed July 14, 2022, https://www.newspapers.com.

4. Hill County Commissioners Court Minutes, vol. D, October 10, 1889.

5. Ibid., December 19, 1889.

6. Ibid., December 21, 1889.

7. "County Bonds," *Austin American-Statesman*, March 12, 1891, accessed July 17, 2022, https://www.newspapers.com; "Wolf Scalps," *Austin American-Statesman*, August 25, 1891, accessed July 22, 2022, https://www.newspapers.com.

8. Hill County Commissioners Court Minutes, vol. D, March 11, 1891, April 7, 1891; Program from the Rededication of the Courthouse, May 1999, Hill County, Texas; Hill County Historical Commission, *A History of Hill County, Texas, 1853–1980* (Waco: Texian, 1980), 146–7; Texas SP Hill County Courthouse, National Register of Historic Places Inventory Nomination Form, 1971, NAID 40972595, National Archives Catalog, accessed March 8, 2021, https://catalog.archives.gov/id/40972595. An NRHP official, giving his approval to the Hill County Courthouse, commented, "And another W. C. Dodson County Courthouse!"

9. Hill County Commissioners Court Minutes, vol. D, December 23, 1890.

10. *Austin American-Statesman*, July 23, 1890, accessed October 19, 2022, https://www.newspapers.com. To get stonemasons, Lovell had offered to pay forty-five cents per hour instead of the usual forty cents.

11. Hill County Commissioners Court Minutes, vol. D, 171, April 7, 1891.

12. Ibid., Vol. D, 217, September 7, 1891,Vol. D, 219, September 1891; *San Saba Weekly News*, September 25, 1891, accessed October 19, 2022, https://www.newspapers.com.

13. Texas SP Hill County Courthouse, National Register of Historic Places Inventory Nomination Form.

14. Hood County Commissioners Court Minutes, vol. C, August 16, 1889.

15. Ibid., August 17, 1889, September 25–27, 1889.

16. "County Bonds," *Austin American-Statesman*, March 12, 1891, accessed July 17, 2022, https://www.newspapers.com; *Austin American-Statesman*, August 22, 1890, accessed October 19, 2022, https://www.newspapers.com; Thomas T. Ewell, *History of Hood County* (Granbury, TX: Gaston, 1895); Granbury Junior Woman's Club, *Hood County History in Picture and Story 1978*, reprint (Fort Worth: Historical Publishers, 1978); Robinson, *The People's Architecture*, 129; Texas SP Hood County Courthouse, National Register of Historic Places Inventory Nomination Form, 1974, NAID 40972605, National Archives Catalog, accessed March 9, 2021, https://catalog.archives.gov/id/40972605; A. B. Crawford, *Hood County News-Tablet* 79, no. 47 (August 11, 1966), accessed January

25, 2022, https://texashistory.unt.edu/ark:/67531/metapth1283127. In 1890, the county sold bonds for $34,500 to the state comptroller.

17. *Wise County Messenger*, May 30, 1891, accessed October 19, 2022, https://www.newspapers.com; *San Saba News and Star*, July 31, 1891, accessed October 19, 2022, https://www.newspapers.com.

18. *Fort Worth Daily Gazette*, September 18, 1890, accessed October 19, 2022, https://www.newspapers.com; *Fort Worth Daily Gazette*, June 1, 1891, accessed October 19, 2022, https://www.newspapers.com.

19. *Galveston Daily News*, August 5, 1891, accessed October 19, 2022, https://www.newspapers.com.

20. *Brenham Weekly Banner*, March 26, 1891, accessed 17 July, 2022, https://www.newspapers.com.

21. "County Bonds," *Austin American-Statesman*, March 12, 1891, accessed July 17, 2022, https://www.newspapers.com; Swisher County Historical Commission, *Windmilling: 101 Years of Swisher County History* (Dallas: Taylor, 1978), 10.

22. "Texas Schools and Churches," *Fort Worth Daily Gazette*, August 20, 1891, July 17, 2022, https://www.newspapers.com.

23. "Notice to Contractors," *Fort Worth Daily Gazette*, September 12, 1891, accessed July 17, 2022, https://www.newspapers.com; "Texas Progress," *Fort Worth Daily Gazette*, October 15, 1891, accessed July 17, 2022, https://www.newspapers.com.

24. *Canyon News*, January 1, 1909, accessed October 10, 2022, https://www.newspapers.com.

25. *Fort Worth Star-Telegram*, March 14, 1909, accessed October 10, 2022, https://www.newspapers.com.

26. Van Zandt County Commissioners Court Minutes, bk. 4, August 14, 1894; Elvis N. Allen, *Building a County: Van Zandt County, 1848–1992* (Fruitvale, TX: Allen, 2007); W. S. Mills, *History of Van Zandt County* (Canton, TX: 1950), 230–31; Wentworth Manning, *Some History of Van Zandt County* (Criswell Park, TX: 1919), 135; *Galveston Daily News*, September 10, 1894, accessed July 30, 2022, https://www.newspapers.com.

27. Elvis N. Allen, Building a County: Van Zandt County, 1848–1992; Van Zandt County Commissioners Court Minutes, bk. 4, September 4, 1894.

28. Mills, *History of Van Zandt County*, 230; Manning, *Some History of Van Zandt County*, 135; Meister, *James Riely Gordon*, 118–22, 285.

29. Meister, *James Riely Gordon*, 117; Robinson, *The People's Architecture*, 134.

30. Texas State Association of Architects Minutes and Proceedings; Robinson, *The People's Architecture*, 134.

31. David Strother, comp., *Building the Denton County Courthouse, 1895–1897*, ed. Bullitt Lowry (Denton, TX: Denton County Historical Commission, 1987), accessed June 24, 2020, https://dentonhistory.net/page25/page50/.

32. *Dallas Morning News*, February 18, 1895, in Strother, *Building the Denton County Courthouse.*

33. *Fort Worth Daily Gazette*, February 16, 1895, February 12, 1896, in Strother, *Building the Denton County Courthouse*; Texas SP Denton County Courthouse, National Register

of Historic Places Inventory Nomination Form, 1977, NAID 40971803, National Archives Catalog, accessed March 8, 2021, https://catalog.archives.gov/id/40971803.

34. *Pilot Point Post-Mirror*, July 12, 1895, in Strother, *Building the Denton County Courthouse*.

35. Ibid.; Denton County Commissioners Court Minutes, July 12, 1895, July 25, 1895, August 9, 1895.

36. "1890 Presidential Address," Texas State Association of Architects Minutes and Proceedings, folio 21, 96.

37. Paul Goeldner, "Central Symbols: Historic Texas Courthouses," *Texas Architect Magazine* (May–June, 1986): 84, accessed August 1, 2022, https://magazine.texasarchitects.org/1986/05/28/may-june-1986. Ogival roofs have curved surfaces forming reverse curvatures. The architectural historian Paul Goeldner thought that Dodson's "assemblage of Romanesque details" revealed "an architect who was clearly uncomfortable with this style."

38. Texas SP Denton County Courthouse, National Register of Historic Places Inventory Nomination Form; *Pilot Point Post-Mirror*, November 1, 1895.

39. Denton County Commissioners Court Minutes, August 27, 1896, November 9, 1896, November 10, 1896, March 13, 1897, May 21, 1897.

40. Ibid., November 9, 1896, December 23, 1896, January 16, 1897; *Pilot Point Post-Mirror*, November 20, 1896.

41. Denton County Commissioners Court Minutes, August 6, 1895, March 13, 1897; in Strother, *Building the Denton County Courthouse*.

42. Commissioners Court Minutes, November 10, 1896, in Strother, *Building the Denton County Courthouse*. Dodson had been a captain during the Civil War. The title "major" was an honorific used widely in addressing veterans during this period.

43. Vivian Elizabeth Smyrl, "Coryell County," Texas State Historical Association, accessed July 4, 2022, https://www.tshaonline.org/handbook/entries/coryell-county; Coryell County Commissioners Court Minutes, bk. E, February 11, 1897; "New Courthouse," *Marshall Evening Register*, March 25, 1897, accessed July 22, 2022, https://www.newspapers.com.

44. Coryell County Commissioners Court Minutes, bk. E, February 18, 1897; "Notes of Improvement," *Houston Post*, March 13, 1897, accessed July 22, 2022, https://www.newspapers.com; "Texas Improvements," *Houston Post*, March 20, 1897, accessed July 22, 2022, https://www.newspapers.com.

45. Coryell County Commissioners Court Minutes, bk. E, November 18, 1897.

46. Ibid., May 1, 1897, May 15, 1897, November 18, 1897; "Texas News Items," *Liberty Vindicator*, May 14, 1897, accessed July 22, 2022, https://www.newspapers.com. For his design work, Dodson would be paid 3.5 percent of the contract price, or an eventual $2,450. As supervising architect he would be paid an additional 1.5 percent, the customary and usual fee.

47. Goeldner, "Central Symbols: Historic Texas Courthouses." For this reason, others have referred to the style as Renaissance revival.

48. Goeldner, "Temples of Justice," 270; Texas SP Coryell County Courthouse, National Register of Historic Places Inventory Nomination Form, 1977, NAID 40971593, National

Archives Catalog, accessed July 21, 2021, https://catalog.archives.gov/id/40971593. "The most unique aspect of Dodson's design," according to the architectural historian Paul Goeldner, "is the color scheme which reverses the common white trim against red brick by the use of red sandstone columns and belt courses with local white limestone."

49. Texas SP Coryell County Courthouse, National Register of Historic Places Inventory Nomination Form; Henry Russell Hitchcock and William Seale quoted in Robinson, *The People's Architecture*, 215–6; Paul Goeldner, "Central Symbols: Historic Texas Courthouses."

50. Texas SP Coryell County Courthouse, National Register of Historic Places Inventory Nomination Form.

51. Coryell County Commissioners Court Minutes, bk. E, May 10, 1897; "Notice to Contractors," *Houston Post*, June 7, 1897, accessed July 22, 2022, https://www.newspapers.com; "Bond Approved," *Austin American-Statesman*, July 10, 1897, accessed July 21, 2022, https://www.newspapers.com. To pay for the bonds, the commissioners levied a tax of fifteen cents on each one hundred dollars valuation of all taxable property in Coryell County, a tax that would remain until the bonds had been retired.

52. Coryell County Commissioners Court Minutes, bk. E, June 26, 1897.

53. Ibid., August 14, 1897.

54. Ibid., May 13, 1897.

55. Ibid., July 10, 1897; "Court House Corner Stone," *Houston Post*, October 8, 1897, accessed July 21, 2022, https://www.newspapers.com; Mildred Watkins Mears, *Coryell County Scrapbook*, rev. ed., Coryell County Museum Foundation (Waco: Texian, 1985).

56. Coryell County Commissioners Court Minutes, bk. E, June 27, 1898, June 30, 1898, July 19, 1898.

57. Ibid., July 18, 1898.

58. "History," Coryell County Texas, accessed July 20, 2020, https://www.co.coryell.tx.us/page/coryell.History.

**CHAPTER 11**

1. "Action in the New Court House Matter," *Waco Morning News*, June 1, 1893, accessed July 18, 2022, https://www.newspapers.com.

2. C. H. Weikel, "Courthouse Plan: Dignity, Elegance," *Waco Tribune-Herald*, July 1, 1967.

3. Dayton Kelly, ed., *The Handbook of Waco and McLennan County, Texas* (Waco: Texian, 1972), 87.

4. McLennan County Commissioners Court Minutes, vol. F, June 30, 1900; For J. Riely Gordon's plans and specifications from December 12, 1900, see "McLennan County Courthouse [undated]," Baylor University Libraries, https://digitalcollections-baylor.quartexcollections.com/Documents/Detail/mclennan-county-courthouse-undated/769766?item=769767.

5. Texas State Association of Architects Minutes and Proceedings.

6. W. C. Dodson, Report to the McLennan County Commissioners Court, McLennan County Commissioners Court Minutes, vol. F, September 6, 1900. The recommended changes were in a separate, accompanying report.

7. Ibid.

8. Ibid.; Kelly, *The Handbook of Waco and McLennan County, Texas*, 87. Dodson collaborated with Gordon to make revisions to his original plans. The plinth is the platform or base on which the drum rests. The drum is the circular wall supporting the dome.

9. McLennan County Commissioners Court Minutes, vol. F, September 15, 1900.

10. "A Big Day for Waco," *Houston Post*, June 28, 1901, accessed July 23, 2022, https://www.newspapers.com.

11. W. C. Dodson, Report to the McLennan County Commissioners Court, September 6, 1900, McLennan County Commissioners Court Minutes, vol. F, 252.

12. McLennan County Contract, December 12, 1900, 7, Baylor University.

13. McLennan County Commissioners Court Minutes, vol. F, December 11, 1900; Gately, "A Tale of Two Courthouses."

14. Weikel, "Courthouse Plan."

15. McLennan County Commissioners Court Minutes, vol. F, September 6, 1900, September 15, 1900; "McLennan County Courthouse, Waco, Texas," 254 Texas Courthouses.

16. *Waco Tribune-Herald*, July 16, 1967. *Harper's Magazine* was referring to the Hill County Courthouse.

**CHAPTER 12**

1. Ed Blackburn, *Wanted: Historic County Jails of Texas* (College Station: Texas A&M University Press, 2006), 2–3, 356.

2. Robinson, *The People's Architecture*, 72.

3. Mason County Commissioners Court Minutes, vol. 3, June 11, 1894. Mason County contracted with Diebold for its complete jail. For a partial list of jails "built complete or equipped with cells," see Pauly Jail Building Company's "Legacy" webpage at https://www.paulyjail.com/legacy. Pauly also has an undated catalogue, "Illustrated Descriptive Catalogue of Steel Jail Cells and Other Steel and Iron Work for County Jails and Other Prisons, manufactured by the Pauly Jail Building and Manufacturing Co."

4. Blackburn, *Wanted*, 123–5.

5. Wichita County Commissioners Court Minutes, vol. 1, August 15, 1889. The Wichita County Jail was built with the plans and specifications of Diebold Safe and Lock Company.

6. Blackburn, *Wanted*, 11.

7. "Another Account," *Dallas Weekly Herald*, March 24, 1884, accessed July 27, 2022, https://www.newspapers.com.

8. "Failure to Negotiate the Hunt County Jail Bonds," *Fort Worth Daily Gazette*, March 5, 1884, accessed July 26, 2022, https://www.newspapers.com.

9. Hunt County Commissioners Court Minutes, Special Session, March 1884.

10. *Fort Worth Daily Gazette*, October 16, 1884, accessed September 17, 2022, https://www.newspapers.com.

11. "Notice to Contractors," *Dallas Daily Herald*, May 16, 1884, accessed July 15, 2022, https://www.newspapers.com; *Fort Worth Daily Gazette*, May 18, 1884, accessed November 21, 2022, https://www.newspapers.com.

12. *Fort Worth Daily Gazette*, October 13, 1884, accessed July 15, 2022, https://www.newspapers.com; *Fort Worth Daily Gazette*, October 16, 1884, accessed September 17,

2022, https://www.newspapers.com; *Galveston Daily News*, May 18, 1884, accessed November 21, 2022, https://www.newspapers.com.

13. *Williamson County Sun*, March 1, 1888, in Jim Dillard, "Building a New County Jail, 1888," *The Noble John Olive*, accessed June 2, 2020, www.georgetown-texas.org/Building_a_new_county_jail.pdf. John Olive was the sheriff of Williamson County.

14. "Notice to Architects," *Austin American-Statesman*, January 20, 1888, accessed July 3, 2022, https://www.newspapers.com; Dillard, "Building a New County Jail, 1888."

15. "Round about Town," *Waco Daily Examiner*, February 21, 1888, accessed April 14, 2020, https://www.newspapers.com.

16. *Williamson County Sun*, March 1, 1888, in Dillard, "Building a New County Jail, 1888."

17. "Notice to Contractors," *Galveston Daily News*, February 26, 1888, accessed July 16, 2022, https://www.newspapers.com.

18. "Fine Jails," *Austin American-Statesman*, November 16, 1888, accessed August 2, 2022, https://www.newspapers.com.

19. Dillard, "Building a New County Jail, 1888."

20. Hill County Commissioners Court Minutes, vol. D, December 22, 1892.

21. "Important Law Suits," *San Saba County News*, January 13, 1893, accessed July 22, 2022, https://www.newspapers.com.

22. Hill County Commissioners Court Minutes, vol. D, January 31, 1893.

23. Ibid., 320.

24. Texas SP Hill County Courthouse, National Register of Historic Places Inventory Nomination Form.

25. Hill County Commissioners Court Minutes, vol. D, April 3, 1893, May 1893, June 13, 1893, July 13, 1893, August 17, 1893.

26. Ibid., October 2, 1893.

27. "Legacy," Pauly Jail Building Company, accessed June 14, 2020, https://www.pauljail.com/legacy. Which company provided the cells for the building is not known. According to a Pauly catalog of the period, Pauly built a jail in Hillsborough, probably the jail from 1876 that burned in 1893.

28. "Texas Siftings," *Fort Worth Daily Gazette*, August 31, 1893, accessed July 22, 2022, https://www.newspapers.com.

29. Blackburn, *Wanted*, 337; Manning, *Some History of Van Zandt County*, 135; *Galveston Daily News*, February 22, 1894, accessed July 25, 2022, https://www.newspapers.com; Margaret Elizabeth Hall, *A History of Van Zandt County* (Austin: Jenkins, 1976). Twenty-year-old James William Dodson assisted his father in writing up the detailed specifications.

30. Coryell County Commissioners Court Minutes, bk. E, May 1, 1897, May 15, 1897.

31. Ibid., June 30, 1897, July 3, 1897.

32. Ibid., July 3, 1897.

33. Ibid., July 8, 1897, August 9, 1897, December 16, 1897.

34. McLennan County Commissioners Court Minutes, vol. H, July 1, 1903; June Rayfield Welch, *The Texas Courthouse Revisited* (Dallas: GLA, 1984), 155.

35. McLennan County Contract with A. Harris, McLennan County Commissioners Court Minutes, vol. H, July 1903.

36. McLennan County Commissioners Court Minutes, vol. H, December 10, 1903; "Short Texas Specials," *Houston Post*, December 9, 1903, accessed July 21, 2022, https://www.newspapers.com; Blackburn, *Wanted*, 232.

37. "The Grand Lodge," *Austin Weekly Statesman*, February 12, 1885, accessed August 18, 2022, https://www.newspapers.com; "The Story of the Widows and Orphans Home in Corsicana," Grand Lodge of Texas, Independent Order of Odd Fellows, accessed August 18, 2022, https://www.ioofx.org/history.

38. *Galveston Daily News*, October 2 1885, accessed August 18, 2022, https://www.newspapers.com.

39. "Corsicana: Odd Fellows' Widows' and Orphans' Home Opened," *Fort Worth Daily Gazette*, January 24, 1886, accessed August 18, 2022, https://www.newspapers.com.

40. "The Odd Fellows' Widows and Orphans Home," *Dallas Morning News*, December 9, 1885.

41. *Galveston Daily News*, March 12, 1886, accessed August 18, 2022, https://www.newspapers.com.

42. Ibid., April 27, 1886.

43. "Girls Leap from Blazing Building," *Fort Worth Star-Telegram*, April 4, 1905, accessed August 18, 2022, https://www.newspapers.com.

44. Pauline Buck Hohes, *A Centennial History of Anderson County* (San Antonio: Naylor, 1936), 96, accessed September 15, 2022, https://hdl.handle.net/2027/uiug.30112049799817. Palestine's minister, S. M. Luckett, was the moderator at the Texas Synod of 1882, which Dodson attended.

45. "About the Church," First Presbyterian Church of Palestine, accessed March 9, 2021, https://www.firstprespalestine.com; Jack Selden, *Seven Score and Ten: One Hundred Years of the Presbyterian Church in Palestine, Texas* (Palestine, TX: Clacton, 1999).

46. Hohes, *A Centennial History of Anderson County*, 137–9.

47. Girls Industrial College of Texas, "Course of Study," *Girls Industrial College Bulletin*, no. 3 (August 1903), accessed August 16, 2024, https://twu-ir.tdl.org/server/api/core/bitstreams/3bea48a8-115b-4187-af66-01f67f465eda/content.

48. Board of Regents of the Girls Industrial College of Texas, First Annual Report, 1902, 4, accessed August 16, 2024, https://twu-ir.tdl.org/server/api/core/bitstreams/f7dd1234-9e18-451e-aa44-c15096af4191/content; "Girls' Industrial Institute," *Austin American-Statesman*, January 7, 1902, accessed July 21, 2022, https://www.newspapers.com; "How It Was Done," *Fort Worth Record and Register*, March 20, 1902, accessed July 21, 2022, https://www.newspapers.com; Bullitt Lowery, *The Historical Markers of Denton County* (1980), 51; E. V. White, *Historical Record of the Texas State College for Women: The First Forty-Five Years, 1903–1948* (Denton, TX: Texas State College for Women, 1948), accessed December 29, 2020, https://twu-ir.tdl.org/server/api/core/bitstreams/b3b6fc4d-6e7e-4407-b801-f58934e5659c/content.

49. Board of Regents of the Girls Industrial College of Texas, First Annual Report, 4.

50. Ibid.

51. W. C. Dodson opening address, "Procedures of the Fourth Annual Meeting of the Texas Association of Architects, Waco, Texas, January 15, 1889," 80, From The Page, https://fromthepage.lib.utexas.edu, accessed December 29, 2020.

52. Waco City Directories, 1876–1923, Texas Collection; Hafertepe, *Historic Homes of Waco*, 6; Amanda Sawyer, "Milton W. Scott," Waco History, February 22, 2021, https://wacohistory.org/items/show/92. The partnership lasted a short time, only the duration of this project. The next year, Scott was listed in the Waco City Directory of 1904–5 as a "draughtman," working for the local architect Glenn Allen. In 1910, Scott partnered with Brooks Pearson. In 1911, Dodson was still a ruling elder at the First Presbyterian Church when the elders chose the firm of Scott, Pearson, and Dean as supervising architects for the construction of their new building. Scott went on to have a long, successful architectural career in Waco, building eighteen public school buildings and a number of college buildings, as well as churches and private homes.

53. Rusticated stonework has beveled or rebated edges emphasizing the joints.

54. Mary Evelyn Huey, "The First Building of the Texas Woman's University," ca. 1974, accessed January 4, 2021, https://apps.dentoncounty.gov/website/HistoricalMarkers/PDFs/The-First-Building-of-Texas-Woman's-University.pdf.

55. Ibid.; "Superintendent Lefever Returned," *Austin American-Statesman*, September 25, 1903, accessed July 21, 2022, https://www.newspapers.com; Girls Industrial College of Texas, "Plan and Scope," *Girls Industrial College Bulletin*, no. 2 (June 1903), accessed August 15, 2024, https://twu-ir.tdl.org/server/api/core/bitstreams/a6624795-176e-4199-a2ce-006cf2e00035/content.

56. *Waco Morning News*, August 2, 1914.

**CHAPTER 13**

1. *Waco Tribune Herald*, July 16, 1967; Terry Jo Ryan, "Brazos Past: Waco Steam Laundry Cleaned Up the Old West," *Waco Tribune-Herald*, November 27, 1910, updated July 10, 2020, accessed January 15, 2021, https://wacotrib.com/news/local/brazos-past-waco-steam-laundry-cleaned-up-the-old-west/article_8ff39427-5a51-5073-93fb-d878e4aa0e1d.html.

2. "Crushed to Death by Falling Wall," *Waxahachie Daily Light*, April 15, 1912, accessed July 27, 2022, https://www.newspapers.com; "Falling Walls Kill Cleburne Marshal," *Austin American-Statesman*, April 15, 1912, accessed August 1, 2022, https://www.newspapers.com; Texas SP Johnson County Courthouse, National Register of Historic Places Inventory Nomination Form; "Johnson County Courthouse, Cleburne, Texas," 254 Texas Courthouses; "Johnson County Will Have New Courthouse," *Fort Worth Star-Telegram*, September 27, 1912, accessed August 2, 2022, https://www.newspapers.com.

3. "Anderson County Courthouse Burns," *Houston Post*, January 7, 1913, accessed August 2, 2022, https://www.newspapers.com; "Pleaded Guilty to Burning Courthouse," *Bryan Eagle*, January 29, 1913, https://www.newspapers.com; "Father of 3 Sentenced," *Houston Post*, November 27, 1913, accessed August 2, 2022, https://www.newspapers.com; Kelsey and Dyal, *The Courthouses of Texas*, 31.

4. "Believe New Court House Will Soon Be Necessary," *Wichita Falls Times*, December 8, 1914, accessed September 5, 2022, https://www.newspapers.com; "Suit Against Railroad on Calendar Monday," *Wichita Falls Times*, March 14, 1915, accessed September 5, 2022, https://www.newspapers.com; "A New Court House," *Wichita Falls Times*, April 14, 1915, accessed September 5, 2022, https://www.newspapers.com; "Court House Bond

Issue Won," *Houston Post*, January 20, 1916, accessed September 5, 2022, https://www.newspapers.com; "Wichita Falls Plan Rest Room," *Fort Worth Record-Telegram*, November 30, 1917, accessed September 5, 2022, https://www.newspapers.com.

5. *Fort Worth Record-Telegram*, March 21, 1917, accessed September 5, 2022, https://www.newspapers.com; James C. White, *The Promised Land: A History of Brown County* (Brownwood, TX: Brownwood Banner, 1941), 11; "Lays Courthouse Cornerstone," *Fort Worth Star-Telegram*, November 5, 1917, accessed October 14, 2022, https://www.newspapers.com.

6. "Palestine, Texas," Texas Escapes, accessed September 23, 2022, http://texasescapes.com/TOWNS/Palestine/Palestine_Texas.htm; Texas MSP First Presbyterian Church, National Register of Historic Places Continuation Sheet, 1998, NAID 40967866, National Archives Catalog, accessed March 4, 2021, https://catalog.archives.gov/id/40967866.

7. *Longview News-Journal*, May 30, 1928, accessed October 10, 2022, https://www.newspapers.com; Camp County History Book Committee, *Camp County, Texas: Customs and Characters, A Sesquicentennial History* (Dallas: Taylor, 1986).

8. "They Demand a Courthouse," *Austin American-Statesman*, September 16, 1927, accessed August 2, 2022, https://www.newspapers.com; "New Hunt Courthouse Contract is Awarded," *Longview News-Journal*, March 22, 1928, accessed August 1, 2022, https://www.newspapers.com; "New Hunt County Courthouse and Jail at Greenville Will Cost $400,000," *Fort Worth Star-Telegram*, April 16, 1928, accessed August 2, 2022, https://www.newspapers.com.

9. "Two Prisoners Escape from Greenville Jail," *Bonham Daily Favorite*, March 28, 1929, accessed August 2, 2022, https://www.newspapers.com; Blackburn, *Wanted*, 173–4.

10. "Work Progresses on Graham Courthouse," *Wichita Fall Times*, January 12, 1932, accessed October 11, 2022, https://www.newspapers.com; Young County Commissioners Court Minutes, vol. 8, October 10, 1932.

11. Nita Miller, "Archway Has Historic Past," *Graham Reporter*, April 20, 1967.

12. "Houston County Plans Courthouse," *Austin American-Statesman*, February 4, 1938, accessed August 4, 2022, https://www.newspapers.com; "Ten More PWA Jobs Are Asked," *Fort Worth Star-Telegram*, June 2, 1938, accessed August 2, 2022, https://www.newspapers.com; "Houston County Courthouse Sold," *Fort Worth Star-Telegram*, October 13, 1938, accessed August 4, 2022, https://www.newspapers.com; Texas SP Houston County Courthouse, National Register of Historic Places Inventory Nomination Form; Aldrich, *The History of Houston County*, 37.

13. *Paris News*, April 9, 1941, accessed September 6, 2022, https://www.newspapers.com; McCoy Collaborative, Kaufman County Courthouse Master Plan, Final Draft, September 8, 2019.

14. "Ground Breakers Attend New Event," *Austin American-Statesman*, March 13, 1955, accessed August 2, 2022, https://www.newspapers.com; *Dallas Morning News*, March 18, 1941, March 22, 1941, May 13, 1954, in McCoy Collaborative, Kaufman County Courthouse Master Plan, Final Draft, September 8, 2019, 19.

15. "History," First Methodist Church of Waco, https://firstwaco.com.

16. Lallie Dodson Gibson to Charles Henry Dodson, March 31, 1963. The author is in possession of the letter.

17. "PWA to Finish 19 Jobs in April," *Fort Worth Star-Telegram*, April 16, 1937, https://www.newspapers.com; "Van Zandt's New Courthouse Paid for at Opening," *Fort Worth Star-Telegram*, June 13, 1937, accessed August 20, 2022, https://www.newspapers.com; "Van Zandt Presents Jail to Scrap Drive," *Lubbock Avalanche-Journal*, February 7, 1943, accessed August 27, 2022, https://www.newspapers.com; "Old Van Zandt Jail Building Being Razed," *Tyler Morning Telegraph*, April 11, 1969, accessed August 27, 2022, https://www.newspapers.com.

18. "Bids for Georgetown Jail," *Austin American-Statesman*, March 14, 1934, accessed August 3, 2022, https://www.newspapers.com; "$40,000 Contracts Let for Georgetown Jail," *Austin American-Statesman*, April 15, 1934, accessed August 3, 2022, https://www.newspapers.com; Texas SP Williamson County Courthouse District, National Register of Historic Places Inventory Nomination Form, 1977, NAID 40973996, National Archives Catalog, accessed March 3, 2021, https://catalog.archives.gov/id/40973996.

19. Texas SP Hill County Courthouse, National Register of Historic Places Inventory Nomination Form; *Fort Worth Star-Telegram*, October 3, 1983, accessed August 24, 2022, https://www.newspapers.com; "Commissioners Approve Cell Block Museum Study," *Lakelander*, September 15, 2022, accessed August 30, 2024, https://lakelander.com/2022/09/15/commissioners-approvecell-block-museum-study.

20. Huey, "The First Building of the Texas Woman's University," 6.

21. Ibid., 7; Official Texas Historical Marker Designation Commemorating the First Building of the Texas Woman's University, Presented by the Past Presidents' Council of the Alumnae Association and the Denton County Historical Survey Committee, April 26, 1974. The author is in possession of the program for the ceremony.

22. Texas MSP First Presbyterian Church, National Register of Historic Places Continuation Sheet.

23. Mildred Watkins Mears, *Coryell County Scrapbook*, rev. ed. (1985; Waco: Texian, 1963), 35.

24. Mears, *Coryell County Scrapbook*, 29.

25. Texas SP Coryell County Courthouse, National Register of Historic Places Inventory Nomination Form.

26. "Courthouse Bell Is Ordered to Close," *Gatesville Messenger and Star-Forum*, May 1, 1986, accessed July 30, 2022, https://www.newspapers.com.

27. *Gatesville Messenger and Star-Forum*, May 29, 1896, June 26, 1986, accessed July 30, 2022, https://www.newspapers.com.

28. Ibid., September 25, 1986, September 10, 1987, February 25,1988, June 2, 1988; "Courthouse Bell Is Ordered to Close," *Gatesville Messenger and Star-Forum*; "One of the Few," *Gatesville Messenger and Star-Forum*, May 1, 1986, accessed July 30, 2022, https://www.newspapers.com; "History," Coryell County Texas; Gately, "A Tale of Two Courthouses."

29. "Coryell County Courthouse 125th Celebration Set for Saturday," *Copperas Cove Leader Press*, July 21, 2023, accessed July 23, 2023, https://www.coveleaderpress.com/news/coryell-county-courthouse-125th-celebration-set-saturday.

30. Texas SP Hill County Courthouse, National Register of Historic Places Inventory Nomination Form.

31. "Hill County Courthouse," 254 Texas Courthouses, accessed July 27, 2020, http://www.254texascourthouses.net/137-hill-county.html.

32. "About the Texas Historic Courthouse Preservation Program," Texas Historical Commission, accessed August 24, 2022, https://thc.texas.gov/preserve/preservation-programs/courthouse-preservation.

33. Texas SP Lampasas County Courthouse, National Register of Historic Places Inventory Nomination Form.

34. "4 West Texas Counties Get Courthouse Grant Money," *San Angelo Standard Times*, May 5, 2000, accessed September 1, 2022, https://www.newspapers.com.

35. "Texas Courthouses," National Trust for Historic Preservation, accessed May 25, 2020, https://savingplaces.org/places/texas-courthouses; "Texas Historic Sites Atlas," Texas Historical Commission, accessed February 4, 2024, https://atlas.thc.texas.gov; Clay Coppedge, "Lampasas County Courthouse Rededicated after 120 Years," *Temple Daily Telegram*, March 3, 2004, accessed August 18, 2022, https://www.tdtnews.com/archive/article_e6474dbe-dfc9-5bf8-b76b-38e8774a66b5.html.

36. Texas SP Denton County Courthouse, National Register of Historic Places Inventory Nomination Form.

37. Strother, *Building the Denton County Courthouse*; "Denton County Courthouse," Architexas, accessed March 14, 2022, https://architexas.com/projects/denton-county-courthouse.

38. Bullitt Lowry, in Strother, *Building the Denton County Courthouse*.

39. Texas SP Parker County Courthouse, National Register of Historic Places Inventory Nomination Form.

40. "Parker County Courthouse, Weatherford," Texas Historical Commission, accessed May 13, 2020, https://www.thc.texas.gov/preserve/projects-and-programs/texas-historic-courthouse-preservation/restored-courthouses/parker.

41. "Wednesday Club Presents Resolution to Commissioners Court on Court House," *Hood County News-Tablet*, November 7, 1968, accessed August 21, 2022, https://www.newspapers.com.

42. Autis McMahan, "Face-Lifting under Way for Granbury's Tilted Tower," *Fort Worth Star-Telegram*, July 17, 1969, accessed August 21, 2022, https://www.newspapers.com.

43. Texas SP Hood County Courthouse, National Register of Historic Places Inventory Nomination Form; "City's History Centers around Courthouse, Downtown Square," *Hood County News*, June 28, 1997, accessed August 21, 2022, https://www.newspapers.com.

44. "Roof Repairs Shoot Up Costs," *Hood County News*, January 24, 1998, accessed August 23, 2022, https://www.newspapers.com; "Up on the Roof," *Hood County News*, March 11, 1998, accessed August 23, 2022, https://www.newspapers.com; "Hood County Courthouse Renovation under Way," *Odessa American*, March 16, 1998, accessed August 23, 2022, https://www.newspapers.com.

45. "Hood County Courthouse," Texas Historical Commission, accessed August 17, 2024, https://thc.texas.gov/preserve/preservation-programs/courthouse-preservation/restored-historic-courthouses/hood-county.

46. "Crown Jewel of Our County," *Hood County News*, February 26, 2011, accessed August 24, 2022, https://www.newspapers.com.

47. *Hood County News*, November 3, 2012, accessed August 24, 2022, https://www.newspapers.com.

48. Mary Saltarelli, "Hood County Courthouse-Granbury," Texas Historical Commission, accessed May 21, 2020, https://www.thc.texas.gov/preserve/projects-and-programs/texas-historic-courthouse-preservation/restored-courthouses/hood-county-courthouse.

49. *Bonham Daily Favorite*, December 3, 1929, Fannin County Historical Society, 1.

50. This limestone, which was buffed to a smooth, silky finish, was mined in the Lueder basin near Amarillo.

51. Scott, "Fannin County Courthouse"; Christina Brown, "The Many Lives of a Courthouse," *Fannin County Leader*, accessed May 18, 2022, https://fannincountyleader.info/the-many-lives-of-a-courthouse-p14158-1.htm.

52. Wikipedia, s.v., "Fannin County Courthouse (Texas)," accessed June 3, 2020, https://en.wikipedia.org/wiki/Fannin_County_Courthouse_(Texas).

53. Alicia Whipple, "Rededication Week at 1888 Fannin County Courthouse," *North Texas e-News*, March 9, 2021. The time capsule buried at the rededication contained an article by the author titled "W. C. Dodson: The 1888 Original Fannin County Courthouse Architect," published in the *Fannin County Time Leader* on March 8, 2022.

54. Texas SP McLennan County Courthouse, National Register of Historic Places Inventory Nomination Form.

55. McLennan County Courthouse, Waco, Texas, Historic Structure Report and Restoration Master Plan, January 25, 2000.

56. Ibid.; J. B. Smith, "McLennan County Courthouse Dome Restoration Has Some Wishing for More," *Waco Tribune-Herald*, November 5, 2012, updated August 16, 2019, accessed August 23, 2020, https://wacotrib.com.

57. The Coryell County Courthouse restoration began in 1986, and the rededication was held in 1988 on the building's ninetieth anniversary. The Hill County Courthouse was restored after the 1993 fire with a combination of public and private money. These restorations were an impetus for the Texas Historic Courthouse Preservation Program created in 1999.

**CHAPTER 14**

1. *Bryan Eagle*, December 9, 1895, May 13, 1898, June 11, 1901, June 3, 1911, accessed June 3, 2019, https://www.newspapers.com.

2. Wesley Dodson to Mollie Bet Board, February 23, 1911. The letter is in the possession of the family of Mary Alice Hall.

3. Wesley Dodson to Mollie Bet Board, October 29, 1893.

4. Wesley Dodson to Mollie Bet Board, July 17, 1910.

5. Oliver Goldsmith's poem from 1770 deals with losses that result from abandoning an innocent, idyllic country life for a corrupt, money-centered urban existence. The poem also might have reminded Wesley of Sarah's college writings on the virtues of country life.

6. Wesley Dodson to Mollie Bet Board, July 17, 1910.

7. "Camp Cleburne Register," Texas Collection, Baylor University Libraries; Waco City Directories, 1876–1923, Texas Collection; Smyrl, "McLennan County."

8. Wesley's granddaughter Lallie Dodson Gibson was in possession of Wesley's handwritten addresses from 1900 and had them typed and bound as "Memoirs of Civil War Battles" by W. C. Dodson. The author is in possession of a copy.

9. *Camp Cleburne Ledger*, 1909.

10. Dodson, "The Battle of Lookout Mountain," 10–11.

11. Dodson, "Events Leading Up to the Battles around Chattanooga," 7.

12. Gaines M. Foster, *Ghosts of the Confederacy: Defeat, the Lost Cause and the Emergence of the New South, 1865–1913* (New York: Oxford University Press, 1987), 6.

13. Alan T. Nolan, "The Anatomy of the Myth," in *The Myth of the Lost Cause and Civil War History*, eds. Gary W. Gallagher and Alan T. Nolan (Bloomington: Indiana University Press, 2000), 11–34. One legacy of the "Lost Cause" myth was the impact on the status of black people in the South. The myth's widespread acceptance in the North as well as the South was followed by the era of Jim Crow segregation, the Ku Klux Klan, and the disregard of the rights of black citizens. See also Foster, *Ghosts of the Confederacy*.

14. "Houston's Gates Are Open," *Galveston Daily News*, May 22, 1895, https://www.newspapers.com; "The Great Reunion of 1895," *Galveston Daily News*, May 23, 1895, accessed July 12, 2022, https://www.newspapers.com. This article was the first time that Wesley Dodson, who had been a captain, was referred to as Maj. Dodson. This designation was part of the movement to honor Confederate veterans as heroes.

15. "The Great Reunion of 1895," *Galveston Daily News*, May 23, 1895, accessed July 12, 2022, https://www.newspapers.com.

16. Ibid.

17. Foster, *Ghosts of the Confederacy*, 6. Historian Gaines Foster notes the reasons for the Confederate celebrations: "In the public commendation of the Confederate cause and its soldiers, veterans and other southerners found relief from the lingering fear that defeat had somehow dishonored them."

18. *Confederate Veteran* (1897): 429, accessed April 13, 2022, https://onlinebooks.library.upenn.edu/webbin/serial?id=confedvet/

19. *Waco Times-Herald*, June 5, 1908, Texas Collection, Baylor University Libraries.

20. *Confederate Veteran* 133, no. 10, 457, accessed April 13, 2022, https://onlinebooks.library.upenn.edu/webbin/serial?id=confedvet.

21. Wesley Dodson to Sarah Dodson, April 24, 1864.

22. Wesley Dodson to Mollie Bet Board, April 23, 1898.

23. *Waco Daily Examiner*, October 7, 1909, https://www.newspapers.com.

24. Application to the Commissioner of Pensions, Form A, For Use of Soldiers, Who Are in Indigent Circumstances. The author is in possession of the document.

25. Wesley Dodson to Mollie Bet Board, June 25, 1912.

26. Wesley Dodson to Mollie Bet Board, March 27, 1897.

27. Ibid.

28. W. C. Dodson, June 1, 1911. The prayer is in the possession of the family of Mary Alice Hall.

29. Wesley Dodson to Mollie Bet Board, October 1, 1912.

30. Wesley Dodson to Mollie Bet Board, April 30, 1914.

31. Ibid. This letter, the last Wesley sent Mollie Bet, is in the possession of Mary Alice Hall's family.

32. Wesley Dodson to Mollie Bet Board, July 19, 1896.

33. Wesley Dodson to Mollie Bet Board, July 17, 1910.

34. W. C. Dodson, *Confederate Veteran* (1897): 429, accessed April 13, 2022, https://onlinebooks.library.upenn.edu/webbin/serial?id=confedvet.

35. Wesley Dodson to John Blackwell, November 21, 1896.

36. Wesley Dodson to Dillingham Dodson, June 21, 1902.

37. *Waco Morning News*, August 2, 1914.

38. *Fort Worth Star-Telegram*, August 2, 1914. Wesley actually served in the 40th Alabama Regiment.

39. "The Death Roll," *Waco Times-Herald*, August 2, 1914.

40. *Waco Times-Herald*, August 2, 1914.

41. Minutes of the Session of the First Presbyterian Church of Waco, vol. 5, 85, accessed January 19, 2021, https://texashistory.unt.edu/ark:/67531/metapth1220987/m1/85.

42. Dodson may have built additional courthouses. In *Confederate Military History: Texas*, Roberts states that Dodson "designed nearly thirty court houses" in Texas. But, no evidence to substantiate that statement has been found. See Roberts, *Confederate Military History*: *Texas*, 375.

43. Robinson, *The People's Architecture*.

44. Robinson, "Temples of Knowledge."

45. Minutes of the Session of the First Presbyterian Church of Waco, vol. 5, 85, accessed January 19, 2021, https://texashistory.unt.edu/ark:/67531/metapth1220987/m1/85.

46. Wesley Dodson to Sarah Dodson, February 5, 1853.

47. Dodson, "Memoirs."

**APPENDIX 1**

1. Dodson, "Memoirs." In today's world, of course, slaveholding and loving liberty are seen as incompatible.

2. "Studies of Southern Colonial Naming Patterns," Bob's Genealogy Filing Cabinet, accessed July 19, 2020, https://genfiles.com/articles/comments-on-naming-patterns.

3. Williams and Lucas, *The Dodson (Dotson) Family*.

4. Williams and Lucas, *The Dodson (Dotson) Family*, 1; Richmond County Records, Deeds: 01–084, 1435, in Williams and Lucas, *The Dodson (Dotson) Family*, vol. 2.

5. Michelle Duval Ule, *Pioneer Stock: The American Ancestors of Ballard Emory Duval* (Maryland: self-pub., 2000).

6. Williams and Lucas, *The Dodson (Dotson) Family*, vol. 2, vi; Wikitree G2G, accessed August 12, 2020.

7. "Richmond Co VA Miscellaneous Record Book, October 1699–September 1724," 4, in Williams and Lucas, *The Dodson (Dotson) Family*, vol. 1.

8. Williams and Lucas, *The Dodson (Dotson) Family*, vol. 1, 1.

9. Old Rappahannock County, VA, deed bk. 6, 112.

10. William Waller Henning, ed. *The Statutes at Large: Being a Collection of All the Laws of Virginia, from the First Session of the Legislature* [ . . . ], vol. 1, 128; Bob's Genealogy Filing Cabinet, accessed July 18, 2020, https://genfiles.com/articles/tithables.

11. Old Rappahannock County, VA, deed bk. 6, 112.

12. Old Rappahannock County, VA, deed bk. 7, 281–3.

13. Williams and Lucas, *The Dodson (Dotson) Family*, vol. 2, 1435, 1438.

14. Williams and Lucas, *The Dodson (Dotson) Family*, vol. 1, 1.

15. Ule, *Pioneer Stock*; Shirley Corbari, *The Guio-Dodson Family* (self-pub., 1986), Sutro Library of San Francisco.

16. Williams and Lucas, *The Dodson (Dotson) Family*, vol. 2, 1437.

17. Ibid., 1438.

18. North Farnham Parish Register in Williams and Lucas, *The Dodson (Dotson) Family, vol. 2, 1445.*

19. Williams and Lucas, *The Dodson (Dotson) Family*, vol. 1, 8; vol. 2, 1435.

20. Williams and Lucas, *The Dodson (Dotson) Family*, vol. 2, 1438.

21. Corbari, *The Guio-Dodson Family.*

22. Richmond County, VA, will bk. 5, 378–9; Williams and Lucas, *The Dodson (Dotson) Family*, vol. 2, 1440.

23. Williams and Lucas, *The Dodson (Dotson) Family*, vol. 1, 15.

24. From the account book of Capt. John Crump, sheriff of Prince William County, Fauquier County, Virginia Genealogy, accessed August 20, 2020, https://www.familysearch.org/wiki/en/Fauquier_County,_Virginia_Genealogy#Taxation.

25. Williams and Lucas, *The Dodson (Dotson) Family*, vol. 2, 1443.

26. Thomas S. Kidd, *The Great Awakening: The Roots of Evangelical Christianity in Colonial America* (New Haven, CT: Yale University Press, 2008).

27. The Broad Run Baptist Church is still located on Broad Run Church Road in New Baltimore (Warrenton), Virginia.

28. Minutes of Broad Run Baptist Church, Fauquier County, Virginia, 1762–1872, Rootsweb, accessed July 24, 2020, http://freepages.rootsweb.com/~gohrpage/genealogy/broadrun.html.

29. Williams and Lucas, *The Dodson (Dotson) Family*, vol. 1, 15–7, 38.

30. Ibid., 12, 22, 33.

31. Ibid., 16, 21.

32. Elias Dodson, "Genealogy of the Dodson Families," cited in Williams and Lucas, *The Dodson (Dotson) Family*, vol. 2, 1462. He also noted that "Thomas Dodson was rich and was called a great gentleman."

33. Williams and Lucas, *The Dodson (Dotson) Family*, vol. 1, 28.

34. Alicia Rennoli, "Welsh Settlers During the Royal Period, 1729 to 1775," July 2019, Royal Colony of South Carolina, accessed July 8, 2020, https://www.carolana.com/SC/Royal_Colony/sc_royal_colony_welsh.html. Later, a number of Welsh settlers moved from the Welsh Tract of South Carolina to North Carolina.

35. *State Census of North Carolina, 1784–1787*, transcribed and indexed Alvaretta Kenan Register (Baltimore: Genealogical, 1987), 148.

36. “The Story of Fort Prince George,” Pickens County Historical Society, accessed August 1, 2020, https://sites.google.com/site/pickenscountyhistoricalsociety/fort-prince-george.

37. David Roach, “Native American Evangelism: Past and Present Examined,” California Southern Baptist Convention, August 1, 2017, accessed August 3, 2020, https://www.csbc.com/news/2017/native-american-evangelism-past-present-examined.

38. “4th North Carolina Regiment,” The American Revolution in North Carolina, accessed July 16, 2020, https://www.carolana.com.

39. Charles L. Davis, “A Brief History of the North Carolina Troops on the Continental Establishment in the War of the Revolution with a Register of Officers of the Same” (Philadelphia: 1896), https://www.carolana.com/NC/Revolution/A_Brief_History_of_the_North_Carolina_Troops_on_the_Continental_Establishment_Davis_1896.pdf; Wikipedia, s.v., “4th North Carolina Regiment,” accessed July 16, 2020, https://en.wikipedia.org/wiki/4th_North_Carolina_Regiment.

40. Wikipedia, s.v., “Battle of Brier Creek,” accessed July 16, 2020, https://en.wikipedia.org/wiki/Battle_of_Brier_Creek.

41. Wikipedia, s.v., “Battle of Ramsour’s Mill,” accessed July 16, 2020, https://en.wikipedia.org/wiki/Battle_of_Ramsour%27s_Mill; Wikipedia, s.v., “Battle of Colson’s Mill,” accessed July 16, 2020, https://en.wikipedia.org/wiki/Battle_of_Colson%27s_Mill.

42. Wikipedia, s.v., “Battle of King’s Mountain,” accessed July 16, 2020, https://en.wikipedia.org/wiki/Battle_of_Kings_Mountain.

43. “Surry County NC Court Minutes” in Williams and Lucas, *The Dodson (Dotson) Family*, vol. 1, 19; *State Census of North Carolina, 1784*–1787, 148, 153.

44. Paul Kankula, “Baptist Church Associations and Conventions.”

45. Leah Townsend, “South Carolina Baptists, 1670–1805,” accessed June 30, 2020, http://www.genealogytrails.com/scar/baptist_churches11.htm.

46. Ibid.

47. John Asplund, *The Annual Register of the Baptist Denomination in North America to the First of November, 1790* [ . . . ], https://books.google.com/books?id=XZtZAAAAcAAJ. The Annual Register of 1790 lists Joshua as serving the Sholl Shoals congregation on the Okony River in Greene County, Georgia. Since Sholl Shoals is about sixty miles from the Pendleton District of South Carolina, it is unlikely that Joshua served that church; more likely, he served the Tugaloo River Shoal Creek Church, listed just above the Sholl Shoals Church in the register.

48. Williams and Lucas, *The Dodson (Dotson) Family*, vol. 1, 53.

49. Ibid., 56–7.

50. “Grants South of Green River (1797–1866)” in Kentucky Land Grants, vol. 1, part 1, 301.

51. 1810 US Census, Warren County, Kentucky.

52. Williams and Lucas, *The Dodson (Dotson) Family*, vol. 1, 54.

**APPENDIX 2**

1. *Waco Daily Examiner*, May 8, 1913, June 15, 1913, August 24, 1913.

2. *Waco Daily Examiner*, October 31, 1911.

3. Waco City Directories, 1876–1923, Texas Collection.

# Bibliography


Aldrich, Armistead A. *The History of Houston County Texas*. San Antonio: Naylor, 1943. Ancestry.

Allen, Elvis N. *Building a County: Van Zandt County, 1848–1992*. Fruitvale, TX: Allen, 2007.

Andrews, Dee. E. *The Methodists and Revolutionary America, 1760–1800: The Shaping of an Evangelical Culture*. Princeton, NJ: Princeton University Press, 2000.

Andrews, Michael. *Historic Texas Courthouses*. Albany, TX: Bright Sky, 2006.

Asplund, John. *The Annual Register of the Baptist Denomination in North America to the First of November, 1790* [. . .]. https://books.google.com/books?id=XZtZAAAAcAAJ.

Blackburn, Edward. *Wanted: Historic Jails of Texas*. College Station: Texas A&M University Press, 2006.

Borden, Robert. *Historic Brazos County: An Illustrated History*. San Antonio: Historical Publishing Network, 2005.

Bradley, Mark L. *The Army and Reconstruction, 1865–1877*. Washington, DC: US Army Center of Military History, 2015.

Caldwell, C. T. *Historical Sketch of the First Presbyterian Church, Waco, Texas*. Waco: Methodist Home, n.d. Accessed April 23, 2020. https://www.genealogycenter.info/search_txwaco1stpres.php.

Camp County History Book Committee. *Camp County, Texas: Customs and Characters, A Sesquicentennial History*. Dallas: Taylor, 1986.

Conger, Roger. *A Pictorial History of Waco with a Reprint of Highlights of Waco History*. 2nd ed. Waco: Texian, 1998.

Crawford, A. B. *Hood County News-Tablet*, August 11, 1966. Accessed January 25, 2022. https://texashistory.unt.edu/ark:/67531/metapth1283127.

Crouch, Carrie Johnson. *A History of Young County*. Texas State Historical Association, 1956. Originally published in 1937.

Davis, Charles Lukens, and Henry Hobart Bellas. *A Brief History of the North Carolina Troops on the Continental Establishment in the War of the Revolution*. Philadelphia: 1896. https://lccn.loc.gov/01000384.

Dillard, Jim. "Building a New County Jail, 1888." *The Noble John Olive*. Accessed June 2, 2020. http://www.georgetown-texas.org/Building_a_new_county_jail.pdf.

Dodson File, The. Allen County Historical Society, Scottsville, Kentucky.

Dodson, W. C. "Errors Concerning Ector's Brigade." *Confederate Veteran*, 133, no. 10 (October 1905): 457.

Elam, Richard. "Johnson County." Texas State Historical Association. Accessed June 24, 2022. https://www.tshaonline.org/handbook/entries/johnson-county.

Evans, Clement A., ed. *Georgia*, 256. Vol. 6 of *Confederate Military History*. Atlanta: Confederate, 1899. https://hdl.handle.net/2027/hvd.hx2n9w.

Fannin County Historical Commission. "Bonham News Annual 1888." https://www.fannincountyhistory.org/bonham-news-annual-1888.

Ferguson, Samuel W. "CSA Battle Report Written at Deer Creek, Mississippi." In *War of the Rebellion: A Compilation of the Official Records of the Union and Confederate Armies*, 460. Vol. 24, bk. 1. Washington, DC: Government Printing Office, 1889.

Foster, Gaines M. *Ghosts of the Confederacy: Defeat, the Lost Cause and the Emergence of the New South, 1865–1913*. New York: Oxford University Press, 1987.

Fox, Stephen. "Heiner, Eugene T." Texas State Historical Association. Updated March 1, 2017. https://www.tshaonline.org/handbook/entries/heiner-eugene-t.

George, Mary Carolyn Hollers. *Alfred Giles: An English Architect in Texas and Mexico*. San Antonio: Trinity University Press, 1972.

Girls Industrial College of Texas. "Course of Study, Girls Industrial College of Texas." *Girls Industrial College Bulletin*, no. 3 (August 1903). Accessed August 16, 2024. https://twu-ir.tdl.org/server/api/core/bitstreams/3bea48a8-115b-4187-af66-01f67f465eda/content.

———. "Plan and Scope of the Girls Industrial College of Texas." *Girls Industrial College Bulletin*, no. 2 (June 1903). Accessed August 15, 2024. https://twu-ir.tdl.org/server/api/core/bitstreams/a6624795-176e-4199-a2ce-006cf2e00035/content.

Girls Industrial College of Texas, Board of Regents. First Annual Report. 1902. Accessed August 16, 2024. https://twu-ir.tdl.org/server/api/core/bitstreams/f7dd1234-9e18-451e-aa44-c15096af4191/content.

Goeldner, Paul. "Central Symbols: Historic Texas Courthouses." *Texas Architect Magazine*, May/June 1986. https://magazine.texasarchitects.org/1986/05/28/may-june-1986.

———. "Our Architectural Ancestor. " *Texas Architect Magazine*, July/August 1974. https://magazine.texasarchitects.org/1974/07/25/july-august-1974.

———. "Temples of Justice: Nineteenth Century County Courthouses in the Midwest and Texas." PhD diss., Columbia University, 1970.

Hafertepe, Kenneth. *Historic Homes of Waco, Texas*. College Station: Texas A&M University Press, 2019.

Hall, Margaret Elizabeth. *A History of Van Zandt County*. Austin: Pemberton, 1976.

Hart, Brian. "Greenville, TX (Hunt County)." Texas State Historical Association. Accessed June 25, 2022. https://www.tshaonline.org/handbook/entries/greenville-tx-hunt-county.

———. "Kaufman County." Texas State Historical Association. Accessed June 26, 2022. https://www.tshaonline.org/handbook/entries/kaufman-county.

Hening, William Waller, ed. *The Statutes at Large: Being a Collection of All the Laws of Virginia, from the First Session of the Legislature in the Year 1619*. Vol. 1, 128. Accessed July 18, 2020. https://babel.hathitrust.org/cgi/pt?id=hvd.hxh5uc&seq=15.

Henry, Jay C. *Architecture in Texas, 1895–1945*. Austin: University of Texas Press, 1993.

Heyrman, Christine Leigh. *Southern Cross: The Beginnings of the Bible Belt*. Chapel Hill: University of North Carolina Press, 1997.

Hightower, Brantley. *The Courthouses of Central Texas*. Austin: University of Texas Press, 2015.

Hightower, C. L., ed. *Hood County in Picture and Story*. Historical Publishers, 1978. Originally published in 1970.

Hill County Historical Commission. *A History of Hill County, Texas, 1853–1980*. Waco: Texian, 1980.

Hohes, Pauline Buck. *A Centennial History of Anderson County, Texas*. San Antonio: Naylor, 1936. https://hdl.handle.net/2027/uiug.30112049799817.

Holt, Michael. *The Rise and Fall of the American Whig Party: Jacksonian Politics and the Onset of the Civil War*. New York: Oxford University Press, 1999.

Huey, Mary Evelyn. "The First Building of the Texas Woman's University." Denton County, 1974. https://apps.dentoncounty.gov/website/HistoricalMarkers/PDFs/The-First-Building-of-Texas-Woman's-University.pdf.

Johnson, Frank W. "Hill County Texas: County History." In *A History of Texas and Texans*, Vol. 2. Chicago: American Historical Society, 1914. Accessed June 7, 2022. https://genealogytrails.com/tex/prairieslakes/hill/history_county.html.

Jutson, Mary Carolyn Hollers. *Alfred Giles: An English Architect in Texas and Mexico*. San Antonio: Trinity University Press, 1972.

Kankula, Paul M., comp. "Baptist Church Associations and Conventions." Accessed June 30, 2020. https://sites.rootsweb.com/~scoconee/church-bapt.html.

Keller, Mabel Covington. "History of Kaufman County, Texas." Master's thesis, North Texas State College, 1950. Accessed July 30, 2022. https://digital.library.unt.edu/ark:/67531/metadc663001.

Kelly, Dayton, ed. *The Handbook of Waco and McLennan County, Texas*. Waco: Texian, 1972.

Kelsey, Melvin P., and Donald H. Dyal. *The Courthouses of Texas*. 2nd ed. College Station: Texas A&M University Press, 2007.

Kidd, Thomas S. *The Great Awakening: The Roots of Evangelical Christianity in Colonial America*. New Haven, CT: Yale University Press, 2008.

Manning, Wentworth. *History of Van Zandt County*. Des Moines: Homestead, 1919.

Martana. *Texas Justice: The Legacy of Historical Courthouses*. Dallas: Red Bandana, 2004.

McFerrin, John B. *History of Methodism in Tennessee*. Vol. 3. Nashville: Southern Methodist, 1879. Accessed August 9, 2020. https://catalog.hathitrust.org/Record/100106774.

McPherson, James M. *What They Fought For, 1861–1865*. New York: Anchor, 1995.

Mears, Mildred Watkins. *Coryell County Scrapbook*. Coryell County Museum Foundation, 1985. Originally published in 1963 by Texian Press.

Meister, Chris. *James Riely Gordon: His Courthouses and Other Public Architecture*. Lubbock: Texas Tech University Press, 2011.

*A Memorial and Biographical History of McLennan, Falls, Bell and Coryell Counties, Texas*. Chicago: Lewis, 1893. Accessed August 25, 2022. https://texashistory.unt.edu/ark:/67531/metapth821501.

Mills, W. S. *History of Van Zandt County*. Published by the author's estate, 1950.

Moneyhon, Carl H. "Reconstruction." Texas State Historical Association. Accessed September 4, 2023. https://www.tshaonline.org/handbook/entries/reconstruction.

Morgan, Bill. *Old Friends: Great Texas Courthouses*. Fort Worth: Landmark, 1999.

Nolan, Alan T. "The Anatomy of the Myth." In *The Myth of the Lost Cause and Civil War History*, 11–34. Bloomington: Indiana University Press, 2000.

Oakes, James. *The Ruling Race: A History of American Slaveholders*. New York: Alfred A. Knopf, 2013.
Pauly Jail Building Company. "Legacy." Accessed June 14, 2020. https://www.paulyjail.com/legacy.
Pickens County Historical Society. "Fort Prince George." Accessed June 29, 2020. https://pickenscountyhistoricalsociety.com/fort-prince-george-2.
Revolutionary War Rolls, 1775–1783. RG 93. National Archives, Washington, DC.
Rhoades, Alice J. "Lampasas County." Texas State Historical Society. Accessed June 26, 2022. https://www.tshaonline.org/handbook/entries/lampasas-county.
Roach, David. "Native American Evangelism: Past and Present Examined." *Baptist Press*, August 1, 2017. https://www.baptistpress.com/resource-library/news/native-american-evangelism-past-present-examined.
Roberts, Oran M. *Texas*. Vol. 11 of *Confederate Military History*. Gulf Breeze, Florida: eBooksOnDisk.com, 2003.
Robinson, Willard B. *Gone from Texas: Our Lost Architectural Heritage*. College Station: Texas A&M University Press, 1981.
———. "Houses of Worship in Nineteenth-Century Texas." *The Southwestern Historical Quarterly* 85, no. 3 (1982): 235–98.
———. *The People's Architecture: Texas Courthouses, Jails, and Municipal Buildings*. Austin: University of Texas Press, 1983.
———. "Temples of Knowledge: Historic Mains of Texas Colleges and Universities." *The Southwestern Historical Quarterly* 77, no. 4 (1974): 445–80. https://texashistory.unt.edu/ark:/67531/metapth117148.
———. *Texas Public Buildings of the Nineteenth Century*. Austin: University of Texas Press, 1974.
Sawyer, Amanda. "Milton W. Scott." Waco History. Accessed February 22, 2021. https://wacohistory.org/items/show/92.
Selden, Jack. *Seven Score and Ten: One Hundred Years of the Presbyterian Church in Palestine, Texas*. Palestine, TX: Clacton, 1999.
Smyrl, Vivian Elizabeth. "McLennan County." Texas State Historical Association. Accessed January 14, 2021. https://www.tshaonline.org/handbook/entries/mclennan-county.
*State Census of North Carolina, 1784–1787*. Transcribed and indexed by Alvaretta Kenan Register. Baltimore: Genealogical, 1987.
Strother, David, comp. "Building the Denton County Courthouse, 1895–1897." Denton History. Accessed June 24, 2020. https://dentonhistory.net/page25/page50/
Taylor, Richard. *Destruction and Reconstruction: Personal Experiences of the Late War*. New York: D. Appleton, 1879. Accessed May 28, 2020. https://docsouth.unc.edu/fpn/taylor/menu.html.
Texas Historical Commission. "Texas Historic Sites Atlas." Accessed June 6, 2022. https://atlas.thc.state.tx.us.
"Texas State Association of Architects Minutes and Proceedings." FromThePage. University of Texas Libraries. Accessed December 29, 2020. https://fromthepage.lib.utexas.edu/katiepiercemeyer/james-riely-gordon-collection/texas-state-association-of-architects-minutes-and-proceedings.

Townsend, Leah. "South Carolina Baptists, 1670–1805." Accessed June 30, 2020. http://www.genealogytrails.com/scar/baptist_churches11.htm.

Ule, Michelle Duval. *Pioneer Stock: The American Ancestors of Ballard Emory Duval.* Published by the author, 2000.

Waco City Directories, 1878–1923. Texas Collection, Baylor University Libraries. Accessed February 24, 2021. https://digitalcollections-baylor.quartexcollections.com/texas-collection-collections/waco-city-directories-1876-1923.

Weeks, Stephen B. *History of Public Education in Alabama*. United States Bureau of Education, no. 12, 1915. Accessed April 24, 2020. https://files.eric.ed.gov/fulltext/ED541810.pdf.

Wells, Jonathan. *The Origins of the Southern Middle Class, 1800–1861*. Chapel Hill: University of North Carolina Press, 2004.

"The Welsh Settlers During the Royal Period, 1729 to 1775." Royal Colony of South Carolina. Accessed July 8, 2020. https://www.carolana.com/SC/Royal_Colony/sc_royal_colony_welsh.html.

Wheeler, Joseph. *Confederate Military History of Alabama*. Edited by Clement A. Evans. Atlanta: Confederate, 1899.

White, James C. *The Promised Land: A History of Brown County*. Brownwood, TX: Brownwood Banner, 1941.

Williams, S., and Silas Emmett Lucas Jr. *The Dodson (Dotson) Family of North Farnham Parish, Richmond County, Virginia: A History and Genealogy of Their Descendants.* Easley, SC: Southern Historical, 1989.

Yeary, Mamie. *Reminiscences of the Boys in Gray, 1861–1865*. Dallas: Smith and Lamar, 1912. Accessed August 7, 2020. https://texashistory.unt.edu/ark:/67531/metapth29786.

# Index

*Page numbers in italics refer to illustrations*